Gerald Fitzgibbon

Ireland in 1868, the battle-field for English party strife;

Its grievances, real and factitious; remedies, abortive or mischievous

Gerald Fitzgibbon

Ireland in 1868, the battle-field for English party strife;
Its grievances, real and factitious; remedies, abortive or mischievous

ISBN/EAN: 9783337733254

Printed in Europe, USA, Canada, Australia, Japan

Cover: Foto ©ninafisch / pixelio.de

IRELAND IN 1868,

THE BATTLE-FIELD FOR ENGLISH PARTY STRIFE;

ITS

GRIEVANCES, REAL AND FACTITIOUS;

REMEDIES, ABORTIVE OR MISCHIEVOUS.

BY

GERALD FITZGIBBON, ESQ.,

ONE OF THE MASTERS IN CHANCERY IN IRELAND.

Semper ego auditor tantum?

LONDON:
LONGMANS, GREEN, READER, AND DYER.
DUBLIN: M^cGLASHAN AND GILL.
1868.

PREFACE.

THE appearance of this book, with my name in the title, will, doubtless, surprise my family and my friends, who know how little I have ever meddled with sectarian controversy or party disputes. Approaching the termination of a life, which, at every stage of it, was, and still is, laboriously occupied in the discharge of duties which no one can, with truth, accuse me of neglecting, no ordinary motive could induce me to undertake the additional labour of writing even this small book. I began it with reluctance, and without forming anything like a resolution to finish it. The first thought of it was suggested by the announcement of a Session peculiarly devoted to the discussion of Irish questions, and the redress of what are called Irish grievances; which, in my view of our national disorders, and of the legislative remedies usually applied, foreboded no good to this unhappy country, condemned as it has been to be the mere battle-field for party combatants. My feeling was still rather a wish that something might be written or spoken, expressive of my views, than a determined design to write anything myself, until the resolutions were announced for abolition of the Irish Church. That party movement attached to my opinions a sense of duty which I never felt before no longer to conceal those opinions, or to flinch from a fearless and public assertion of them. What my sentiment was upon that announcement, and what it is at this moment, I cannot better express than by citing from a report which came under my notice in a newspaper on Wednesday last, after I had prepared my last pages for the press. At the great meeting which was held on Monday last in London, Sir W. Baynes began his able speech by saying: "I appear before you as the partisan of no political side. I come here only as the exponent of Protestant feelings. I am one, I believe, of many laymen who, avoiding the arena of politics, and endeavouring quietly to pursue the duties of their respective callings, shun public notice, till drawn forth by feelings of conscience in an all-important matter, like the present, when, in the calmness of our comparative retirement from public life, we discern in a measure like that now before the country a signal danger threatened to our civil and religious liberties, by what is nothing short of (though guarded at the moment) an attempt to undermine that glorious pillar of our constitution, the union of Church and State, and the supremacy of the Crown in all matters civil and ecclesiastical, in this Kingdom." How perfectly this expresses my sentiments, and how clearly it describes my motives, in writing this book, will abundantly appear in every page.

The book itself will be the most convincing proof that I am not, and never could have been, a partisan of any political side. The remarkable coincidence between many passages in the pages which I had previously printed and the views expressed by the distinguished men who spoke at this meeting, is a corroboration of my resolution to publish the book which I had not expected, and gives me some confidence that I will not be considered obtrusive or impertinent when I submit it to the public, without other motive than a faint hope that it may not be useless.

I must beg of the Presbyterians, and other Dissenters from the Romish Catechism, to bear in mind, when reading some passages in which I claim for Protestants the principal share in the improvement of Ireland, that I mean to include all denominations of Dissenters from that intolerant creed, although I have inadvertently, in some places, only designated Protestants of the Church of England. As an instance of this, I refer to page 27, where it is stated that "To the Protestant Church of England the majority, in Ireland, of the class just mentioned, belong." When writing this, I had in my mind the three southern provinces only, and did not perceive the inaccuracy until it was too late to correct it. I hope this explanation will be applied with kind indulgence to all similar passages.

10, Merrion Square, N., Dublin,
25th May, 1868.

CORRIGENDA.

Page 58, line 30, *for* principles *read* principle.
—— 80, —— 6, *for* suits *read* pursuits.
—— 128, —— 1, *omit the words* already adverted to.
—— 208, —— 8, *for* 1863 *read* 1853.
—— 256, —— 17, *for* pole *read* poll.

IRELAND IN 1868,

&c. &c.

CHAPTER I.

GENERAL REFLECTIONS ON THE CONDITION OF IRELAND.

Rich and poor, wealth and poverty, are words in common use; and their general meaning is, for ordinary purposes, correctly enough apprehended. A man is called rich in proportion to the amount of money which his property in land or goods, convertible into money, would, if sold, produce. A man who has no property convertible into money may be properly called poor, as contrasted with one who possesses an estate in land, or who has goods or rights marketable, and, by sale, exchangeable for money.

A nation every individual of which is possessed of accumulated wealth, and therefore rich, in the sense here expressed, may be truly called a wealthy nation. But no nation of which every one is thus a man of property has ever existed, and no nation wealthy in this sense ever can exist. There are numberless operations and works which must be performed, if human society is to be maintained; and very many, if not the great majority of these, are such as no rich man will submit to perform. Toil and labour have ever been, and ever must be, disagreeable to the great bulk of mankind, and nothing but necessity will compel men to labour and to drudge in the way which God and nature have made essential to their existence.

Wherever man has been found in what we call the savage state, wandering and unassociated with his fellow-men, his state and condition have always been, not merely poor and destitute, but precarious, wretched, and often miserable to the last degree of human suffering. This has been called a state of nature, but it is not properly so called. Nature has given faculties to man by which to discover that association is essential to his security, his happiness, and his comfort. To live without using these faculties is no more the natural state of man than to lie down and die, neglecting the use of those powers of bodily action with which nature has endowed him, and which, by the strongest instincts, she prompts him to exercise. Association in civil life, under laws and government, is, therefore, the normal state of man, and more properly his natural state, than that of the wandering savage. The number of the human race existing in the savage state of independent misery has never at any time, of which we have authentic history, been any greater than a small fraction of the whole : plain proof that such is not the natural state of man.

It requires very little reflection to see that, in every form of civilized society, the multitude must be destitute of accumulated wealth, and made dependent for bread upon their daily toil. This dependence forces each individual to seek and find the kind of work which his education and habits enable him to perform; and he soon becomes reconciled to this, however disagreeable or even loathsome it may appear to those of better cultivated faculties or more fastidious tastes. This it is which practically insures the execution of all the offices of social life, innumerable and varied as they are, from the Sovereign on the throne, descending by steps of infinite variety and number, and of imperceptible degrees of degradation, to the working classes and lowest functionaries in the community, who, by natural law, must form the wide-spread basis of the pyramid, into which a civilized nation must form itself if it desires to stand.

The multitudinous classes which thus form the basis and support of every human community depend, and ever must depend, for the necessaries of life on the sale of the only vendible commodity which they possess, and that is their labour. As every article in which what is called wealth can be invested and preserved for the use of its owners is the product of human skill and labour, a market will never be wanted for these; and he who has, and is willing to apply them, will have a sure means of living, so long as he has strength and health and is willing to work. Compared, therefore, with that of the wandering unsocial savage, the condition of the poorest member of a civilized community is not miserable or precarious, although by no means exempt from many and great perils, and sometimes sufferings.

The amount of wages, or, in other words, the amount of enjoyable goods which the labourer can earn and get, depends on the ratio of the demand for his labour to the quantity of such labour in search of employment at any given time. When the demand is great, and those out of employment few, the competition of employers will soon and certainly raise the rate, and nothing is so important to the labouring classes to know as the causes which increase or diminish the demand for their services.

In the present discussion, those whose labour is reproductive are alone considered; first, because, as compared with them, all others are but a small fractional quantity; and, secondly, because the prosperity and the contentment of this great class necessarily imply the general prosperity and well-being of the whole nation; as their pauperism, misery, and discontent, are sure to disturb the peace, and destroy, or at least injuriously affect, the tranquillity and happiness of all the classes above them.

The great majority of the labourers who come within the scope of this inquiry work under employers who calculate the value of the expected return, and compare it with the outlay for wages and materials. If the outlay be, by experience, found greater or even equal to the return, the employer's interest will soon suggest to him to discontinue the work. If the profit be large, he will just as certainly be prompted to extend his operations and seek for additional hands, even at advanced wages. The employer's profits are, therefore, the great cause of high wages, as his losses and disappointments are the cause of diminishing the demand for labour, and reducing the workman's wages, and throwing numbers out of employment.

There being but few operations of the working man which produce an immediate return, and the pennyless labourer requiring his wages to supply the wants of the day that is passing over him, it follows that capital, viz., accumulated property in the hands of employers, is essential for the support and security of the workers, who have nothing to vend except their labour. When the number of capitalists bears a large ratio to the whole population, and when the amount of their capital is also large, the nation deserves to be ranked as a wealthy nation, and it is in this sense that England is truly denominated a wealthy nation. When, on the contrary, the number of capitalists bears a low ratio to the whole population, and when the total amount of capital possessed by them is small, the nation so circumstanced may properly be called poor; which, however, as well as the word wealthy, has a comparative, and not a positive signification. It is in this latter sense that Ireland is called a poor nation.

Although it is true to say, that the English, in the sense here expressed, are a wealthy nation, and that the Irish are comparatively a poor nation, yet it would not be true to say, that there are not many, nay, multitudes of individuals in the English nation suffering all the miseries incidental to the extremes of destitution and poverty. It may, probably, be truly said, that greater sufferings from poverty, in certain classes, are endured in England than could be found in any part of Ireland. It would probably also be found, that the number of those who are enduring in England the last extremities of want and destitution, bears a larger ratio to the whole population of England than the poorest classes in Ireland bear to its entire population.

In Ireland it is perfectly certain, that the great majority of the suffering poor belong to the class of small farmers and agricultural labourers. Wretched and ill fed, ill clad, and badly housed, as multitudes of these are, yet but a small fraction of them will consent to enter the poorhouse, certainly proving, that they believe the condition of the pauper in that abode is less tolerable than their own condition outside.

The want of employment in Ireland chiefly exists in the class of agricultural labourers. The skilled labour of tradesmen, and also the work of common labourers who serve in cities and towns, for many years last past, has been in great request, and very highly paid for, in all the cities and towns in Ireland. The only complaints I have heard, in respect of these skilled tradesmen and town labourers, have come from their employers; and the substance of these complaints has been, that the workmen, finding the wages of three, four, or five days of the week sufficient to supply their wants, and to gratify their appetites, they idle for one, two, or three days, to the great injury and inconvenience of their masters, and that the competition for them is so great, that the employers find it difficult to govern their men; and are obliged to connive and be silent at misconduct, which would not be endured under a different state of things.

Discontent in Ireland, founded on poverty and privation, exists chiefly, if not exclusively, amongst the agricultural labourers, and the small farmers, who are but little above the condition of labourers. I speak here of real discontent, and not of that wanton seditious discontent ostentatiously exhibited and heralded with outcry by those who trade upon the assertion of it, and who make it the topic of speeches, letters, and pamphlets for sectarian and party purposes. To say that a man who is only half fed, who is scarcely clad at all, and whose hovel is no shelter from the pitiless storm, is, or ever could be contented, would be a self-evident and palpable falsehood. The natural, necessary, and painful discontent of men in such plight is the discontent here alluded to, and the existence of which in Ireland is here admitted and asserted. To investigate and expose the causes of the destitution which necessarily occasions this discontent in Ireland is one great object, if not the principal object, of the writer of these pages.

There is no proposition more generally believed in Ireland by holders of land than that the tillage of the land is not a paying operation, in which to embark capital. The holder of land who has capital, that is, who has wherewithal to live without mere drudgery and toil, will not submit to rise himself half an hour before the bell calls his men to work. He will not submit to stand over his men, in all seasons, during the whole working day; and without doing this, the employer who expects a fair day's work from agricultural labourers, in Ireland, will certainly be disappointed. Here is the true foundation of the assertion that Ireland is a pastoral, and not an agricultural country. Here lies the cause why the poor working farmer of five, ten, or twenty acres, of which he tills, and can live only by tilling, every perch that will yield a crop, can, for this small farm, pay the landlord a higher acreable rent, than the most skilful farmer on an extensive scale could, in Ireland, pay for the same land, if it were added to the large tract which he farms by hired labourers. Capital, however, is beginning to profit by the implements and improvements of modern invention. The small farmer tills badly; his fences are wasteful; his haggard is slovenly and wasteful; his crops are scant and light; and yet he pays a larger rent by the acre than the landlord could get for the same land, if he threw it into a large consolidated farm, manageable only by a capitalist. The explanation of this apparent paradox is yet simple and easily understood.

The small farmer does the work of his little holding principally, if not entirely, with his own hands, and the hands of his sons, his wife, and daughters. If, in spring or harvest time, he is forced to bring hired labourers to assist him, he himself, or his sons, or both, will work beside the hirelings, and compel them to give value for their wages; and he finds this no difficult task, for the hired labourers are prompted by a feeling that is almost universal amongst them in Ireland, especially in the agricultural class, to work with a will for the poor man, when they will not work for the rich man one jot harder than they consider necessary to avoid dismissal.

This is the true explanation of the fact, that a very large proportion of the tillage land of Ireland is held by small farmers. I believe this fact will not be denied or doubted by any one who knows this country. If a proof of it be wanted, the following unquestionable facts will be admitted as a fair if not a conclusive proof.

There are receivers, under the Court of Chancery, over 655 estates, which are situate, I believe, in all counties and parts of Ireland. The total of the rents of these amount to about £500,000 yearly. The total number of tenants on them is about 29,000, shewing an average annual rent of about £17 for each tenant. The rentals of these estates vary from £100 a year, to £20,000. One estate, the total rents of which amount to over £13,000, has over 2,400 tenants on it, whose average yearly rents amount, therefore, to about £5 6*s.* for each.

It is quite certain that the ability of those small farmers to pay as high or higher rents by the acre than extensive farmers of superior skill and capital could, in Ireland, pay for the same land, does not arise from the production of superior crops. As a general rule, their crops are much inferior to the crops which the same lands would produce to an extensive and skilful farmer of adequate capital. Of the produce also, such as it is, of these small farms a larger proportion goes to waste, and is wholly lost, than would be lost if the produce were properly harvested and prepared for market by a farmer of capital. This waste is caused by the want of corn-stands; the want of barns, the want of proper implements for threshing and winnowing, the want of necessary offices for the storage and preservation of the produce when brought home. All this excess of waste, as well as the deficiency of produce, is so much lost to the public stock, and commonweal of the nation; although no part of it apparently falls upon the immediate landlord, for he gets, in Ireland, the highest rent that any tenant could pay for the land. It follows, and it is the fact, that the ability of the poor man to pay this rent entirely arises from diminution of expenditure in the cultivation of the land, and in the diminution also of expenditure in maintaining the wretched cultivator and his family, who consume but a small part of the produce, and sell the chief part, to provide for the rent, and avoid eviction.

This system of small farms, cheaply and badly cultivated, greatly militates against the production, and accumulation of capital and national weath. Machinery is not used; therefore no demand is created for mechanical skill and labour. The farmer and his family are in rags; therefore, no market is created for manufactures of home or of foreign production. Hired labourers are employed but sparingly, and the small farmer can hardly be considered as a competitor amongst employers. His cattle are ill fed, and, if housed at all, are placed in dens, dark, filthy, and unwholesome, whereby the value of the cattle is proportionably lessened, and this part of the national wealth is, therefore, by so much diminished.

The proposed legislation to secure to the tenant the value of his improvements, if his tenancy be determined by the landlord, can have no possible application to these small farmers. They have no capital to expend in improvements. They can scarcely produce a scanty, and, in most cases, an almost famine allowance of the necessaries of life, over and above the rent which they must pay, or quit the land, and go to the workhouse. A clear, strong, and terrible demonstration of this was made by the blight of the potato, in 1846. The destruction of this single item of the poor farmer's produce hurled him over the precipice, on the brink of which he had been living; and death by starvation was the consequence to thousands in the frightful years which followed.

A similar calamity in all essential particulars befel Ireland in 1739, 1740, and 1741, and that visitation arose from the same cause, destruction of the potato in the winter and spring of 1739, 1740, not by blight, but by frost, an equally destructive agent. This calamity of the last century will be more particularly noticed in the sequel.

In due proportion to its extent, this system of small farms is a cause of national poverty as well as individual misery. It is impossible that these poor people can be contented, and they are not contented. Many, perhaps the great majority of them, are resigned, and their discontent does not exhibit itself in seditious agitation. It is certain that they are religious, and a prominent tenet of their religion, to them the most consolitary, is, that those who innocently suffer privations and miseries in this life are, like Lazarus, all the more secure of happiness and glory in the life to come. Nothing is farther from my intention than to make any question as to the soundness or unsoundness of this doctrine, theologically considered, or to raise any discussion whatever on the truth of it. The temporal and social effect of it upon those who implicitly believe it is wholly beside, and independent of its truth or falsehood ; and obviously, must be the same, whether the tenet itself be orthodox or not. One effect is to reconcile the believer to the tribulations to which he is subjected, and to keep him resigned and quiet while he suffers them, in the sure and certain conviction that they are inflicted for his ultimate good. To the magistrate in all probability this will appear a useful effect. Another effect, and an effect quite as certain and more general, is to slacken energetic exertion. The utility of this will be denied by the political economist, and no one can doubt that it prolongs and aggravates the temporal suffering. This applies not alone to the class of small farmers; it equally affects the still more numerous class of agricultural labourers, and both together form a very large section of the Irish nation.

To these two great classes we must add the vagrant tribe of mendicants, the lazy and despairing paupers, who never did, and never would submit to labour; whose number in Ireland is great, and whose means of existence is more of a mystery to those who behold them, than that of the fowls of the air, or the wild beast of the forest.

To the same category belong all whose efforts in life have failed, and proved abortive, who have lost heart and lost cast, and have fallen out of employment, who are all the more numerous, by reason of the difficulties which, in Ireland, are greater and more numerous than in most other countries, in the way of the active, diligent, and intelligent labourer, in all the useful vocations of life.

There is another class of malcontents in Ireland, who have no just cause to complain of the present state of things, and who are yet more prompt and ready to disturb the peace of society than any of the classes before mentioned. These are tradesmen, working in cities and large towns, and labourers employed attending them, and in other works carried on in those cities and towns; porters engaged in loading and unloading ships and canal boats, carting to railways and otherwise in a great variety of town works and employments. These, both tradesmen and labourers, for many years last past, have been very highly paid, and fully employed. They are much better off than they could possibly be in any revolutionary change, such as they shout for. The discontent of these men is purely seditious, and wantonly expressed. From amongst these come the men who exhibit themselves in processions ; make noise at meetings ; utter threats of revolution by physical force ; attack the police, and seize every opportunity for disturbing the peace, and substituting riot and confusion for the order and quiet essential to the progress and well being of the country, and to nothing more essential than to the sources of their own prosperity.

These four classes, whatever may be their ratio to the whole Irish nation, as to the three first, must be, and as to the last, are discontented, and see nothing to fear, and imagine they have much to hope from any change. Their ears are open to every man who tells them that their sufferings are unmerited and unjust; the result, not of their own defaults, but of oppression and misgovernment. No matter to whom or to what the blame is imputed, they are ready to listen, to assent, and to believe, and they with alacrity join in the outcry against the asserted cause of their sufferings, without any the smallest examination of the arguments, or the sophistry addressed to them. They inquire not into the motives or the character of any one who preaches condonation of faults, and misconduct to themselves, and condemnation of others. Whoever tells them that the English have always been, and still are, brutal invaders and oppressors ; that the English legislature has been and is partial and unjust; that Ireland has been and is misgoverned and oppressed, and who abuses all the institutions connected with the government, is, at once, and without question, admitted to the rank of a patriot. They meet for him, they listen to him, they shout for him, they canvass for him ; if they have a vote, they vote for him, if not, they threaten, or even beat those who have votes, unless they support him ; in their view, the agitator and the patriot are confounded and identical, and their favour and clamour give a mischievous power and influence to the crafty and unprincipled orator, who flatters and cajoles them, while he pursues, unsuspected, some selfish object for his own sole benefit and advancement.

The agitators, and their multitudinous and noisy dupes and abettors, are the only part of the Irish nation conspicuous to foreigners, in which category of foreigners, most unfortunately, our English fellow-subjects stand. In their eyes, and to their understandings, the public orators, public writers, tumultuous assemblies, who meet and pass violent and seditious resolutions, marauders, who assail property and life, and processionists, who beard the police and constituted authorities, make up the total of the Irish nation, and stamp it with the vilified character which it has attained in England and abroad. The orderly and industrious are silent, and consequently ignored, as if they had no existence in this troubled and troublesome community. The character which the nation has thus established abroad and in the sister island, bears hardly and most injuriously upon this peaceful, industrious, and unnoticed portion of the people; that any such exist in Ireland, I do believe, is a matter of question and grave doubt to a large and powerful part of the English people.

To say that there are no manufactures ; no profitable

commerce; no industrial establishments; both mercantile and agricultural, even in the West and South of Ireland, is by no means true: no one asserts it of the north, although, even there, the existence of these effects of civilization and thrift is admitted, or believed, in England, only to a limited and a qualified extent, far short of the truth. The founders and proprietors of these establishments, great and small, and numerous as they unquestionably are, and the working people employed in them, constitute the efficient and truly respectable portion of the Irish nation. Surrounded with difficulties, the proprietors and conductors of these establishments, by laborious thought and persevering industry, create and employ capital. They hold no meetings, make no speeches, publish no letters or pamphlets, are candidates for no places, in or out of parliament. They read newspapers; and feel some alarm at the changes which are threatened, and which, vague and undefined as they are, create a just apprehension and dread of coming events in all reflecting minds. To this sound and virtuous part of the nation, nothing is so agreeable, nothing so much desired, nothing so essential as peace and tranquillity. The most reflecting amongst them regard changes with doubts and fears; and do not readily believe that alteration imports improvement. They look upon long established laws, and firm institutions, with affection and favour; and they are averse from legislative empiricism, however plausibly recommended. When they see and dread, and, in many instances, clearly understand, the mischief of proposed and so-called reforms; they find themselves powerless to resist the agitation and clamour with which such projects are pursued. Publicly to speak or write in opposition to a patriotic orator, or a radical reformer, is sure to draw down unmeasured personal abuse from some practised calumniator, and the volunteer champion of established laws and ancient institutions is sure to become an example well calculated to deter all others, in like case offending.

Tenant right, which no man has yet defined; fixity of tenure, which no one has yet defined; compensation for tenants' improvements, which no one has yet proved to be practicable, consistently with the rights of property, plainly have no tendency to relieve the poverty of the small farmer; to reform the laziness of the agricultural labourer; to reduce the vagrant tribe to a life of useful industry; or to raise the fallen and desperate to hope, and renewed exertion. This proposed remedy for the alleged grievances of Ireland, therefore, leaves wholly untouched the sufferings of that multitude, upon whose discontent the busy agitator trades and thrives, and to a moral certainty will acquire new powers for mischief, from every concession, which he will accept as, and be sure to call, an instalment of justice to Ireland, extorted by his exertions.

Abolition of the Church Establishment, on the assumption that its existence is an Irish grievance; and the confiscation of the property which supports it; how will this affect the discontented multitudes before described, over whose passions their sufferings, or their seditious propensities, give to the agitator the same power which the tempest has over the waters of the ocean? No reflecting man, who knows Ireland, can believe that the abolition of this Establishment, and the confiscation of its property, will have any other effect upon agitation than that of a powerful and enduring stimulus. It will be a palpable and an admitted concession to agitation and clamour. As such it will be received; as such it will operate; and, since the concession to agitation made in 1829, no such grave error will have been committed by the English rulers of Ireland, as that of yielding up this Establishment.

The Protestants of the three southern provinces of Ireland, though numerically a minority of the people, are yet in rank, in property, in knowledge, and in governing influence, and ability, the more powerful and important section of the population. Take away from these the property, and the consequent dignity and prestige, of the Established Church, to which they belong, and to which they resort for worship, and their religion and worship will soon be made, and will become, objects of derision to the multitude, who now justly respect them, in spite of sectarian hostility.

In 1825 a bill for Catholic Emancipation was passed by a considerable majority in the House of Commons. It was accompanied by two other bills, then called its wings, by one of which the old forty shilling freehold franchise was to be abolished; and by the other, an independent provision was to be made for the Roman Catholic clergy. To the former wing, O'Connell and his followers had agreed; and, by this agreement, it was believed that their popularity and their power of agitation would receive a death blow. The Roman Catholic clergy had also, it was understood, consented to take the provision proposed by the State. By this provision they would have been rendered independent of the voluntary contributions of their flocks, and thenceforth the loss of a member of their congregation, by conversion, would no longer import a loss of income. They would have been thus placed, more than they had ever been before, on a level with the clergy of the Protestant Church, and a great stimulus to polemical zeal and exertion of ecclesiastical power over the religious fears of illiterate and ignorant congregations would have been taken away—a stimulus, too, which, had never been applied to their antagonists, the Protestant clergy of Ireland, who were at all times made independent of their congregations, by an impost which, in former times was justly detested.

Emancipation, which had been long and loudly called for, and the claims to which were supported by every principle of humanity, policy, and justice, would have been then accepted as a concession to constitutional petitions and arguments, founded upon and supported by the eternal principles of equity and good government. It would have been then accepted as a wise and voluntary concession, made by a considerate and a provident majority of the legislature, with the consent of a liberal and benevolent sovereign. The day that this great and necessary measure was defeated by a majority of the Lords, was the day of Ireland's greatest calamity, and the day on which the difficulties of England, in the government of Ireland, were, I fear, for ever perpetuated.

The passing of the bill, by a substantial majority of the Commons, turned hope into certain assurance. The subsequent rejection of the measure, by the Lords, was a maddening conversion of this assurance into despair. The insulted Roman Catholics, as one man, rallied round their leaders; the popularity of these, which had been shaken, was not merely restored, but renewed with enthusiasm. Agitation spread, and became apparently irresistible. The Clare election of O'Connell followed, and the organization of the people, exhibited at this unprecedented scene, impressed the mind of the firm Duke, then the Prime Minister, with the conviction, that Ireland was ripe for a better organized rebellion than had ever taken place before. His humanity (and he was a truly humane man) inpulsively recoiled from the horrors of such an event. He believed that the immediate concession of Emancipation was the only means of preventing it; and, accordingly, a bill was introduced for the purpose, as a Government measure, by those who had all their lives strenuously opposed Emancipation. One of the wings, and the most essential for every pacifying purpose, was lopped off, for it required no wings, thus supported by Government, to give the measure velocity through Parliament. Thus, this great and just measure of relief, which had been long refused to the humble petitions of oppressed subjects, was yielded to the clamour and violence of a well organized agitation. No Roman Catholic, no matter what his rank, no matter what was the measure of his intelligence, or capacity, has ever since regarded that act of the Legislature in any other light than as a concession made to, and extorted by, violent agitation and open threats, suggesting that recourse to physical force was then an imminent danger.

No such danger did, in fact, then exist. The Clare election, and the scenic exhibition of the organization and discipline of the peasantry at it, were the result of clever and artful management. Had the truth been known in England, and had consequences been wisely considered, no concession would or should have been then made to demands supported by threats of sedition and violence. Regard to consequences would have suggested a peremptory rejection of claims so enforced ; and wisdom would have dictated all possible efforts to regain, as soon as practicable, the position, which, by the decision of the Lords, had been rashly abandoned in 1825. But the superiority of legitimate power should have been first asserted, and the clamour of agitation should have been reduced to a tone of respectful solicitation and constitutional petition ; and this was perfectly practicable, notwithstanding the excitement which then prevailed.

From the moment that a Government, with such a man as the Duke of Wellington at its head, had been, as was then believed, intimidated, and forced to yield to threats, and to the apprehension of force and violence, after the rejection of prayers and petitions, agitation was regarded as an Archimedean lever by which the political world could be thenceforth moved, with the gods who ruled it. It was soon applied, and successfully applied, both in England and Ireland, to force the reform of 1832. Agitate !—agitate !—agitate ! was the concise exhortation used and addressed to the Irish people, at that time ; and, from that hour to the present, agitation has been in the ascendant, and the sun has never risen upon the day, when topics for agitation did not crop out in the most luxuriant abundance.

The fulcrum upon which this lever rests, and from which it exercises its power, is the marvellous ignorance of the English people and their representatives of the actual condition of society in Ireland. Their belief that the Irish nation is made up of an impoverished and oppressed tenantry; of starving labourers, willing to work, but who cannot get employment; of vagrants who are ready for any mischief; of daring processionists and Fenian conspirators, and of noisy demagogues, who derive importance from the real, and from the factitious discontent of the several classes before described, gives power and disastrous importance to all the enemies of tranquillity and peace.

The tenantry, thus brought under the notice of the English Government and English people, are no other than the small tenants before alluded to, whose existence in Ireland was not caused, and is not continued, by any misgovernment, and the amelioration of whose condition is not in the power of any government, or of any legislature, suddenly to accomplish. It is probable that some of these small tenants originated by the creation of votes in the time of the forty shilling franchise; but, as a class, they were created by a pre-existing cause, before that franchise was created, and multiplied by their ability, in the way before described, to pay higher rents than tenants of capital, farming by tillage on an extensive scale, and employing Irish agricultural labourers, could pay for the same land, thus making it the immediate interest of landlords to prefer the small farmers as tenants.

Nothing that can be done by government or by law can enable a man who farms five or ten acres of land, and who has no other source of income than what he can make his petty farm produce, to have anything beyond a stunted and wretched provision for his family after payment of a rack-rent.

As long as the rights of property are respected, no Government, no legislature, can prohibit the owner of land from letting it in small farms, for which he can get a higher rent than he could get for the same land let in extensive tracts to tenants of capital. It is idle, and it is unjust, to rail at and abuse landlords for thus dealing with their property. As long as the tenant of capital is not able to compete, in tillage, with the small mere labouring farmer, who does the work himself; who supports himself and family on the potato crop alone ; who sells all the corn crop ; who feeds a pig or two on the small potatoes and the mere waste, and who sells the pig, as well as the corn, to make up the rent, these poor farmers will always be successful competitors for possession of the tillage land. As long as the farmer of capital has to compete in the market with foreign corn, produced in countries where the habit of the hired labourer is to work with more energy and diligence than he does, or can be forced to do, in Ireland, the capitalist, who depends on hired labour, must continue to be an unsuccessful competitor of the small working farmer, for tillage land.

What is here stated of the Irish agricultural labourer is founded partly on personal experience of twenty-two years, and partly on the observation of more than fifty years, with much favourable opportunity for acquiring knowledge on the subject. For the first eight of those twenty-two years, I farmed 217 statute acres, of which about two-thirds were tilled in a four-course rotation of roots, heavily manured, followed by wheat, oats, or barley, sowed with Italian rye-grass and clover, which was twice mowed in the summer of the third year, and broken for oats in the fourth year, the tilled land being thus divided into four nearly equal sets.

The wages paid during those eight years, including the wages of the steward and carpenter, and cost of smith work for the farm, amounted to over £700 in the year. For the last thirteen years the farm was reduced to 140 statute acres—one holding of seventy-seven acres having gone out of lease—and for which the landlord preferred, for about forty acres, a poor tenant of no capital, and for the residue, an ordinary farmer of adjoining land who had sufficient means, but working very much upon the common Irish system of farming. Although unable to bestow any personal attention beyond occasional visits, I was desirous to have the land, having offices, implements, and an ample staff to work it, and I offered what I believed to be a full rent. How much more the tenants who got it undertook to pay I am not able to say. Since that, for the last fourteen years, the part of the remaining land under tillage amounts to about ninety statute acres, cultivated in the same four-course rotation, and the residue in pasture. The wages for these fourteen years amount to about £500 a year; if not more, certainly not less. Some four or five of the men have been in the employment from the commencement, in June, 1846; five or six are the sons of men who were in it from 1846 until they died, and several are in it for from five to ten and twelve years. I have very seldom discharged a labourer, except to let him into what he thought a better employment, on some railroad as a porter.

With the exception of diligence in work, I can truly say of these men, that they are honest, sober, well conducted men; that they are, without exception, skilful, expert, and able agricultural labourers; fit to compete, in all sorts of farm-work, with any in Scotland, or in England. I have seen no better crops than I have had. I have not seen, in Scotland, or in England, a stack-yard as tidily and as skilfully made up, for its extent, as mine has been every harvest from the commencement to the present. Being by professional avocations fully occupied myself, I have always had a first-class steward. No better stall-fed cattle go to market than those from my farm; no better wheat, oats, and barley; no better turnips, mangolds, and potatoes. Here must end my praises of my farming operations. The result is an annual loss, to an amount that would have destroyed an ample capital in the three or four first years of my experiment. This loss, however, has been taken out of a large income from sources independent of the farm; and reluctance to give up some enjoyments flowing from this source, and an habitual dislike of change, bind me to persevere in my unprofitable operations, by which I avoid the necessity of discharging a number of men who have so long depended on me for employment.

With full knowledge of every kind of agricultural work, acquired in early life, and long before I had this farm, I have used my opportunities of estimating the ratio of the work done for me, to the work which, with fair and ordinary diligence, ought to be done; and my conclusion is, that, from every man, I get certainly less than one-third of the work which, without any undue exertion, he should perform. These men get wages varying from eight shillings to twelve shillings a week. Nine of them have their houses rent-free. They are paid for full six days of every week in the year, and never lose a day's wages, unless they choose to keep a holyday beyond some four or five on which they are excused from work, without losing wages.

If the wages thus paid be multiplied by three, it will be obvious that their employer must lose his capital; and I believe this to be the experience, with rare exceptions, of every man of capital who tills extensively in Ireland. This is sufficient to account for the very general preference of pasture to tillage. It is, in my opinion, erroneous to say, that pasture is more profitable than skilful tillage, with proper implements and diligent labourers, would be in Ireland, notwithstanding all that is said about the climate. A farmer confining the extent of the tillage to a just and proper proportion of the whole farm would quite certainly make more profit than by pasturing the whole. This proportion must, in each case, depend on the facility for obtaining manure, on the character of the soil, and other circumstances. But reasonably willing labourers are essential.

I doubt not that, in Ireland, as elsewhere, there are men of extraordinary energy and ability to make others subservient to their will; and that some of these gifted men have turned their attention to the cultivation of land on an extensive scale, and on an approved system of farming. In proportion to the personal attention devoted; to the sagacity used in selecting labourers; to the good temper, tact, and skill exercised in the treatment of these labourers; and to the firmness and justice with which their faults are corrected, and the liberality and certainty with which their merits are rewarded, their employers will succeed, and their experience will dictate a favourable report of Irish labourers. But as such gifted men must ever be a small number of the class to which they belong, successful tillers, upon an extensive scale, are few in Ireland. In proportion to their number, they are certainly foremost amongst the operative causes of the vast improvement which, in spite of all obstructions, has taken place in the present century. They have all the more merit, by reason of the peculiar difficulties that surround them in this country. An extensive landholder who has capital, and who prefers attention to the good management of his land to field sports and town amusements, is, however, an exception to the general rule. He is not in fashion, nor quite sure to be respected in the ratio of his merit. If he sows in time, his seed is in ground weeks before that of his neighbours, and all the birds in the country are down upon it, and will eat it up, unless he incurs extraordinary expense in protecting it. He is in like case when harvest approaches, and when his corn is yellow, while that of his neighbours is green. His soil is well tilled, and clear of weeds; the land which surrounds him, and all the roadsides, headlands, ditches, and wastes of his neighbours, produce a plentiful crop of thistles, rag-weed, grounsel, dandalion, and other weeds, whose seeds are borne on wings, and are sure to light upon and strike root, and thrive in his good tilth, unless he incurs the constantly recurring expense of interrupting their growth. If he is in easy circumstances, and able to pay his rent, the landlord, as a general rule, is ready, and too frequently pressed by his wants, to make a prompt demand, while the inability of the unthrifty tenant forces the landlord to indulge him with time. These are but a few of the instances in which the rule of justice is inverted in Ireland. Still there are men who have courage to encounter, and ability to conquer, all these disadvantages, and whose example, beyond all doubt, has, sooner or later, a good effect upon their slovenly neighbours. Men of this class and character do not come into public notice, and to the English eye they are not a visible part of the Irish nation. For redress of their grievances, no one agitates—no one thinks of legislating.

In every calling of life there are men of this useful stamp, whose energy commands success, and whose exertions, mental and bodily, produce the good effects which are, more or less, conspicuous in all parts of Ireland. Good general and permanent laws, well administered, form the sum and substance of all the benefits which any Government can confer upon them; and, beyond the enactment of these laws, and the impartial and due administration of them, the less legislators, and governors meddle with these people, the better for all the best interests of society. They dread litigation, knowing that human laws are a net of such texture that great ones can break through, little ones creep through, and the middle class alone are caught. New laws require new interpretations, and create a necessity for suits; and the most reflecting men, of the useful type here alluded to, look on the most plausible reforms with doubt and apprehension.

To the Protestant Church of England, the majority, in Ireland, of the class just mentioned, belong. The right of private judgment, and freedom of conscience, recognized and admitted by that Church, are congenial to them.

The domination and dogmas of men assuming to be a heaven-appointed, and an infallible hierarchy, they detest, and abhor; and this detestation and abhorrence are entirely and bitterly reciprocated by a hierarchy which assumes divine right and infallibility. The Church Establishment in Ireland gives not only protection and the means of religious worship, and congenial religious instruction, to this independent body of men, but attaches to them a countenance and prestige which attract and command the respect of their Roman Catholic neighbours, to which respect their intelligence, their energy, their orderly conduct, and their thrift entitle them, and are the foundation of that prestige. In localities where they are few, in comparison with the Roman Catholic population, the Protestant clergyman, with an income sufficient to maintain him in the respectable rank to which he properly belongs; the Church built and maintained from the property of what is called the Church Establishment; and the expenses of decent worship, defrayed from the same source, keep up the dignity of the smaller congregation, and protect them from the derision of the spiritual rulers of the multitude, to which, beyond all doubt, they would be exposed, if their clergyman, their Church, and their worship, were reduced to a beggarly scale, proportionate merely to their number. If, by confiscation of Church property, this reduction shall ever take place in this country, a class of men will be frowned down, who, even in the districts where their numbers are least, are now the most influential part of the population, for every purpose of national improvement. Asserting the right of private judgment; ignoring the doctrine that the poverty and suffering, in this life, which are consequent on sloth, ignorance, and want of thrift, constitute any title to retribution in the life to come, these men regard activity, knowledge, and thrift as duties; and they set an example which produces the most salutary effects; and, to some extent, counteracts the temporal bad effects of that lazy acquiescence in misery, produced by the assurance of future retribution in the life to come.

It is difficult to describe, and make intelligible to strangers, who know little of Ireland, the exact relations of this minority of Protestants to their Roman Catholic neighbours, and the feelings with which they and their neighbours reciprocally regard each other. In the last century, and beginning of the present, the line which separated them was much sharper, and was blackened with more ill-will and hatred than it is at present. It may be relied on as a fact, that, to nearly the end of the last century, it was not an uncommon thing, amongst the lower orders of Roman Catholics, to scrub the chair on which a Protestant visitor had sat, as soon as he left the house. No such monstrous feeling of aversion now exists, in any part of Ireland.

To sharpen, and to blacken with gall, the line of separation between Roman Catholics and Protestants, is the plain tendency, if it be not the purpose and object, of much of the agitation now carried on, under colour of redressing alleged grievances. This agitation is not regarded with favour by the educated, the reflecting, the intelligent, and, least of all, by the independent portion of the Roman Catholic people. They love, they cultivate, and they seek a friendly intercourse with the Protestants of their respective ranks. It is perfectly obvious, that this agitation is promoted chiefly by the Roman Catholic hierarchy; and that the great majority of the laymen, of any position, who join it, are dependent on the influence of this hierarchy for seats in Parliament, and other benefits, which that influence has power to bestow, operative, as it is, not merely downward, upon those who have votes, but, in the ascending line, upon those who exercise the patronage of the Government, to whatever party they belong. How much of the Irish difficulty emanates from the high bidding of leading statesmen of both parties, for the countenance and support of the Roman Catholic hierarchy, is a subject well worthy of inquiry.

The notion of appeasing, or mitigating this agitation, by concessions to it, is entirely visionary. Priestly power and uncontrolled domination are its purpose and object; and as long as one layman, who spurns and defies this domination, exists in the country, the hierarchy who claim it will have a grievance to complain of. The concession now in contemplation, and most ignorantly insisted on by some public writers and speakers in England as a tranquillizing measure for Ireland (viz. that of abolishing the Church Establishment in this country,) will not only encourage and stimulate this pernicious agitation, but will break down one of the strongest existing barriers against encroachments upon the natural and legitimate liberty of the Irish people, both Protestant and Roman Catholic. The Act of Parliament which shall command and accomplish the destruction of this barrier will not be a year in operation, when its bad effects on the peace and progress of Ireland will be as plain and evident, as the expected benefits from it are now obscure and unintelligible. But no one can prophesy all the possible, or even probable, effects of such an enactment.

The jargon by which this Institution is assailed, and asserted to be a grievance to Ireland, produces nothing but disgust in the mind of any man who knows the true condition of this country. It is no more a grievance to a Roman Catholic or a Presbyterian owner of a chargeable estate in land, to pay to the minister the tithe rent-charge, to which the old vexatious impost of tithe has been reduced, than it is to pay a head rent or rent-charge to a Protestant owner of it; or to pay quit-rent to support a Protestant throne; or to pay the same tithe rent-charge to a lay impropriator.

CHAPTER II.

ON THE CLAIM FOR A ROMAN CATHOLIC UNIVERSITY.

Another grievance loudly complained of by the Roman Catholic hierarchy, and their dependent associates, is the want of a purely Roman Catholic University, where Roman Catholics may obtain learned degrees, and distinctions of equal value with those now attainable only in our Protestant University. Nothing is more obvious than the forbearance of the very class of Roman Catholics assumed to be suffering from this grievance, from any participation in the cry for this new University. They do not, however, raise their voices in opposition to the cry for it ; and the cause of their silence, and apparent neutrality, is evident enough to those who know them, and know the circumstances which surround them.

Let a Roman Catholic University be once established in Ireland, and, from that hour, no Roman Catholic family will be at liberty, without offending the Roman Catholic hierarchy, to send its young members to the Protestant University. This they clearly foresee, and this they as certainly dread, and dislike.

The new University will be one of the most powerful agents in sharpening, and darkening that line of distinction between Protestants and Roman Catholics before alluded to. In this new University the Roman Catholic youth of this country, in the higher ranks, will be subjected to the sole teaching, to the religious discipline, and to the uncontrolled power and influence of the hierarchy, unchecked and unmitigated even by the presence of a Protestant fellow-student. What effect this will have, and how it will, of a certainty, propagate religious prejudice, and sectarian aversion and bigotry, can be no matter of doubt to any reflecting mind, whether of Roman Catholic or of Protestant. Many, if not all, the educated Roman Catholics see this, and dread it.

I passed through Trinity College five or six years before Catholic Emancipation. I had many Roman Catholic fellow-students. Nothing could be more friendly or sincere than the intercourse between these and their Protestant cotemporaries. Some of the warmest friendships I ever knew were then formed between Protestant and Roman Catholic students, friendships, too, some of which lasted until death put an end to them ; and some of them continue to the present hour. I say, with perfect truth, that I never knew one instance in which a Roman Catholic student was regarded as an inferior by any Protestant fellow-student, nor one instance in which any Roman Catholic had the least suspicion that he was so regarded on account of his religion. They attended lectures with their class-fellows ; competed for, and often obtained premiums and medals ; and left college well educated, and qualified for the profession of their choice. At the bar, many of them became distinguished men ; and when emancipated, in some instances, not few in proportion to the total number of Roman Catholic competitors, succeeded to the Bench. It is reasonable to presume that men educated, as here described, in harmonious and friendly union and intercourse with those who differed with them in religion, were better qualified to dispense impartial justice, in this mixed community, than they could possibly have been, coming from an exclusively Roman Catholic University.

Educated Roman Catholics of sagacity and foresight must, and do see the subject in this aspect of it. The power of annoyance, which the hierarchy have over them, and their unwillingness to offend those whom they consider it a duty to reverence, sufficiently account for their silence, and the reflections here suggested explain their absence from the ranks of the agitators.

It is, therefore, gravely to be considered, whether the concession of a charter, to establish an exclusively Roman Catholic University, will conduce to the freedom and the happiness of Roman Catholic families, to the tranquillity and peace of society, or to the moral improvement of any class in the community, or have any possible good effect upon the material interests of Ireland. Being a concession made to agitation, and above all, to clerical agitation, it cannot have any other effect upon the peace of the country, than that of increasing, and perpetuating this evil, under which all the best interests of the country have been, and still are, so extensively suffering.

For any other purpose than that of separating the Roman Catholic from the Protestant youth, during their collegiate course, there is no necessity, or even pretence of necessity, for a new University. It was some assumption, that the Protestant constitution and character of Trinity College raised an objection to it in the minds of Roman Catholics, that led to the creation of the Queen's

University, founded on the principle of perfect religious equality, and entire freedom from sectarian disabilities, and sectarian advantages. Three handsome buildings were erected in Cork, Belfast, and Galway, for the Colleges of this University. Governors, and Deputy Governors, Professors, and other learned functionaries were chosen, and appointed; a course of study was arranged, and everything practicable was done, to give an impetus and successful progress to this Institution.

So far as royal countenance and state power can confer estimation and current value upon Academical degrees and honours, the degrees and honours bestowed by this University have upon them the stamp of proper authority. Comparing the number of honours conferred, with the total number of students on the books of the University, it cannot be said that there was a niggardly measure of encouragement held out to diligence and exertion. If the honours represent positive, as well as comparative merit, the small number of unsuccessful competitors ought to constitute some evidence of progress, and be an effective attraction to the Colleges of this new University. Yet, it cannot be denied, that those who can afford to make choice, whether Protestant, Roman Catholic, or Presbyterian, prefer the ancient institution of Trinity College, notwithstanding the expense and the facility for obtaining honours deducible from the high ratio of successful candidates for honours in one, and the difficulty deducible from the very low ratio of them in the other, to the total number of students. But collegiate erudition, and the reputation consequent upon it, are plants of slow growth. No human power, without the aid of time, nor time itself, without proper cultivation, can bestow erudition upon a collegiate body.

The most powerful monarchs in Europe have found it impossible, unless in rare instances, to induce men of established fame for scientific and classical learning, to leave the institutions in which they acquired their reputation, and transfer their labours to a new University. Such men are generally far advanced into the vale of years, and much better suited to the guidance of the established course of education in their native college, and to the production of successors therein, worthy of its reputation, and competent to extend and perpetuate its fame, than to the work of arranging a new college, and of training an efficient staff, for the cultivation of learning in it.

Everything that money, royal countenance, and state patronage could accomplish, has been done for the Queen's University, in Ireland; and yet, when we estimate the results, and compare the educational powers of this new institution with those of the old University, the magnificent effort to raise it to eminence must, to any impartial mind, appear a failure; and a strong experimental proof of the principles before mentioned, derived from the nature of such establishments, and the historical experience already had of them.

The Fellows of Trinity College have been, for a long succession of years, elected from candidates encouraged to the contest by successful competition for honours in the undergraduate course. The ability, and known impartiality of the examiners, give full assurance to conscious merit, upon an investigation conducted in a theatre open to the public. The result is an all-sufficient staff of fully qualified men, for all purposes of Academical education.

There is a School of Divinity in Trinity College, and a professor for the instruction of those intended for the Protestant Church. There is also a School of Medicine and Surgery, with full means for anatomical study, and study in chemistry and botany, and qualified professors in all departments. There is a Law School; and professors of English and Civil Law. These are quite separate and distinct, not only from each other, but they are all distinct from, and entirely unconnected with the general course of education in the Arts, which undergraduates are required to learn, for whatever profession they may be intended, or to what religious persuasion soever they may belong. No Protestant student intended for the bar, or for the medical profession, thinks of attending the divinity lectures; and the notion of a Roman Catholic student attending them, or being in any manner affected by them, never enters the head of any one connected with the University. It is a danger just as remote from Roman Catholic students in Trinity College, as that arising to Protestants from the teaching of Roman Catholic doctrines in the College of Maynooth. Protestant students of the Church of England, and these alone, are required to attend a certain course of catechetical lectures in the College chapel, and they do so unheeded by other students. They are also bound to attend for worship in the same chapel, and other students resort to their several places of worship in town; and no colour of scandal or controversy has ever arisen from these arrangements.

Trinity College, it is truly said, is a Protestant institution; and it is so, in all practical aspects, only as regards its head, and the constitution of its truly liberal government. It is asked, why should Roman Catholics be left in the dilemma of being obliged to resort to it, Protestant as it is, or else lose the benefits of an University education? The same question may be as forcibly asked in respect of Presbyterians, Unitarians, Methodists, or any other dissenters from the Church of England; and the answer to the question will be equally pertinent to all; and that answer flows from the rational consideration of the many shades of religious opinion existing in the people of these islands; and the social wants, social arrangements, and social treatment made necessary by the existence of these various, and, in many points, conflicting opinions upon the subject of religion. The state policy suitable to a nation having one universal creed would be inpracticable in a community compounded of so many different religious sects.

The final result of all the contests, and all the mortal strife on this subject of religion, which heretofore deluged, not only Great Britain and Ireland with the blood of their inhabitants, but in like manner every other country in Christendom, now happily is, that universal toleration is not only sound state policy, at least in England, but has become there an imperative state necessity. If there was nothing more than an enforced toleration of each other, accomplished amongst these heretofore jarring, and fiercely warring elements, the result would be no other than a temporary truce; and established peace, and cordial social intercourse, would still be as distant as ever.

That those who embraced the reformed religion of England were the chief, and most efficient human agents in this final settlement of religious contests into toleration, and mutual forbearance, no one can, with the least semblance of truth or candour, deny, or even question. In the bloody wars and struggles, so far as these islands are concerned, theirs was the final and decisive victory; and to them alone resulted the power of quelling the pugnacity of other sects. That they, at all times, and in all places, and under all circumstances, used this power with perfect humanity, and moderation, I do not assert; nor is any such assertion a necessary premiss for any one conclusion at which I arrive. But after having established an exclusively Protestant Throne; after having attached to this Throne the Church of England, as a State Church; after reducing, no matter by what means, all other sects to a subordinate position, in which they were compelled, and are still compelled, to let each other live; this dominant power has, step by step, relaxed the fetters imposed upon the raging forefathers of the present generation, until every subject of their Protestant Throne is perfectly free to worship God according to conscience. No torture to scare, no bribes to seduce any one, of any sect, from the Church of his free choice, or the creed of his ancestors.

In the war which has terminated in this settled state of things, the Roman Catholic hierarchy, with the Pope at their head, were the great antagonists of this victorious, and now reigning body of Protestant men. This hierarchy now acknowledges temporal allegiance to our Protestant Throne; and submits to the laws of this Protestant Constitution; and it is not, for any argument of mine, necessary to inquire whether they do this from choice, or from compulsion.

That they are still the same organized and living body, with the same head, the same limbs, the same mind, the same opinions, the same claims to at least the spiritual government of mankind, founding these claims upon authority from Heaven, is so self-evident, that I confess my inability to find any proofs as clear as the proposition itself. The preamble to a resolution of the Roman Catholic Archbishops and Bishops of Ireland, to which I shall have occasion, on another topic, shortly to refer, makes this proposition so undeniable, that it is only necessary to read the terms of it to understand what it claims, viz.: Resolved,—" That, appointed, as we have been, by Divine Providence, to watch over, and preserve the deposit of Catholic faith in Ireland; and, responsible as we are to God for the souls of our flocks," &c. This divine commission, to watch over and preserve the deposit of faith, and this assumed responsibility to God for human souls, is, by the terms of this resolution, apparently restricted to Ireland. But it has been, at all times, construed by the Church which pretends to have it, as giving spiritual jurisdiction over the whole human race. Under this commission have been held all the inquisitions by which those who denied its authority were condemned to the rack and the fagot, and cruelly executed by thousands, in all parts of Christendom.

The repudiation of this pretended commission is the great distinctive and governing principle of Protestant men; and to restrain all exercise of temporal power, under pretence of it, is the salutary principle of Protestant Government, salutary no less to Roman Catholic subjects of that Government than to all others.

In those countries and times which prostituted the temporal power to enforce obedience to the spiritual authority usurped under pretence of this commission from Heaven, it was necessary to do something to reconcile the natural feeling of human beings to the horrible executions daily exhibited under its jurisdiction. The creation of social hatred and abhorrence towards recusants was the most obvious means to this end, and the expediency and necessity of segregation followed as a corollary, and prohibition of social intercourse was a consequential policy.

Under the free and tolerant Protestant Government of England, good will and brotherly love amongst subjects of all creeds are the feelings most conducive to every end and every purpose of the Sovereign. To promote, and, by every means, to encourage social intercourse and reciprocal good offices amongst the members of different sects, must be, and is the true policy of such a Government. Everything tending to diminish this friendly intercourse, or to throw difficulties in the way of it, runs counter to this benevolent policy. That denominational schools, and denominational universities have this tendency to obstruct intercourse between the youth of different persuasions and creeds, in the rising generation, is obvious, and they thus operate most powerfully in opposition to the conciliating policy of the tolerant Government, and act with equal force in furtherance of the segregating policy of those who would reduce all mankind to surrender the care of their souls to those who assert this divine right to take charge of them.

It is no answer to say, that Trinity College is denominational, being Protestant. So the English Throne and Government are Protestant; and, as yet, essentially Protestant, as every lover of liberty and peace hopes they will continue to be. As such, this may be called a denominational Sovereignty and Government; but it is the only denomination as yet found able and willing to dispense, with perfect impartiality, the blessings of toleration and protection to all subjects, regardless of their creeds.

In exact analogy to this Government, Trinity College, with its Protestant Provost, its Protestant Board and Governors, and Protestant clerical Fellows, was established, and still flourishes in full vitality. Governed by the laws which a Protestant Legislature has enacted, and the regulations, habits, and practice which have emanated from free, tolerating, and liberal Protestant minds and principles, it has become an institution most favourably, if not affectionately, regarded by all classes, and well qualified as a helpmate to this Government for the reception, the liberal education, and the training to humanity and social virtue of its pupils, according to the universal and eternal principles of right and wrong, without tampering with, and wholly regardless of, their different creeds. Within its walls they can meet, and for long years have been meeting, in constantly reciprocated feelings of friendship and collegiate association, and in pursuit of knowledge equally useful to, and equally desired by all.

The Protestant Governor of this National University is selected by the Government, whose ruling principle is peace and toleration; and, as far as my memory for over fifty years extends, the power of selection has been wisely, and consistently exercised. The present head of this great Institution stands, in the eyes of Europe, a conspicuous instance of the right man in the right place; and his father, with like reputation, filled the same place.

This University, and its reputation, are now the growth of 275 years. The degrees and honours conferred by it have, in public estimation, a value which no sovereign, no legislature, no power under Heaven, can attach to degrees and honours of the same denomination, however bestowed by any newly-created Univer sity. The competition for fellowships, and the public and scrutinizing examination by which the contest for them is determined, are well known. Long and universally known as they have been, they have created a traditional respect and prestige, which nothing but time and merit can bestow.

Let any one who has lived in the University of Dublin, or in one of the old English Universities; or any one familiarly acquainted with their academical discipline, their studies, and their joyous sports, and friendly intercourse, pay a visit to any one of the colleges of the modern University, and candidly describe the chilling effect of everything that he sees, and of the many things which he cannot see, because they do not exist.

Good and useful lectures may be, and, I believe, are given in them, and any diligent and apt student, by study at home, if his home be near, or in the lodging which he hires in the town, may profit by the lectures, and may obtain distinction at a competitive examination in London; but that his degree in the Arts is equally prized as a like degree conferred by one of the old Universities, few, I think, will assert.

The magnificent and all-sufficient scale upon which the educational arrangements have been made and conducted in the old seat of learning; the known erudition and scientific attainments of its governors and teachers; the facility with which ancillary instruction and aid can be there obtained; the ample accommodation afforded to resident students; the mild and humanizing discipline to which the pupils are subjected; and the calm and firm dignity with which collegiate laws are administered, upon the assumption, that a ready obedience is to be expected, as of course, from gentlemen who are too proud to deserve, or to provoke even a rebuke; these and many other attractions peculiar to the ancient University of Dublin have secured to it the unhesitating preference over any newly created college, wherever the power of free choice exists.

That it is perfectly adequate to the demands of the country, is capable of demonstration. At the end of the long war in 1815, a great number of youths, who had contemplated a military life, were suddenly directed towards the professions, and after two or three years devoted to necessary preparation, they entered college in great and unusual numbers; and no difficulty was found in the enlargement of its capacity for the reception and accommodation of all who demanded, and were qualified for entrance. There is, therefore, and there was, no necessity for any new University; and it was not, and is not, in the power of the Government to create anything but a puny rival to the ancient establishment which exists, all-sufficient as it is.

Although the majority, and a large majority, of the whole people of Ireland are Roman Catholics ; this is not the case if we confine the division to the ranks which alone supply candidates for collegiate education. A very large majority of these belong to the Church of England, and other Protestant communities. By the statutes of the College, a certain number of the Fellows should be clergymen : a smaller number are allowed to be laymen. At present there are ten lay Fellows, of whom two are on the Board, as senior Fellows. I believe ten lay Fellows transgresses the legal limit. The greater number of the scholars are undergraduates, and scarcely any enter the Church before their scholarship expires. Some duties connected with religious worship in the College chapel are performed by scholars, and a sufficient number of these must, therefore, be of the Church of England. The number required for these duties does not exceed six, whereas the total number of scholars on the foundation is seventy, to which nine newly created scholarships have been added. If to the present number some lay Fellowships were added, and if all the scholarships and lay Fellowships were open to candidates of all creeds, without preference or distinction, there would still be a sufficient number secured of clerical Fellows, and successful Protestant candidates, in the contest for lay Fellowships and Scholarships, to secure a substantially Protestant government for the College, and Protestant scholars sufficient for discharge of religious duties. This would give a liberal share of the temporal advantages to

Roman Catholics and dissenters of ability to compete successfully for them.

Still it is objected, that this would not raise Roman Catholics and dissenters to an exact religious, however it may to an academical equality with the Protestants; and it is insisted that until such equality shall be established, Ireland will have a grievance to complain of. Under a monarchy and constitution essentially Protestant, it should not, for one moment, be admitted, that a Protestant government for the Universities, liberally and impartially conducted, as it has been, and as it is conducted in Trinity College, can possibly be a grievance, or anything resembling a grievance, to any class of subjects whatever.

If it be once admitted that such a Protestant constitution of the Universities inflicts the grievance of inequality, and disparagement on other sects, it will be impossible to deny, that a similar, and in all respects an equally disparaging grievance, is inflicted by exclusion of all but Protestants from the throne; from the Privy Council, and from offices necessarily reserved for the maintenance of a Protestant throne, and Protestant constitution. The claim of equality, pushed to this extent, is nothing less than a demand upon victorious Protestant men to surrender the victory obtained by their ancestors; and the power of enforcing toleration, and maintaining rational liberty, transmitted to them by those ancestors, a power which for over forty years has been not merely impartially, but liberally exercised. If such a surrender be made, it will, most assuredly, be followed, sooner or later, by battles and bloodshed, and by a revival of the horrors of past centuries.

It would be injustice to the memory of the men who expelled James II., and excluded his posterity from the throne, to suppose that his religious creed, theologically considered, was the motive to that revolution. It was because that creed bound and subjected him to the Papal hierarchy, and because the Papal hierarchy was not, and it was believed, could not be tolerant, that the men who repudiated the pretensions of that hierarchy expelled the hereditary sovereign who acknowledged and submitted to its supremacy; and, as a consequence of that submission, had prostituted the organized force of the nation, placed under his command, to enforce a like submission from his subjects, in derogation of national liberty, and in violation of the rights of conscience.

It was not because of his creed, theologically considered, that the same men invited William of Orange to fill the vacant throne. The Church of England Protestants, in whose hands the power then was, dissented from what they knew to be the religious creed of the sovereign so selected by them. It was because he, and the clergy, whose religious instruction and doctrines he respected, did not pretend to any "appointment by Divine Providence, to guard the deposit of faith on earth; or to any responsibility to God for the souls of their fellow-men," that he was chosen as a monarch qualified to govern a free nation of subjects widely dissenting from each other, on the topic of religion. He was the successor, and the worthy and faithful representative of William the Silent, whose life had been gloriously passed, and finally sacrificed, in the contest with the Papal hierarchy, and their cruel and bigoted tool who filled the throne of Spain. That contest was not founded on any theological question of orthodoxy. It was a life and death struggle for the great principle of universal toleration, and liberty of conscience, against the Papal hierarchy, and its pretended commission from Heaven to impose shackles on the human race, and on the freedom of human intellect, under pretence of responsibility to God for the souls of mankind, as precious treasure committed to their charge.

The Revolution of 1688 was effected by the men who had repudiated this enslaving pretension, and had waged successful war against those who had admitted it, and had prostituted the civil power to maintain it. In assertion of this Papal assumption, the King of Spain slaughtered by the sword, and cruelly tortured and burned 100,000 of his subjects in the Netherlands, guilty of nothing but the manly assertion of rational liberty, in opposition to tyrannical and debasing bigotry. By the attempt to force this same Papal assumption on his revolting subjects, James II. lost his throne. To guard the nation permanently against this tyrannical assumption, that vacant throne was offered to, and was filled by William of Orange, for no other reason than that he was the most conspicuous, and the most resolute opponent then existing in Europe, of the Papal hierarchy, and of the villanizing principle which they asserted.

It is against this principle that the congregations of the English Church persistently protest. To guard the Throne from the intrusion of this odious pretension of the Papal hierarchy, the coronation oath of the sovereign is administered. Yet in the face of these historical records, fresh in the recollection of every educated British subject, the Papal hierarchy boldly come forward, and, with the most astonishing plainness, in unequivocal terms, address the Government of England thus established, and say: "Appointed, as we have been, by Divine Providence, to watch over and preserve the deposit of Catholic faith in Ireland; and, responsible, as we are, to God for the souls of our flocks," we demand a charter for establishing, and an endowment for supporting, an University, in which to propagate this our doctrine, and in which to enforce this our divine right upon the minds of educated and wealthy Roman Catholic youths in Ireland, subjects though they be of this recusant Protestant Constitution and Government of England, whose principle is, freedom of conscience, repudiation of this our asserted commission and authority from Heaven, and whose policy is, the promotion of friendly and humanizing social intercourse amongst all its subjects, of every creed, and the discouragement of everything which may prevent or obstruct that happy intercourse. We, the Roman Catholic hierarchy, with the Pope at our head, for and on behalf of the Irish Roman Catholic gentry, whose title to social liberty the Government admits, whose right to religious equality all liberal orators proclaim, now demand the erection of a closely-fenced and well protected fold, in which to segregate our own flock, and there to teach them what a damnable thing it is to deny the divine right and claim of the infallible Church to take charge of all human souls, and to prescribe proper limits within which to exercise the human intellect. Our lambs and their parents are aggrieved by the liberty of associating in collegiate amity with their fellow-subjects, who deny and repudiate our divine right; and we therefore demand a redress of this grievance, by the erection and fortification of this fold, into which the youths of Roman Catholic gentry may be driven, and in which they may be protected from contamination by continuing to associate with Protestant friends, and Protestant class-fellows.

This is the plain, undisguised statement of an Irish grievance, and of the remedy for it suggested to, and demanded from, the English Legislature and English Sovereign.

I imagine that I hear some of my old class-fellows, with whom, nearly half a century ago, I associated and contracted a friendship, which I value to the present hour, blurting out, with alarm at this clerical intercession for the redress of a grievance which they never felt, and which they do not believe that their sons will ever feel—" Oh, save us from our pastors ! Do not, ye Protestant governors of this free nation, lend your aid to the erection of this prison for our sons. Assist not in the establishment of an intolerant school in derogation of all the principles of toleration and liberty which you and your forefathers professed ; in assertion of which they exposed, and often sacrificed their lives; the establishment of which has given to our age the enjoyment of a full measure of rational liberty, and uncontrolled freedom of conscience; the recognition of the right to which blessings by your statesmen too loquaciously expressed, has suggested and encouraged this most unnecessary and mischievous demand, made by our pastors without our concurrence or assent.

If any of the Roman Catholic gentry of Ireland be blind to this view of the subject, I most sincerely pray, that they and their posterity may not soon be exposed to a painful lesson in the dear school of experience.

The influence of the Roman Catholic clergy over the minds of the wealthy and educated portion of their congregations is not, I do believe, greater than that of religious instructors and diligent well-conducted pastors ought to be. But the power which they have over the minds and religious fears of the poor and illiterate, who form the great multitude of their flocks, gives them temporal power also over those who are above the influence of superstitious terrors. The prostitution of this clerical influence to party and electioneering purposes has provoked competition for the countenance and favour of the Roman Catholic hierarchy amongst leading statesmen of all parties. This has given that hierarchy a dogmatical control, and dictatorial power over every Ministry, which operates most injuriously on the peace of the country, by exciting and keeping up a never-ceasing agitation against the stability of the laws and institutions of the realm. The Ministry, who have no hope of obtaining their active co-operation and support, still expect, by professions of respect, often degenerating into flattery, to mollify and soften the violence of their opposition. Concessions are made, when great public interests would be served, and peace would be promoted by a firm denial of attention to unreasonable demands. Those who hold seats in Parliament, subject to the power of this clerical body, must be an united and campacted force, sufficient, in the equilibrium of English parties, to turn the scale, and thus to assume an importance in the discussion of political questions disproportioned to their abilities or just pretensions.

How many of the factitious grievances of Ireland emanate from this source, and are forced upon the attention of the English public, and are made the subject of barren discussions in the legislative assemblies; how many of the real wants and grievances of the country are, by this system of misrepresentation, unnoticed and unredressed, may form a subject worthy of inquiry, preparatory to a measure of practically useful reform for Ireland. No one can witness those elections, wherein the landlords are marshalled on one side, and the Roman Catholic clergy on the other, without deploring the demoralizing effects of such contests, and without being sensible of the utter indifference of the result, as regards the true interests of the nation. I cannot believe that the Roman Catholic gentry of Ireland desire to see this power and influence of their clergy augmented. The influence which they already have, being thus abused for sectarian, and for party purposes, after a fashion which every man of cultivated mind, who values the peace and social happiness of the community, must censure and condemn. It is on behalf of these gentry, and their posterity, that a charter is solicited by the ultramontane hierarchy, to propagate upwards a power and influence, which at present press only on the lower classes of the people. I have in vain looked for any expression of a desire for such a charter emanating from the Roman Catholic gentry themselves.

Whatever ingenuity may be exercised in concealing the sacerdotal nature of this contemplated institution, and by the admixture of laymen, or other contrivance, painting a complexion of healthy constitutional liberty upon it, the practical effect of it will remain unmitigated, and unaffected. It will be a separate and distinct school to which Roman Catholic youths will be driven; in which prejudice against Protestant principles and British institutions will be propagated, unobserved, and apart from all control; a school in which the growing freedom of intellect will be repressed and shackled, by a discipline hardly tolerable in the dark ages in which it was invented, and over which the English monarchy will have no more power of supervision or correction, than it has over the congregation of the Propaganda at Rome.

It is not possible to conceive anything more antagonistic, in all points, than this University must be to the policy of a tolerant and paternal government, by which it aims at the social fusion of all its subjects into one compacted mass of national union, national strength, and national prosperity. This is quite evidently a movement, suggested by thirst after priestly power; and intended to counteract the effect of collegiate association in restraining the growth of that power within proper limits. The grant of this charter is palpably a retrograde step, leading directly to the revival of fading prejudices, and evanescing antipathies.

CHAPTER III.

NATIONAL EDUCATION.

Another grievance, which occasions much of the clamour and outcry of our time, is the system of education pursued in what are called the National Schools of Ireland. This grievance is distinguished from all others, in this, that the clergy of the three great sects, each in their turn, rail at it. The Roman Catholic clergy who, in the three southern provinces, and in little less than two-thirds of all the schools, have it very nearly all their own way, are still much dissatisfied with it, and proclaim it as one of their grievances. The Protestant clergy of the Established Church are indignant, and, many of them, highly disgusted at it; and occasional strong remonstrances against some of the proceedings of the Board, either taken or threatened, are expressed by the Presbyterian ministers.

This institution is maintained at a great national expense; and the cost of supporting it is taken from the fund created by the general taxation of all subjects, whatever may be their religious persuasions. This would seem to give it a good title to be, in fact, as it is in name, a National Institution. To be such, and truly such, it ought to be equally accessible to the children of all who contribute to support it.

No parent, whatever may be his opinions on the subject of religion, should get any fair or just reason for objecting to send his children to this National School.

The clergy and teachers of every form of Christianity, require from their disciples a profession of implicit belief in the truth of the doctrine which they teach. Many of them insist upon the public avowal of this belief at every congregation for worship; and some peculiar solemnity, expressive of earnest conviction, is commonly used in making this avowal. The religious obligation sincerely to entertain this belief is enforced by the hopes, and the fears resulting from the contemplation of a future state; and the profession of it, whether sincere or not, is suggested, if not exacted, by the more immediate, and, therefore, more effective consequences to temporal interests. The clergy of every Christian sect impress on the minds of their congregations the necessity for an unreserved and unqualified profession of belief in the truth of their religion. All spiritual teachers agree in this, that truth is an essential attribute of every religion, which it is allowable to teach; and that some evils, temporal or eternal, if not both temporal and eternal, must inevitably fall upon the believers in a false religion. The innocence of error is not admitted by the clergy of any sect. The teachers of false doctrine are by all denounced as leading their votaries to perdition.

Of all forms of Pagan worship, practised throughout the Roman Empire, when it extended over the civilized world, a great historian said, "that by the people they were regarded as equally true; by the philosophers as equally false; and by the magistrates as equally useful." It followed that, not only toleration, but religious concord, as a general rule, prevailed over the Pagan world.

This cannot be said of any two forms of Christianity, if the truth of one be inconsistent with the truth of the other. It follows, that, although we may have toleration, we cannot have concord. The teachers of every system, if they be sincere, must regard the teachers of all other systems, inconsistent with the truth of their own, as workers of mischief to their misguided followers. To the ignorance of these followers, whatever sect they belong to, what is called blind devotion to a false religion is attributed by the clergy of other persuasions. Therefore all religious teachers, however contradictory of each other their doctrines may be, concur, unanimously, in the utility of, if not the necessity for, a sound system of early instruction, to enlighten the mind of the rising generation, comprehending the youth of all persuasions. They will probably, if not quite certainly, concur in admitting the necessity for a sound system of instruction; and they will concur in this admission before they approach the consideration of the important question, what that system must be, which deserves to be termed a sound system of instruction.

One might reasonably expect, in this enlightened age, that no clergy of any sect would, in a civilized community of the present day, assert that true knowledge, in any useful branch of learning, or of science, could have the effect of destroying or weakening the proofs of any true religion. No teacher of any creed would assert that learning to speak correctly, learning to read and write with ease and correctness, learning to use the elementary rules of arithmetic, and to calculate correctly, according to them, could be dangerous to religious faith, no matter what that faith may be. With one who could make such an assertion, I decline all attempts to reason.

A man may be a learned theologian, and an excellent teacher of religion; and yet be an indifferent, or incompetent teacher of the rudiments of common science. There is no connexion between the boy's school task and his catechism. While he is learning his lesson from the schoolmaster, there is no necessity for the presence of his spiritual instructor, if all danger be removed that the schoolmaster will tamper with his faith. But if the clergy of any denomination have a title to be present at the school lessons; if they have any right to direct what those lessons shall be; if any amount of religious instruction is to be, in any way, combined with the course of instruction, in the school to which children of different creeds are expected to resort, then, at once, arises, to the clergy of each denomination, the duty of guarding against attempts to proselytize.

It has hitherto been found impossible, and it will, to the end of time, be impossible to get the clergy of the different sects to agree as to the nature and amount of the religious instruction which all will consent to combine with the school lessons. This will clearly appear from the experiments already made.

On the 4th of June, 1824, a commission was issued to five Commissioners, to inquire into the nature and extent of the instruction afforded by the several institutions in Ireland, established for the purpose of education. These Commissioners made their first Report on the 30th of May, 1825, in which they appear to have been unanimous. To this Report is appended a full statement of the evidence on which it is founded.

Two fundamental principles were adopted by the Commissioners, and steadily adhered to from the commencement to the end of their labours.

First, that no system could, or ought to obtain general and cordial support in Ireland, which should not, in addition to elementary knowledge of a literary character, afford the opportunity of religious instruction to persons of all persuasions (p. 91).

Two corollaries resulted from this proposition, viz., First, the necessity for introducing the Scriptures into all institutions for the education of the people, as a fundamental part of the instruction (p. 98). Secondly, the necessity for compiling a volume from the four Gospels, in the manner which the Commissioners adverted to in their conference with the Roman Catholic Archbishops, adding certain portions of the Pentateuch.

The second fundamental principle was, that such a system should be established, as should unite children of all religious denominations in the same schools, except when it should become unavoidably necessary to separate them for the purpose of religious instruction, (p. 95).

They considered this a point of great importance to the interests of the State, as it was only by training the youth of all persuasions in habits of early intercourse and attachment, that they could hope to establish among them those reciprocal charities upon which the peace and harmony of society must depend. With this principle every reflecting, charitable man must agree, its incompatibility with their first principles, when applied to Ireland, remained to be proved by experience. Without attentively perusing the first, second, and ninth Reports of the

Commissioners, it is impossible adequately to estimate the labour, the ability, the imperturbable temper, the unflinching firmness, yet, the delicate deference to the opinions and prejudices of men over whom they had no control, with which they proceeded—their untiring efforts to mollify the antipathies, and to reconcile the differences of those who had the power of promoting, or of defeating the objects of their inquiry, are evident in every step which they took. In short, those Commissioners performed the great and important duties imposed upon them, with a diligence and impartiality which cannot be too highly estimated. With incalculable labour, they compiled three ponderous volumes, which may at all times be confidently resorted to, as an abundant, and an authentic source of information, on the subject of education in Ireland.

When their first Report was made, on the 30th of May, 1825, and the system of education thereby recommended was practically considered, and the difficulties of carrying it into execution contemplated, the Government found it necessary to solicit from the Commissioners, a continuation of their labours, in accomplishing the work which yet remained to be done, of constructing a system, such as would secure some practical benefit from what they had already performed.

This request was communicated by Mr. Goulburn (the then Secretary for Ireland) in a letter of the 28th November, 1825. They were, by that letter, informed that Parliament had placed at his Excellency's disposal what were considered to be ample funds for the commencement of the experiment, which the Commissioners had recommended, viz., to institute by way of trial a certain number of schools, on the system which they had devised. The difficulty of selecting individuals properly qualified for the duty of framing regulations for the conduct of such schools, was urged as a reason for asking the Commissioners to undertake that task.

The Commissioners readily undertook this new duty, and their ninth Report, made on the 2nd of June, 1827, is an enduring record of the skill and perseverance with which they, for fourteen months, laboured to perform it; and it is also a clear and able exposition of the difficulties which they found insurmountable, and by which all their efforts were made abortive.

Adhering to the first of the two fundamental principles before stated, they called upon the bishops and clergy of the Established Church, and on those of the Roman Catholic hierarchy, to agree in the compilation of a volume from the sacred Scriptures, which all would allow to be read in mixed schools, without objection. The correspondence, and the evidence on this subject, set forth in the third volume of the Reports, afford ample proof of the labour, the ability, the candour, and the perfect honesty and sincerity with which the Commissioners endeavoured to accomplish this preliminary, and apparently simple portion of their task. That *they* failed in overcoming this first obstacle should have been taken as a conclusive demonstration, that the task itself was impossible.

At a meeting of the Roman Catholic Archbishops and Bishops, held on the 21st of January, 1826, resolutions had been passed, and they had been transmitted to the Commissioners, and a copy of them had also come to the hands of the Lord Primate. The sixth of these resolutions was in the following terms :—

"6. RESOLVED,—That appointed, as we have been, by Divine Providence, to watch over and preserve the deposit of Catholic faith in Ireland; and, responsible, as we are, to God for the souls of our flocks, we will, in our respective dioceses, withhold our concurrence and support from any system of education which will not fully accord with the principles expressed in the foregoing resolutions."

By the second of these resolutions it was resolved, that the master should be a Roman Catholic, appointed upon the recommendation, or with the express approval of, the Roman Catholic Bishop of the diocese, in each school in which the majority of pupils should be Roman Catholics ; and, where these were a minority, the master should have a Roman Catholic assistant, chosen in like manner. There was no suggestion of a Protestant assistant for the minority in the schools for which they insisted on a Roman Catholic master.

In a letter from the Lord Primate to the Commissioners, dated 28th of August, 1826, commenting on these resolutions, the views of the Primate and Protestant clergy are thus expressed:—

"I have already expressed an opinion in my former letter, and I do not think it too much to repeat it now, that the State, and particularly a State like ours, in which so much depends upon public feeling, has an immediate interest in the moral and social principles of all its members; that this interest gives it a right, or rather imposes upon it an obligation, of providing a system of national instruction ; and that the trust of superintending this system is most consistently reposed in an Established clergy. Circumstances would guide me in determining the degree in which the clergy should be ostensibly engaged in this superintendence; but no circumstances could induce me to sacrifice the rights of the Church, or the future prospects of the nation, by an entire surrender of it. I should therefore feel it my duty to object to any plan of national education in which the co-operation of the clergy, in preparing books, visiting schools, and overseeing the teachers, was pointedly excluded. I have seen many reasons to believe, that the Roman Catholic hierarchy have similar views of the rights of their order, and that they claim to themselves, as the true Church, what I consider due to the Established Church from its union with the State."

In support of this last proposition, His Grace referred to the resolutions of the Roman Catholic prelates, before mentioned, and transmitted a copy of them to the Commissioners, with his letter, not knowing that the Commissioners had got them before.

Thus the Commissioners had before them a claim by the Roman Catholic hierarchy of the right (founded on a commission from heaven) of superintending the education of the children in the schools, expressed in the most unequivocal terms, and insisted on with dogmatical resolution ; and, at the same time, they had this right claimed by the Established clergy, in equally clear and positive terms, and pressed with a determination no less resolute, supported by the law of the land.

It requires but little reflection on the subject, even in the absence of experiment, to convince any reasoning mind that agreement and concord amongst the clergy of different persuasions, in any system of united education, in mixed schools, is impossible. The first suggestion of an effort to accomplish such a purpose was made in the fourteenth and last Report of the Commissioners who were appointed in 1806 to inquire into the subject of education in Ireland. They, in that Report, made in 1812, stated "that they had applied their efforts to the framing of a system which, whilst it should afford the opportunities of education to every description of the lower classes of the people, might, at the same time, by keeping clear of all interference with the particular religious tenets of any, induce the whole to receive its benefits, as one undivided body, under one and the same system, and in the same establishments."

After stating their confident expectation that such a plan would be cordially accepted by those to whom it should be presented, "if all interference with the particular religious tenets of those who are to receive such instruction should, in the first instance, be unequivocally disclaimed, and effectually guarded against," they add, "We conceive this to be of essential importance in any new establishments for the education of the lower classes in Ireland; and we venture to express our unanimous opinion, that no such plan, however wisely and unexceptionally contrived, in other respects, can be carried into effectual execution, in this country, unless it be explicitly avowed, and clearly understood, as its leading principle, that no attempt shall be made to influence or disturb the peculiar religious tenets of any sect or description of Christians."

After suggesting the appointment of a Board to carry this new system into execution, they expressed their "confident persuasion, that in such selection of bo oks as they recommended, it would be found practical to introduce, not only a number of books in which moral principles should be inculcated in such a manner as is likely to make deep and lasting impressions on the youthful mind, but also ample extracts from the Sacred Scriptures themselves, an early acquaintance with which it deems of the utmost importance, and indeed indispensable, in forming the mind to just notions of duty, and sound principles of conduct; and that the study of such a volume of extracts from the Sacred Writings, would form the best preparation for that more particular religious instruction, which it would be the duty and inclination of their several ministers of religion to give, at proper times, and in other places, to the children of their respective congregations."

A voluntary association had been formed in 1811, under the name of "The Society for Promoting the Education of the Poor of Ireland." The Committee of this Society was composed of gentlemen of various religious persuasions. They promoted the establishment of schools, of which the governors and teachers should be chosen without religious distinction, and pupils of all creeds be admitted. In these schools the Bible was to be read, but without note or comment, by such of the scholars as were suitably advanced in reading. All catechisms and books of controversy were excluded.

In 1814 the Government, conceiving that this was a Society already formed on the principle which had been so confidently recommended by the Commissioners in 1812, made a grant to it of £6980, which the Society applied in obtaining a site for a Model School, and in erecting the building at Kildare-place, to which they removed in 1817; and the system so adopted by them got the name of the Kildare-place System; and the association was called the Kildare-place Society. Annual grants were continued to it, until 1831, when, having been accused of departing from the original principle of total abstinence from all tampering with religious convictions, the support and confidence of Government were withdrawn from it.

In October, 1831, Lord Stanley, the then Chief Secretary for Ireland, addressed a letter to the Duke of Leinster, stating the intention of Government to constitute a Board for the superintendence of National Education in Ireland, of which the Duke, with his consent, should be the president: and the letter sets out an elaborate programme of the rules and principles according to which the Institution was to be conducted. A Board was accordingly elected, with the Duke at its head. Dr. Whately, then Archbishop of Dublin, Dr. Murray, the Roman Catholic Archbishop, Dr. Sadleir, a Senior Fellow of Trinity College, Mr. Carlile, a Presbyterian Minister in Dublin, Mr. Anthony R. Blake, the Chief Remembrancer of the Court of Exchequer in Ireland, a Roman Catholic, and Mr. Robert Holmes, a lawyer of the first eminence, and, I believe, an Unitarian, but of whose manly and upright character, and high moral principles, no Irishman of any class or creed had, or could have, any doubt. The Board has since been kept up by the addition of new members, not only to fill vacancies caused by death and resignation, but to supplement its number, as occasion seemed to require. In selecting persons for this important office, every Government appears to have carefully acted on the principle of having every sect and every party fully and fairly represented.

From the day it was constituted to the present, I have never seen reason to doubt that this body has faithfully and anxiously laboured to attain the objects proposed, according to the spirit and intention of the government programme originally framed for their guidance. That they have been in turn assailed by every sect and every party; that they have had to defend themselves from calumnies and false imputations, is sufficiently notorious.

To remove suspicion, and create general confidence, it was thought necessary to place on the Board men of conflicting opinions, both on the subject of religion and politics. That a Board so constituted should be unanimous in all, or even in many of their proceedings, could not reasonably be expected. But what differences of opinion existed; what discussions, what divisions and disagreements took place; what concessions and compromises were made; and what subjects were abandoned, or never discussed, in despair of a decision, in this mixed body, in the course of their proceedings, no one can know who was not present at their meetings.

That disagreement, bordering on discord, sometimes occurred, may be fairly inferred from resignations and other facts which, from time to time, became public. Yet the fundamental principles before mentioned were adhered to, and, accordingly, religious instruction was combined with the course of literary education adopted in the schools, and the utmost care was taken from time to time in framing and amending rules to prevent the perversion of it to the disturbance of pre-existing convictions.

Such rules were accordingly published, and from time to time, modified, by which the option was allowed to all children to accept or to decline the religious portion of the course; and to give an opportunity of exercising this option, notice was to be given a sufficient time before Scripture reading, and religious instruction should commence, to enable every pupil who did not desire to receive it to leave the school. When Protestant doctrine was about to be taught, it was expected that Roman Catholics would depart; and when Roman Catholic instruction was announced, it was, of course, assumed that Protestants would leave the school.

Religious instruction was thus introduced in deference to the opinion, "that no system of education could or ought to obtain general support, which should not, in addition to elementary knowledge of a literary character, afford an opportunity of religious instruction to persons of all persuasions." The warning notice was given to remove all apprehension of attempts to proselytize, and to render the schools, if not attractive, at least unobjectionable to the youth of all persuasions.

The first obvious effect of this warning was to separate religious from secular instruction, as completely, and as effectually, as if it were imparted at a different time, and in a place at a distance from the school, suppose on Sunday, or some other day, in the church, or other place appointed for the purpose.

In a school attended by children of only one persuasion, the utility and convenience of combining spiritual instruction with some of the literary lessons, is easily understood, and such a combination would certainly be generally approved. But in the mixed schools of Ireland, the experiment of the National Schools, if an experiment were necessary, has proved this kind of united instruction to be distasteful to all parties, and it is admitted to be impracticable.

Another effect of the warning notice, not quite so obvious, but equally certain, is the impression which it must make upon the susceptible minds of children. Take a school in which, perhaps, three-fourths of the pupils are Roman Catholics. When the Protestant catechism, and reading of the Bible is announced, the Roman Catholic children are sure to be under a strict injunction to vanish from the school, as from a place in which heretical doctrines leading to perdition, are about to be taught. Can they, at that moment, when starting from their seats, exclude from their minds and memory those questions and answers, in their own catechism, which were quoted by the Lord Primate in his letter to the Commissioners 28th August, 1826, and printed at page 17 of their 9th Report, viz. :—

"*Question.* Is there but one true Church?

"*Answer.* Although there be many sects there is but one true religion, and one true Church.

"*Q.* Why is there but one true Church?

"*A.* As there is but one true God, there can be but one true Church.

"*Q.* How do you call the true Church?

"*A.* The Roman Catholic Church.

"*Q.* Are all obliged to be of that true Church?

"*A.* Yes.

"*Q.* Why are all obliged to be of that true Church?

"*A.* Because none can be saved out of it.

"*Q.* How many ways are there of sinning against faith?

"*A.* Chiefly three.

"*Q.* What are those three ways?

"*A.* First, by not seeking to know what God has taught; secondly, by not believing what God has taught, &c.

"*Q.* Who are they who do not believe what God has taught?

"*A.* Heretics and infidels."

To say that Protestants do not come within the category of heretics, in the minds and understanding of those who learn this catechism, is to deny a manifestly self-evident proposition. In what light, therefore, must these Roman Catholic children view those who remain behind them for instruction in the tenets of one of those many sects who belong not to the one and only true Church, except as heretics doomed to perdition? It is impossible to conceal from the Protestant children this feeling and opinion of their Roman Catholic school-fellows; they are well aware of its existence. The flight from the school is an unequivocal expression of it, perfectly understood by the Protestant children. These naturally and necessarily resent it. The operation of daily severing the two classes, by this warning notice, deepens these sad and dismal impressions on the minds of both, and effectually defeats what the Commissioners considered of such importance to the interests of the State, viz., "training the youth of all persuasions in habits of early intercourse and attachment, in the hope of establishing among them those reciprocal charities upon which the peace and harmony of society must depend." Pity is the only charitable feeling with which Roman Catholic children can regard their Protestant school-fellows, when leaving them behind, to learn heretical doctrines, by which they are to be excluded from salvation. The reciprocal feeling of the Protestant children, in self-defence, will also be pity, for what they are sure to consider as ignorant bigotry and superstition, and this sort of pity is not as nearly allied to charity as the other ; it must evidently be much more akin to contempt, than to charity.

To bring children of these different persuasions together in the morning, and thus to sever them in the afternoon, creates an intercourse not leading to attachment, but to reciprocal contempt, hatred, and all uncharitableness; and the effects produced by it must be, and are, diametrically opposite to those desired and intended by the institution of mixed schools. The parents and the clergy of both persuasions, knowing that the doctrines to which they are opposed, are to be taught in the schools, and that a warning notice is to be given, are quite sure to send their children carefully armoured with sectarian prejudices, and bound by injunctions to fly the moment the warning is given ; and thus the salutary effect of meeting under the same roof, learning from the same teacher lessons upon subjects in which they hold no conflicting opinions, and the knowledge of which must be the common object of their pursuit, is most sadly and certainly defeated. So to meet in the morning, so to bestow their undivided attention during the day, and to break up all together in the evening, and be turned out to play, without being reminded that their creeds are different, must and would mitigate antipathies, must create friendships, and soften prejudices, and would eventually spread out that dark, sharp line which had before separated them, into a gradually fading shade of difference, untainted by hatred or ill-will, and perhaps seldom thought of at all, in their intercourse with each other.

I have no intention of denying, or at all calling into question, the utility and propriety of combining, in public schools, a due amount of religious instruction with the literary course. I have not expressed, and shall not express, any doubt of this whenever it is possible to accomplish it. The only question I have raised, or intend to raise, or in any shape to discuss, is, whether it is, in Ireland, practicable to combine any amount of religious instruction with secular teaching, in schools which will be resorted to by the children of all persuasions; and, whether this combination can be continued in the National Schools, without destroying the character imported by that name, and finally converting them into strictly denominational establishments.

It is fifty-four years since the Government made a liberal grant of £6980, in the benevolent hope that a system of combined spiritual and secular education might be made acceptable and attractive to all the different classes of Christians of which the Irish nation is composed. The fund was placed in the hands of a voluntary association of honourable men, comprehending members of as many creeds and opinions as existed in the community at large. For seventeen years the donation was repeated, and the experiment carried on with persevering tenacity, and it resulted in failure.

An energetic effort was made in 1825 to devise a system to serve the purpose and end so anxiously desired; and for fourteen months, the co-operation of Protestant and Roman Catholic prelates and clergy was diligently and persuasively solicited, and was, by both, most sternly and positively refused; on which refusal, the design was abandoned in despair.

After more than four years' acquiescence in this result, the Government, without further effort to obtain the concurrence of the discordant hierarchies, set up the present system of National Education, and appointed a Board of its own nomination.

After thirty-seven years of persistent experiment and anxious exertion to succeed, the concord and peace so ardently pursued appear more distant, and less likely to be arrived at, than they were in 1814.

A new commission to inquire after them, and to discover the means of attaining these evanescent blessings, is the result of this benevolent and philanthropic effort to please everybody, which, in fact, has pleased nobody; and the labour of fifty-four years, and the expense of millions, like the ass in the fable, have been lost into the bargain.

For the purposes of this investigation, I suggest the convenience of dividing the schools in Ireland into two classes, viz., one class comprehending all free schools, whether connected with the State, or supported and controlled by societies; and the other, pay schools, unconnected either with the State or with societies, and subject to no control of any extern authority, but opened and conducted by individuals, as profitable speculations, solely dependent for support upon their reputation for efficiency in the business of instructing the pupils who should resort to them.

According to the second report of the Commissioners, dated 16th September, 1826, at page four, the total number of schools in Ireland, in the year 1824, was 11,823. The total number of children attending these, on an average of three months, in the Autumn of 1824, was 560,549. According to the same Report, at page 18, the pay schools, included in this total, were 9352, attended by 394,732 pupils, according to the Protestant clergy's returns; and by 403,774 pupils, according to the returns of the Roman Catholic clergy. Taking the mean of the two returns, the pupils were 399,253. Deducting these schools from the total of 11,823, the result is, that there were in Ireland, of dependent free schools, 2471, attended by 161,296 pupils; and at the same time there existed more than three times as many independent pay schools, attended by twice and a half as many pupils.

The independent schools here mentioned, numbering 9352, attended by 399,253 pupils, may be divided into three classes, viz.:—head schools, for the children of wealthy parents, who could afford to give them what is called a liberal education, and to send their sons to one of the Universities, on leaving school. The greater number of these were boarding schools, to which also some day-boys resorted, whose families resided near enough to the school.

The second class were almost exclusively day schools,

opened and kept by men who professed learning and ability to teach pupils who could pay such stipend as the independent master, in his discretion, thought it his interest to demand. About half a guinea per quarter was a very general amount, with additional charges for instruction in branches of learning not included in the common curriculum of the school. These schools may be distinguished by the name of intermediate schools, standing, as they did, in respect of expense, between the head schools and what were called hedge schools. The number of these intermediate schools was regulated solely by the demand. In every locality which promised a sufficient number of pupils to support a school, some man, professing ability to teach, was sure to open one, as a profitable speculation, and means of living.

The third class were called hedge schools, from a common custom of adjourning from the poor cabin of the master, when a fine day invited, to the shade of a neighbouring hedge, where the poor children had the double advantage of inhaling fresh air, and learning their task. These are the schools poetically, and graphically described in the "Deserted Village," kept by masters "severe and stern to view, whom Goldsmith knew, and every truant knew." They were pay schools, to which children resorted who could pay twopence per week; and who, in winter, could also daily bring one or two sods of turf, to keep up a fire in the school. There was, in Ireland, a sort of vagrant youths, called poor scholars, to be met very commonly on the highways, with a copy book under the arm, preferring a supplication for charity to the poor scholar. These wandered from place to place, begging a night's lodging at the nearest cabin in the evening, a meal, where they entered at meal-time, and instruction at the hedge schools at which they arrived in their travels.

From this enumeration Sunday schools are excluded; but what were called hedge schools are comprehended.

It is certain that the national schools, and the sectarian free schools, set up in opposition to them, have entirely abolished the hedge schools; and have greatly diminished the number of the pay schools, which were intermediate between the hedge schools and the superior and expensive head schools.

From the fourteenth Report of the Commissioners, appointed in 1806, it appears that, in 1812, the total number of schools in Ireland was only 4600, attended by about 200,000 pupils, which numbers, in the twelve years, from 1812 to 1824, were more than doubled. The Commissioners of 1824, in the conclusion of their first Report, observe that education was then still, in a great degree, administered in the pay schools of the country, unconnected with societies; and, generally speaking, not subjected to any particular control or superintendence: and they concluded their Report by stating, that they could not more fully express the conclusion which they had come to upon this part of the subject, than in the words of the fourteenth Report of their predecessors, above quoted, viz.:—"Were it therefore even admitted that the benefits of education are not to the lower classes of the people as great as we conceive them to be, yet the necessity of assisting in obtaining it for them in this country would not be diminished, but increased; for such education as has been objected to, under the idea of its leading to evil rather than to good, they are actually obtaining for themselves; and though we conceive it practicable to correct it, to check its progress appears impossible; it may be improved, but it cannot be impeded."

In corroboration of this opinion, we have the fact that, in the twelve years which immediately followed this Report of 1812, the schools in Ireland had increased from 4600 to 11,483, as before stated.

Both the Commissioners of 1806 and of 1824 animadverted on the pay schools which then existed, observing, that the instruction afforded by them was extremely limited, and the masters, in general, very ill-qualified to give even that instruction, having themselves been taught in schools of a similar description. That, instead of being improved by moral and religious instruction, the minds of the pupils were corrupted by books calculated to incite to lawless and profligate adventure, to cherish superstition, or to lead to dissension or disloyalty (*vide* Report of 1825, p. 38).

This stricture on the schools and the books was founded on evidence, that certain books mentioned by some of the witnesses were used in those old schools; among them the lives of two Irish highwaymen, named Freny and O'Hanlon, which appear to be the books alluded to as inciting to lawless and profligate adventure. It should have been noticed, that no one of those books, so objected to, ever was a school-book, in any school. They were two-penny romances, which boys bought with their pocket-money, and read for mere amusement; and many of them, if not all, were of a very harmless character. Being voluntarily read, in addition to the school tasks, they promoted ability to read, which was some set-off against the assumed moral ill effects of them.

The amount of instruction, no doubt, was extremely limited, and necessarily limited, the great majority of the children, and nearly all those resorting to the hedge schools, being forced to leave school, and become labourers at the age of thirteen or fourteen. As to the qualification of the masters of these hedge schools, no one could reasonably expect to find it anything but humble. Judging from the few instances in which I visited National Schools of the present day, the same observation may be as justly made on them as on most of the masters in the old pay schools. The qualification of the modern masters is, in some cases, sought to be secured by teaching them, and their diligence is enforced by a system of inspection. The sufficiency of the old masters depended on competition. The National system takes away this stimulus; for the parents have now no choice of schools, and it may be fairly doubted that the modern security for qualification and diligence is at all superior to that which the public had before.

That the National Schools have imparted to a great number of children the ability to read (but it must be admitted, in most cases, to read awkwardly, and with hesitation and difficulty), also the ability in a smaller number of cases, to write, but in most instances slowly and clumsily, and in still fewer cases also, the ability to cipher to a very limited extent, must be admitted. To the amount of the knowledge thus imparted, their positive utility is not to be denied or questioned. But whether they have done more in this respect than the people would have done for themselves, through the agency of the old-fashioned schools, is worth inquiry. It cannot, with truth, be asserted, that the good which the National Schools have done is anything but a balance, after deducting from the sum of it the good which they prevented the people from doing for themselves; and which it is by both sets of Commissioners admitted the people were fully determined to accomplish, whether aided or not. It is perfectly certain that the old hedge schools, being unable to compete with the National free schools, vanished altogether. The National Schools, by attracting pupils of a class higher than those who formerly resorted to the hedge schools, came into competition with those intermediate schools before alluded to, and took from them many of their pupils, to whose parents the saving of the stipend, although moderate in amount, was a sufficient motive of preference.

How many of those intermediate schools, by this abstraction of their pupils, were left without sufficient support, and driven out of existence, it is not easy to determine, and forms a subject of useful, if not necessary inquiry, if the benefits conferred by the National Schools are to be fairly estimated. After deducting the value of all the hedge schools, and the value of the injury done to the intermediate schools, the question remains yet to be determined, whether the remainder will be a positive or a negative quantity, i.e., whether the balance be in favour of, or against the National Schools. Whatever that balance may be, a further question remains—whether the good, assuming the result to be positive good, has not been too dearly purchased?

It is also worth inquiry, whether the people would not have set a higher value upon the instruction which they should be obliged to pay for, than they have set upon instruction not only offered to them gratuitously, but which has been importunately pressed upon them; and whether both parents and children would not have used more exertion to profit by what they had to pay for, than they have applied in using what they got for nothing, and what was, therefore, too likely to be undervalued and neglected. This consideration does not apply to the poor, who are destitute of means to pay for any sort of instruction. The humanity and utility of providing accessible day-schools for these are not to be denied or doubted.

But the difficulty is to arrange such schools upon a system equally attractive to children of all persuasions, and above all suspicion of danger to the religious convictions of any. To secure this, all discussions of, or even allusions to sectarian difference must be scrupulously excluded, and the precincts of the school must be protected from everything that could remind the children, that any such differences exist. This is clearly impossible, and experience has proved it impossible, if religious instruction in any shape, or to any amount, is to be combined, or taught in the school. The intermediate schools, between the two-penny hedge schools and the expensive head schools, existed in all parts of Ireland. In them some boys were taught classics and mathematics, as well as reading, writing, and ciphering. From these schools some lads even entered the University, and became distinguished men. A still greater number obtained that modicum of Latin which was, and still is, necessary to qualify them to pass at examinations of candidates for army surgeons, for becoming apothecaries' apprentices, and many other pursuits requiring a knowledge of one or two Latin classics. These intermediate schools were supported, not only by those who learned Greek, Latin, and mathematics, but also by children of a more humble class intended for clerkships, and mercantile suits, some of them humble, who, by rigid saving in other things, were just able to pay the moderate stipend of the intermediate school. To a large number of these, the saving of this stipend was sufficient to determine their choice in favour of the free National School. Their departure from the intermediate schools left many of these without adequate support; and they soon disappeared from many localities, leaving a large, and important section of the community (who are too proud to send their children to the free schools) absolutely powerless to obtain for them, not only the humble measure of classical and mathematical teaching which they require, but that amount of English learning, essential to their progress in life.

In those intermediate schools there was much useful teaching. The want, which their disappearance from many localities has created, was recently strongly illustrated. The Benchers of the Honourable Society of King's Inns, a few years ago, instituted a preliminary examination, in school literature, including arithmetic, geography, and a little Latin, as a test of qualification to become an attorney's apprentice. The course prescribed, as to Latin, consisted of Sallust, one book of Cæsar's Commentaries, and two books of the Æneid. Nothing could be more lamentable than the ignorance and deficiency of the lads who presented themselves at these examinations, in every branch of the course prescribed to them. No critical knowledge was required, no difficult passages were presented to them, or difficult questions asked, and, in the greater number of examinations, more than half the candidates were rejected; at one, the whole, being fourteen in number, failed to pass. It was obvious that nearly all had depended upon a short feverish effort, with the aid of a translation, and some temporary assistance from what is called a grinder, to cram them for the occasion, without any attempt to learn anything systematically or fundamentally, and neglecting the most elementary rudiments of what they endeavoured to learn. In the common ability to spell English, too, they were, in many cases, woefully defective. These were lads who could not afford to enter an expensive, and, perhaps, a distant boarding school, supported by students for entrance at the Dublin University; and no other school existed, in which they could learn what it was essential to know.

Is it possible, is it practicable, in Ireland, to devise schools adequate, and more than adequate, to supply for the poor the amount of instruction which they can receive, but for which they are unable to pay, without destroying the demand for self-supporting schools, suitable to the wants of the people, in the various localities in which they may be required?

On the subject of education, this is a great problem which yet remains to be solved. Whether the Government of a free country should undertake to supply school instruction at the expense of the State, to any class of subjects, who have ability to pay for this as for anything else they may want. If such schools can be established for the poor who have not this ability to which they will cheerfully resort, and which will not destroy or injure self-supporting schools, such free schools will be a benevolent supplement, and the benefits conferred by them will no longer be a mere balance of good: it will be an integer quantity on the right side of the equation.

If we suppose a free school, open only to the children of poor people, wholly unable to pay for their instruction, making the title to admission nothing but inability to pay, there would be very little difficulty in the investigation of this title, so as to exclude from the free school all who could pay a moderate stipend for instruction. Place in these free schools masters well qualified to teach reading, writing, and arithmetic, as far as the rule of proportion, and including a perfect understanding of that rule. To this should be added some instruction in simple mechanics, sufficient to enable the children to understand how much muscular power is wasted by the use of ill-constructed implements. The use of plates, and simple models, in primary schools would greatly contribute to this kind of instruction, which, to the Irish labourer, is the most essential. The most obvious distinction between English and Scotch agricultural labourers and the Irish, is the different implements, and the different mode of using them. Every mechanical advantage is taken by the former; the latter seem to study that which requires the exertion of the most muscular power. This difference has passed into a proverbial definition of the Irishman's purchase, which is ironically called, "main strength." The defect in this particular of the primary schools is demonstrable, and the remedy for it is easy. Let the limited curriculum be clearly defined, be well and efficiently taught by the master, and effectually learned by the children. Keep a boy at the first page of his book, and let him not advance farther, until he can read that page, and deliver the sense of it with clearness and propriety, and let some exertion be used to correct his brogue, and induce him to speak without being ridiculous, remembering Juvenal's maxim, "Nil habet infelix paupertas durius in se quam quod ridiculos homines facit;" a truth no more clearly illustrated than in the case of the poor Irish, who cannot open their lips in England without being laughed at.

The child who has conquered this first page of his book has gained a substantial benefit. The child who has mumbled over the whole book, and reads the last page as badly as he read the first, has gained little or nothing. Let the same care be used in teaching how to write; and in teaching the elementary rules of arithmetic, and the expert use of them.

Leaving prodigies of natural talent out of consideration, the course here defined is as much as can be learned by children who must leave school and become labourers for their bread at fourteen. The boy who has acquired ability to read with ease and understanding, to write with facility and reasonable rapidity, and to calculate expertly, enters upon his path of life, no matter how humble, with incalculable advantages over an illiterate competitor. The habit of docility to which he has been broken (care being used to do it kindly and judiciously) at school, is likely to serve him in afterwards learning to work, whatever may be his calling. His power of being useful is largely increased; and the power of further improvement, by solitary effort, is effectually conferred on him. So treated, he leaves school with a debt of gratitude, of which, if his nature be not essentially base, he is not likely to be insensible.

Amongst the children at these free schools there must be some of superior natural ability, who will be easily distinguished from the rest. Suppose the inspectors were instructed, in their official visits, to mark, and, in due time, to pick out these, with the aid of the master; and, being bound in the selection, to estimate conduct and diligence, as well as ability. Assume the existence, within a reasonable distance, of a good, self-supporting pay school, at which a superior course of instruction is followed; at which Greek and Latin, geometry, grammar, and other higher branches of school learning are taught to, at least, some of the pupils; book-keeping, algebra, mensuration, and other such subjects, which were formerly taught, and often very effectually taught, at the old-fashioned half-guinea schools. By excluding from the free schools all who could pay a moderate stipend, room would again be made, and the market restored, for the several classes of self-supporting schools, and they would soon come into use. The free school, for poor children, would not be in competition with them; and much of the present expenditure of public money upon the National Schools would be saved. If a part of this saving were judiciously applied in advancing the poor talented children, selected from the free schools to a place in some superior school, paying for them out of the public fund; and also giving them something for decent clothes, and something to indemnify the poor family from loss in feeding them, for a probationary time, longer or shorter, according to conduct and industry, and consequent progress, the free school, from being a competitor, would be thus converted into a feeder, and a supporter of the cheap intermediate schools; and it is impossible to estimate the effects of such a stimulus as this system would apply to the excitable minds of the Irish people. The number of such selected pupils being restricted, as it should be, to boys of exceptional talents, never could be so great as to create an intolerable public burthen. The legitimate ambition which it would create must, and I have no doubt, would soon spread, and elevate the hopes and the character of the Irish poor. If the number of candidates for promotion, who came up to the adopted standard of merit, should become too great, it would be easy to raise the standard, and keep down the number.

The Government should no farther interfere with paid, self-supporting schools, than by the location in them of boys selected as here suggested. These should be so located as day boys, paying the ordinary stipend, and living at home. This is merely a suggestive outline of what, by careful management, may grow into a useful National Institution, without provoking contention or interfering with the efforts of people possessing ability to help themselves.

The question still remains unanswered, Would such free schools, in which nothing but secular instruction is allowed, be resorted to by the children of the poor, of whatever religious persuasion? Suppose the clergy condemned them for defect of religious teaching, would their opposition be effectual?

In answering these questions, I assume that a diligent and competent master, without regard to his creed, will be placed in every free school, and kept to his duty by vigilant, frequent, and unexpected visits of well qualified, well paid, and respectable superintendents, bound to visit, and faithfully to report the condition of, at least one school every day, except Sundays; and to transmit these reports daily to an office in Dublin, in which a competent number of persons (under the control of a commissioner of dignity and station) should be employed to examine these reports; and to which office should be also attached a sufficient number of occasional inspectors—ready to start, at an hour's notice, to visit any school to which a report had directed attention. These occasional inspectors should also be frequently sent to pay unexpected visits, of which neither the regular inspector nor the schoolmaster should have any intimation. The visits, both of the regular inspector and occasional inspector should not be formal, careless, and, therefore, worse than useless visits, of a few minutes' duration, merely to look at a few copy-books and other papers; but they should involve a sound and careful examination of the several classes, and a superintendence also of the master himself, while teaching, at least one or two of his classes, in presence of the inspector.

Under such a system of control, it may be rationally expected, that the free schools would be efficient working establishments. Assuming them to be such, I believe, that no condemnation of them by opponents would be effectual to keep the poor children from them, unless other more attractive schools were made accessible to them, which, without Government aid, I am morally certain never would happen.

The Irish are a sharp and sagacious race. Let all

danger of tampering with religious convictions be removed, and they will soon estimate the schools according to their usefulness and intrinsic value. Guard these free schools carefully against the interference of all who would use them for sectarian purposes. Prohibit strictly and quietly, and firmly discountenance, all discussions on the subject of religion amongst the children; confine their attention to the proper business of the school, and all reluctance to resort to them will be speedily overcome, and will soon vanish.

If those who insist on using the school as a means of propagating their own religious views and opinions be able to found, without aid from the State, and to maintain sectarian rivals to the National free schools, and make them more attractive, and thus draw away the children from the purely secular State school, let them be at full liberty to do so, but give them no aid from the public funds. If they succeed, by offering what the parents of the children think better schools, the cause of education is sufficiently promoted; and the National School, if deserted, may, and should be shut up, as a thing unnecessary, whereby the tax of maintaining it would be saved. But I do not apprehend any such event; and such event is not to be desired; for the predominance of denominational schools would certainly be, and to the extent of their existence is, a corroding social evil in Ireland.

If not supported or countenanced by the State, denominational schools could exist only by voluntary contribution, made by zealous members of the several rival sects, desirous to propagate their own peculiar faith and views. If there were no free schools for the poor, to give either secular or spiritual instruction, the necessity for, and the inducement charitably to institute, and, by voluntary contribution, to support such schools, would, in such circumstances, be most obvious and pressing, and certainly greater than it would be if efficient schools existed in which the secular instruction of the poor should be adequately provided for; leaving spiritual teaching to be administered by the clergy of the different persuasions, with such aid as they could get from benevolent members of their several congregations.

Such was the state of things before 1831, when the Government intervened, and instituted the system of National Schools. Four-fifths of all the educational establishments in the country were independent pay schools, in which nothing but secular instruction was given. Even the hedge schools demanded payment, however small; and thus the children whose parents could not pay two-pence a week, and the modicum of turf daily for the fire, were left without the means either of secular or religious instruction in school; the latter, however, they got from their clergy.

This was the most favourable state of society for evoking the charity and benevolent activity of the zealous laity of every persuasion; and if denominational free schools, supported by voluntary contributions, could spring up and flourish under any circumstances, one should think they would have done so in Ireland before the Government interfered. Yet, in 1825, the Commissioners found, that the chief part of the educational business of the country was performed in the independent pay schools, for which the people themselves had created a market, and at which their children were getting instruction; which, however open to the criticism of fastidious moralists, was by no means ineffectual for the literary improvement of the people. The denominational schools, supported by mere voluntary contributions, were few; and, if left without aid from the Government, very few, if any, of them could continue to exist. The old-fashioned half-guinea schools, and the two-penny hedge schools, still not only maintained their ground, but multiplied, until the Government, by instituting the National Schools, eventually extinguished them, whether for good or for evil, is a question on which sensible men are by no means agreed. If the old schools were as defective as their severest censors represent them, there is no ground for asserting that they would not improve with all the other institutions of the country.

Any one who will take the pains to investigate this subject historically will find, that, from the earliest period, since religious controversy began in Ireland, the cry for religious instruction in *schools* was at all times, as it is now, very much confined to the Protestant clergy and a small fraction of the laity, who were more religious than their neighbours, and who joined the clergy in their efforts to create proselytizing schools.

For every purpose of fair discussion on this subject, the Irish nation may be divided into two opposing creeds —the Roman Catholic, and the Protestant. The clergy of the former were, and still are, left dependent on the voluntary support of their congregations. Every member lost is income lost; and the same motive which prompts the shepherd to guard his flock, operates on them, and it is quite natural it should. Their opposition and unmeasured hostility to proselytizing schools was, therefore, prompt, vigilant, and effectual. No candid man will impute this as a fault, or as any just ground of reproach. It may co-exist with every higher motive; and I have no intention of insinuating that it does not. To these dependent pastors belong the most numerous, the poorest, the most uneducated, and ignorant part of the nation. Any one who knows this great majority of the Irish people must know, that at least the poor and uneducated amongst them (and these are ninety-nine hundredths of them) firmly regard the Protestant faith as a heresy, which leads to eternal perdition. In this they are so firmly convinced, and steadfast in the conviction, that the death of a child is, by its parents, regarded with less horror, than his desertion of what they believe to be the true and only saving faith. The propagation of this conviction was the means to which the Roman Catholic clergy resorted for protection of their flocks.

To invite people holding such a conviction (no matter how irrationally) to send their children, or to permit their children to enter a school, in which what they believe to be a damnable doctrine is taught, at any hour, in any way, or in any form, is mocking, and insulting them. No precautions that human ingenuity can contrive will induce them to let their children enter the building, in any corner of which this doctrine is taught, at any hour of the day, to any children whatever, unless effectual provision be made, that these children shall not be present at such teaching. They must be secure that due notice shall be given to the pupils, and they and their clergy will effectually warn these children to fly the moment the religious instruction for Protestants is announced. Roman Catholic children, therefore, go to these schools forewarned of danger to their eternal salvation, and deeply prejudiced against Protestant doctrine, and Protestant religious instruction. Scripture reading they regard as a part of this forbidden teaching; and they must leave the school the moment it is commenced. The Protestant children must also attend under a strict injunction to leave as soon as Roman Catholic instruction is about to commence. The clergy of either persuasion are not satisfied with this cautionary arrangement, and they insist on having a more direct and immediate control over the schools to which they will allow the children of their respective congregations to resort. Hence it is that of 6600 National Schools, in Ireland, 4000 are under the direct patronage—that is subject to the direct influence and control of Roman Catholic clergymen. Whatever may be the number of Protestant children in the 4000 localities, where these schools exist, they must forego all benefit from them, or be exposed to the danger of being tampered with in a school, the patron and controller of which believes that he has been, by Divine Providence, appointed to preserve the deposit of Roman Catholic faith in Ireland, and responsible to God for the souls of these Protestant children, if he fails to convert them. If the resolution of the Roman Catholic Archbishops and Bishops means anything, it means this, and nothing less. It may be inferred that 2600 of the schools are in like manner under Protestant patrons.

The Protestant clergy, on the other hand, for centuries, have claimed, and still claim, as their legal right, the privilege of teaching to all the children in the schools, whether Roman Catholic or Protestant, the Word of God, according to what they assume to be the true interpretation of it. To deny them this privilege is to take from them, and as they assert to take also from the children, the inestimable benefit, and the inalienable right of teaching and reading the Scriptures; which right of teaching the clergy claim by the statute law of the land, and feel bound to exercise by their duty towards God and their flocks. To ask them to take part in any system of instruction from which the exercise of this privilege is excluded, is inviting them to commit what many of them believe to be a sin. They regard the schools as the great means of effectually performing what they profess to feel as a sacred and imperative duty.

If this be their feeling, if this be their solemn public profession, what greater absurdity can be proposed than the task of getting these and the Roman Catholic clergy (who claim the same privilege by direct authority and command from Heaven) to agree upon any plan of school education, to be administered in seminaries to which the children of both persuasions are expected to resort?

That such is the view taken of this subject by the Protestant clergy, both in ancient and modern times, must be known to every one who has read even a moderate portion of what has been published for the last two centuries.

On the 5th of May, 1730, Primate Boulter wrote as follows to the Bishop of London:—

"The great number of Papists in this kingdom, and the obstinacy with which they adhere to their own religion, occasion our trying what may be done with their children, to bring them over to our Church; and the good success the Corporation established in Scotland, for the instruction of the ignorant and barbarous part of the nation, has met with, encourages us to hope, if we were incorporated for that purpose here, that we might likewise have some success in our attempts to teach the children of the Papists the English tongue and the principles of Christian religion; and several gentlemen here have promised subscriptions for maintaining schools for that purpose, if we were once formed into a corporate body. This has set the principal nobility, gentry, and clergy here on presenting an address to his Majesty, to erect such persons as he pleases into a Corporation here for that purpose, which we have sent over by the Lord Lieutenant to be laid before his Majesty. The copy of this address I have here sent your Lordship, in which you will, in some measure, see the melancholy state of religion in this kingdom; and I do, in my own name, and that of the rest of my brethren, beg the favour of your Lordship to give it your countenance. I can assure you the Papists are here so numerous that it highly concerns us, in point of interest, as well as out of concern for the salvation of those poor creatures, who are our fellow-subjects, to try all possible means to bring them and theirs over to the knowledge of the true religion.

"And one of the most likely methods we can think of is, if possible, instructing and converting the young generation; for instead of converting those that are adult, we are daily losing many of our meaner people, who go off to Popery.

"I am sure your Lordship will be glad of any opportunity of advancing the glory of God, and promoting

His service and worship among those who at present are strangers to it."

Such was the claim of the Primate of Ireland, in the name of himself and the rest of the Protestant clergy, made one hundred and thirty-seven years ago, to have a corporate right to govern the schools to which the children of Roman Catholics were to resort, and to use those schools as the means of converting those children to the Protestant faith.

In the 28th year of Henry VIII. an Act had been passed for the establishment of schools, to teach the English language, propagate English manners, and enforce the wearing of English dress. These were to be pay schools. What schools, if any, were established under this Act, it is now difficult, if not impossible, to ascertain. An Act for erection of free schools had been passed in the 12th year of Elizabeth; and by 7 William III. c. 4, it had been enacted, that the two previous Acts should be strictly observed. From these several Acts, what are called parochial schools derived their origin. How many of these existed, or how they were conducted, or what effects they were producing, at the time when Primate Boulter wrote this letter, does not appear in any record that I am aware of. But, that many schools were established, in obedience to them, is certain; for in 1824 the Commissioners found 782 schools existing, which they trace to these Acts; at which 21,195 pupils of the Protestant Church, and 15,303 of the Roman Catholic Church, were attending; and for support of which, the Protestant clergy annually contributed £3,299 19*s.* 4*d.* (see first Report, 30th May, 1825, pages 3, 4, 37, and Appendix, No. 2).

Contemporaneously with Primate Boulter's letter, a petition was presented to George II., signed by all the prelates, and many of the other dignitaries and clergy of the Protestant Church, and by many men of rank in the laity of Ireland, praying for a Charter of incorporation, as mentioned in the letter. This was granted in the year 1733; and schools, which acquired the name of Charter Schools, were accordingly established.

The professed object of these schools being the conversion of Roman Catholic children to the Protestant faith, it was soon found that this would be impossible, unless the children were severed from their parents, and their homes; and to accomplish this, the schools were turned into boarding schools, where the pupils were fed and clothed.

It was then found necessary to set up nurseries for such infants as could be procured, in order to provide pupils for the schools.

By a petition to Parliament, in 1769, it appears that 52 schools, and five nurseries, then existed, in which 2100 children were maintained. An Act was then passed imposing a duty on pedlars and hawkers, and giving the proceeds for support of the Charter Schools, and nurseries.

In 1775 the Incorporated Society passed a resolution not to admit any children, except those of Roman Catholic parents. This resolution continued in force until 1803, when it was rescinded.

In 1787 and 1788 the justly venerated John Howard, in his anxiety for the helpless sufferers of the human race, visited thirty-seven of these schools, and the four nurseries which then existed. The condition in which he found each of these is stated, in a separate paragraph of his work, from page 100 to 118 of the 2nd volume. He had previously visited them in 1784; but it does not appear that he took any active steps until after his second round of visits. In 1788 a Committee of the House of Commons was appointed to inquire into the state of these schools, and Howard was examined by them. What was done, or whether anything effectual was done, to reform the shocking abuses and inhuman cruelties which Howard discovered, in most of these earthly purgatories for the torture of poor helpless children, does not appear; and the next light let in on them emanates from the first Report of the Commissioners, made in May, 1825. The savage cruelties in the romance of "Dotheboy's Hall" are thrown into the shade by those inflicted on the pupils in Charter Schools in Ireland, up to and in the year 1825, some of which are described in the Report, from page 7 to page 19. They describe the wretched and squalid appearance of starved, imprisoned, and brutally-beaten and tortured children of tender years; the sullen and dogged faces of these victims; the vicious, useless, and eloping apprentices into which these maltreated children were converted.

The Commissioners, at page 14 of their first Report, set out a passage extracted from a Report made to the Incorporated Society, by the Rev. William Lee, on visiting the Charter Schools in 1819 and 1820. This passage, read with the light thrown on these schools by Howard, and by the Commissioners themselves, is certainly most remarkable. Mr. Lee, in his Report, stated as follows :— "I was led, in the course of my official visitations, to compare the Charter Schools with those of the foundation of Erasmus Smith, and of the Association for Discountenancing Vice and promoting the Knowledge and Practice of the Christian Religion, both of which came under my authorized inspection. The two latter, it is well known, consist exclusively of daily and parochial schools; the children attending them are, for the most part, clothed in rags, and fed upon the scanty and homely fare afforded in the cabin of an Irish peasant. In the Charter Schools, on the contrary, the children are comfortably lodged, well clad, and abundantly fed. No pains are spared to preserve their health. On the first appearance of disease, medical aid is procured, and their teachers are, in all cases, equal, and generally far superior to those employed in the daily and parochial schools. Yet, I was invariably struck with the vast superiority, in health, in appearance, in vivacity, and in intelligence, of the half naked, and, one would suppose, half starved children, who live in their parents' cabins, over those so well maintained, and so carefully instructed in the Charter Schools. The reasons of this striking fact, it might not be difficult to assign. In the Charter Schools, all social and family affections are dried up; children, once received into them, are, as it were, the children, the brothers, the sisters, the relations of nobody! They have no vacation; they know not the feeling of home; and hence it is primarily, whatever concomitant causes there may be, that they are so frequently stunted, in body, mind, and heart."

Read the statements, "that in the Charter Schools the children are comfortably lodged, well clad, and abundantly fed, &c., with the light let in on them by John Howard, vol. 2, page 108.

"County of Mayo: Castlebar school is situated on a fine eminence, just out of the town. No pump, no vault. September 12th, 1787, the master received from the Dublin nursery five girls, and from that of Monasterevan nine: several of them without shoes or stockings. At my visit, March 31st, 1788, there were twenty girls, and the number had not been greater for a year past, though in the account which the Society last published the number, on the 29th September, 1787, is stated forty-one. These children were puny, sickly objects, almost naked; seven had scald heads, and almost all the itch. With these disorders they came; and having no clothes, but such as were in rags, the apothecary was afraid to give them physic. The master said they could not earn him a halfpenny. They had never been at church since they came. The following is an extract from a letter sent to the Society in Dublin, signed by six gentlemen of the local committee, and the surgeon. '2nd November, 1787. The clothes of the 12th of June are of so bad a quality, that the children who have been here since Nov., 1786, are now naked, and unable to attend the church. A set of sheeting is much wanted.' No answer to this was received from the Society in Dublin till Friday before my visit, and then only a printed receipt for the cure of scald heads." Having allowed the scald heads, for five months, to take the chance of getting better without the medicine, and having allowed the five coldest months in the year to operate on the naked children, the Society, by this tardy letter, conveying no comfort beyond the receipt for cure of scald heads, throws light upon Mr. Lee's statement, that no pains are spared to preserve their health, and that on the first appearance of disease, medical aid is procured: that they are well clad, and comfortably lodged, &c., &c.

At page 109 of vol. 2, Howard reports:—"Loughrea School, April 3, 1788; forty girls. These dirty, sickly objects, without shoes and stockings, were spinning and knitting in a cold room, paved with pebbles. The usher stood, as at some other schools, with a rod in his hand, to see the children work; but there was not a book to be seen. There were only sixteen beds; sheets much wanted; the infirmary a potato-house. The children were sadly neglected by their drunken mistress. But I observed that her own children, by the fire-side, were fresh and clean."

So it was observed by Squeers to Mr. Newman Noggs of that renowned master's own son, Master Wakford Squeers, that he had on him the fatness of twenty boys, provoking the cynical pity of honest Newman for the twenty whose fatness had been transferred to the pampered son of their cruel master.

Read Mr. Lee's praise by the light let in by the Commissioners themselves at page 20 of their first Report:—

"At Clonmel, in 1817, the boys appear to have been punished with great severity by the usher, who used, on all occasions, a common horsewhip. It is stated that he often gave four dozen lashes, with his utmost strength, and that the boys had been beaten until the blood ran down upon the flags. A boy was once knocked down by the usher and kicked so severely that two of his ribs were broken; and the ear of another boy was nearly pulled off. For this last offence the usher was reported to the catechist by the master."

In a note to this passage of the Report, it is stated that "this usher was dismissed from this school in December, 1817, on the representation of Mr. Thackeray, as unfit, and incompetent; but no notice of his cruelties seems to have been brought forward."

At page 21 of the Report it is stated, that, "at Strangford the same severity appears to have prevailed, previous to the appointment of the present master. His predecessor was dismissed in 1819, on the ground of incapacity; but he was afterwards appointed to the day-school at Newport."

(Page 21). "At Shannon-grove it is stated that the children were improperly fed; and the tubs used in the boys' bedrooms at night were used in the morning for washing, and also for fetching potatoes from the field. The same disgusting practice prevailed at New Ross, and even in the Model School at Santry."

"No offence that a Charter School child can commit seems to be less pardonable than daring to utter a complaint. We have already mentioned the severe punishment of two boys at New Ross school, for a similar offence; and in the examination of William Lewis will be found a statement of a severe beating which he received with a horsewhip, for having, as was suggested, advised another boy to complain to the Rector of the parish."

The New Ross case is stated, at the end of the preceding page of the Report, thus:—"At New Ross, the same severe mode of punishment is stated still to exist [i. e., in 1825]. Two boys have been punished for complaining, one of them with peculiar cruelty. The boys appear to have been employed to carry dung in hand-barrows, and to have been kept at work at unusual hours, and to have been left without due instruction. Many boys eloped from this school during the time the witness, Thomas Moyle, was there: he thinks nearly fifty in nine years ending in 1822, and he states that the boys were in constant fear and alarm. The return of elopements from this school, supplied to us by the Society, states twenty-nine as having taken place within the period above mentioned."

These are merely a few of the instances given both by Howard and the Commissioners, and they amply explain a phenomenon which seemed to puzzle Mr. Lee. In his Report, printed in the Appendix, at page 125 of the Commissioners' First Report, he stated as follows:—

"In the first place, then, I have found it generally the case that, among the lower classes, a rooted and an inveterate prejudice exists against the Charter Schools; that nothing but entire destitution will induce them to seek in them an asylum for their children; and that the fact of having been educated in one of those seminaries is very commonly brought forward, and received as the bitterest reproach that can be offered. There can be but one opinion as to the unreasonableness and injustice of this prejudice. The causes of it I do not mean to investigate, I simply state what appears to me to be the fact; and I think it demands the attention of the Society, were it only in order that the best means may be devised and employed, for meeting and counteracting this unpleasant feeling."

It is stated at page 14 of the Commissioners' first

Report, "that Mr. Lee had been, for many years, a regular visitor and catechist of a large Charter School."

At page 30 of the Report is given a summary of the expense, and of the results, of these Charter Schools, for ninety years of their existence, viz., that they had cost an expenditure of £1,612,138; that 12,749 pupils had been bound as apprentices; that 1155 had received the marriage portion of £5, given to all apprentices duly serving their time and marrying Protestants,—showing that 7905 children apprenticed cost £1,000,000 sterling, being about £126 each.

Such was the sequel of that petition of all the Prelates and Protestant clergy, backed by the noblemen and gentlemen who solicited the Charter in 1731, and obtained it in 1733, "as one of the most likely methods of instructing and converting the then young generation, of advancing the glory of God, and promoting His service and worship among those whom Primate Boulter assumed to be strangers to it." The scheme of this Charter School system had been devised by the Primate and clergy of that time. The conduct of it, from the beginning to the end, was very much in their hands. The Kildare-place system, from 1814 to 1831 (although they affect to complain that it was not sufficiently left in their hands), was subject to their control and influence in a high degree. The Association for Discountenancing Vice and Promoting the Knowledge of the Christian Religion, incorporated in 1800, was also an essentially religious and Protestant Institution, and very much subject to clerical supervision and control. After 137 years of unavailing efforts, and vainly, if not most mischievously, expended treasure, the same claim to the management of National Education, at the expense of the State, set up in 1731 by Primate Boulter, is now as peremptorily made and as strongly urged by the Protestant clergy of the present day, as if it were yet an untried experiment, or rather as if it were recommended by an experiment, with a result in their favour.

We have seen that the Roman Catholic clergy claim the same power of supervision, and direction of the education of all the rising generation, by right divine; and that this right was claimed by the Lord Primate and Protestant clergy, by force of their union with the State, in 1826. That the claim is still set up by them, as strongly as it ever had been before, is very clearly apparent from what follows.

At the annual meeting of the Church Education Society, held in the Round Room of the Rotundo, in Dublin, on the 11th of April, 1866, which, according to the newspaper report, was crowded in every part by a most respectable and influential assembly: the Report stating, also, that the platform was filled to excess with clergymen, a speech of the Bishop of Ossory is reported in "Saunder's Newsletter" of April 12th, 1866, in which the sentiments of the Lord Bishop on this subject are very diffusely expressed, and warmly applauded by the whole assembly. After adverting to a charge of the Archbishop of Dublin, in which his Grace had commented on the conduct of the Protestant clergy, consequent upon the change made in 1831, whereby they saw the whole education of the people of Ireland suddenly taken out of their hands, the Lord Bishop of Ossory, according to the Report, proceeded as follows:—

"But, then, that they (the clergy) should have acted

in this so serious a matter—that they should, under the influence of their feelings, reject the system of education, as proposed by the State for the people of this country; and that they should reject it, not under the impression that they were actuated by very different, and by holier sentiments—by a zeal for the honour of God, and by a zeal for the good of the souls of the young committed to their care—this would be not merely base, but blasphemous hypocrisy." [Applause.] After stating that the Archbishop could not have intended this meaning, the Lord Bishop quoted from a former speech of his own upon the subject, as follows : " After saying that the profession of the clergy was, that it was their duty to aid the Government in educating the people ; and a duty from which they could not be relieved, unless by conditions annexed to the discharge of it which would render it necessarily contrary to that high and holy duty, he said, that in that former speech he had gone on to say, such has been the uniform language of the clergy. Nor was it mere profession on their part. They had an opportunity of evincing the sincerity of their professions, and of giving a very conclusive proof that they would not suffer themselves to be prevented from rendering such assistance to Government by any minor objections, or by any selfish considerations. I do not mean to claim credit, in this way, for their co-operation with the State in the earliest attempts which were made in this country to extend the blessings of education to the poor, because the Church then enjoyed a monopoly of State favour, and no conditions were laid upon it, with reference to this matter, except such as it was easy to bear. But this state of things did not continue up to the introduction of the National system of education. It was altogether changed when the Government adopted the Kildare-place system. The clergy then saw themselves deprived of the prominent place which they had heretofore held, and which many thought, and still think, it was their right to hold, in devising, directing, and conducting the state system for the education of the poor. The Church was wholly set aside in the new system. It was not, that it had not the principal place in the system—it had no place at all. This was a very great change, and one not very easy to bear. But though, in taking up the Kildare-place system, the State seemed to have overlooked what was due to the Church, it did not overlook what was due to the honour of God's word, and to the best interests of the people. The Kildare-place system did not rob the children whom it educated of the inestimable blessing of an early acquaintance with the word of God. It did not aid or countenance others in robbing them of it. On the contrary, it embodied and set forth the great principle, that the word of God is to be the basis of the education of the people, and that, not merely because it is the depository of all saving truth, and the source of all sound religion, but because it is the foundation of all pure morality. This was one principle set forth by the Kildare-place system; and there was another—namely that it is the right and duty of all to read God's Holy Word; and that no man, or set of men—no power, civil or ecclesiastical, has a right to forbid the reading of God's Word." Farther on in the Report the Lord Bishop is represented as saying, "He (the Archbishop) thinks that the clergy should have accepted the aid offered by the State, in the conduct of these schools, and on the conditions which the State offered, without committing a sin; and they thought they could not do so without commiting a sin —not a sin, in the narrow, and false sense, but a sin, in the proper acceptation of the term. Now I must say, that this, under the circumstances, seems to me a most unreasonable expectation."

After forcibly laying down the principle, that the duties of a clergyman, with respect to their eternal interests, are infinitely more important and direct, and, in fact, his primary duties, with respect to his flock, he goes on to say: "Now the most important part of a clergyman's office, is his duty as a spiritual teacher, but that duty would be most imperfectly discharged, particularly as regards the young and ignorant, if there was not instruction given in a different way, and under different circumstances. Now I suppose, that if every clergyman in Ireland, with the exception of a certain class, were asked, which of all the means at his command, as regards the young, he considered the best to supply this needful supplement to the discharge of his public duty; to prepare for it, to second and force it; which of all the means would be regarded as the most important; there would, in my opinion, be scarcely an exception to the answer—the schools."

Thus, the Protestant clergy, a century and a half ago, insisted; and, to the present day, they persistently still insist, on the right of devising, directing, and conducting the State system of education of the poor (of course, including Roman Catholics), and on what they describe as the sacred duty of teaching; and forcing to be read and learned in the State schools the Holy Scriptures;

and teaching them in their own way, and according to their own interpretation. They seem to ignore the fact, that the parents of the children over whom they claim this prerogative of teaching, would, as a general rule, prefer to see their children cast into the sea, rather than have them subjected to this teaching, which they have learned to regard as the teaching of a heresy which it is damnable to learn.

Any system, therefore, which, in Ireland, proposes to combine spiritual with secular instruction, in a mixed school, attended by children of different persuasions, is, and ever must be, visionary, mischievous, and impracticable. Such combined instruction is impossible, in any other than denominational schools, and these denominational schools will effectually propagate and perpetuate the religious antipathies by which this country is afflicted.

Any one acquainted with the constantly published opinions, claims, and views of the Roman Catholic clergy, must see that they assert, as their inalienable right, and regard as their most sacred and imperative duty, not merely to guard Roman Catholic children from the contagion of Protestant doctrines, and all teaching in the least degree tinged with any countenance of those doctrines, but that they also consider it a high and holy duty imposed upon them by Heaven itself, to use all means in their power to convert and reclaim Protestants, and especially Protestant children, from what, without any hesitation or delicacy, they stigmatize as a damnable heresy, leading to the perdition of souls. They do not hesitate to assert, that all this is done by them, or desired to be done, "for advancing the glory of God, and promoting his service and worship; and out of concern for the salvation of those poor creatures" (meaning Protestant children). And no terms could be more appropriate to the expression of the sentiments which they profess, than these words of Primate Boulter. Every one of them would also claim credit for sincerity, when he professes, that in all this "he is actuated by high and holy sentiments, by a zeal for the honour of God, and by a zeal for the good of the souls of the young committed to his care;" and he could find no language better suited to the expression of his professed motives, than that which the report ascribes to the Bishop of Ossory. The Roman Catholic clergy would also be unanimous, and (unlike the Protestant clergy) without the exception of a certain, or any class, in regarding the schools as the best means of discharging the duty of reclaiming the young from the paths which they say lead to perdition. It is not a violent, or absurd imagination, to fancy that while the Protestant Bishop of Ossory, on the 11th of April, 1866, was addressing a crowded meeting of Protestant clergy and their supporters in the Protestant laity; at the Rotundo, a Roman Catholic Bishop was, in precisely equivalent language, exhorting a crowded meeting of Roman Catholic clergy, and devout Roman Catholic laymen, in Marlborough-street Roman Catholic Cathedral, claiming for the Roman Catholic clergy the inalienable right to use the schools for the propagation of Roman Catholic doctrine. In such a meeting also, the Roman Catholic principle might with equal plausibility be insisted on, that it is the right and the duty of all Roman Catholics, in obedience to their Church, to forbear from reading the Scriptures, except so far, and unless in the way permitted by their pastors, and aided by the infallible interpretation sanctioned by the Holy Church.

It is, therefore, fully as dangerous to the faith of Protestant children to attend schools in which Roman Catholic clergymen are allowed the privilege of "devising, directing, and conducting the State system for the education of the poor," as it was for Roman Catholic children to attend those schools when so controlled by Protestant clergy. It is even more dangerous; for the same care and pains are not used to infuse into the minds of Protestant children the belief and conviction that the Roman Catholic religion is a damnable heresy, leading to inevitable perdition.

The secret armour by which Roman Catholic children are protected in Ireland is illustrated by an humorous incident which took place, not long ago, in one of the police courts in Dublin. At Glasnevin, to the north-east of Dublin, is the great Roman Catholic cemetery, in which no one is allowed to be interred except those who die in communion with that Church. At Harold's Cross, to the south-west of Dublin, in the opposite point of the compass, is the cemetery called Mount St. Jerome, used exclusively for deceased Protestants.

A child was produced before the magistrate, so young, that he considered it his duty to examine her on the *voir dire*, in order to ascertain whether her belief in a future state of rewards and punishments was sufficiently established to render her a competent witness; and to make the question intelligible to her childish capacity, he addressed her in these words: "Now, my little girl, can you tell me where the *good* people go when they die, and where the *bad* people go? Her ready answer was, "The good people go to Glasnevin, and the bad people go to Harold's Cross." Will any one, who knows the passionate affection with which the poor of Ireland regard their children, believe that parents, deeply impressed with these terrifying convictions, would willingly expose their offspring to the remotest danger of being attracted to a creed of which they entertain such an opinion as this child expressed, in the simplicity of her heart?

To the system of secular education before suggested, it is probable, the clergy of every creed and order, and the laymen who advocate the combination of spiritual with secular instruction in all schools, will object, that the notion of omitting spiritual instruction in the State schools savour of impiety; and, perhaps, they will impute to the proposer of this omission an intention of denying the utility and the propriety, not to say the necessity, of religious instruction. My answer is, that nothing is farther from my intention than to deny, or call in question, the utility, or the propriety of, or even the necessity for a full measure of religious instruction. It does not follow because spiritual instruction is not to be combined in the free schools of the State with secular teaching, that no such instruction is to be given at all.

Before the National Schools were thought of in Ireland the Irish people were a religious people, and were earnest believers in the several creeds which they professed. Yet, in the old two-penny hedge schools, and in the half-guinea intermediate schools (which then executed more than four-fifths of the education business of the country) there was no mixture of religious instruction. Both Protestants and Roman Catholics promiscuously resorted to them, and especially to the intermediate schools; for there were greater numbers of Protestants in the class of children who attended these intermediate schools than in the humble rank who frequented the hedge schools. These intermediate schools were indifferently kept by Protestant and Roman Catholic masters; and they attracted pupils in the direct ratio of the reputation of the master for his ability and diligence as a secular teacher. Nothing was more common than Protestant boys leaving a Protestant master, and changing to a school, in the same locality, kept by a Roman Catholic master; and, *vice versa*, Roman Catholic boys frequently changed from the school of a Roman Catholic to that of a Protestant master, solely on the ground of greater ability or greater diligence in the conduct of the school. It was not uncommon, in those schools, to begin and close the business of the day by repetition of the Lord's Prayer, in which every pupil joined without objection, whether Protestant or Roman Catholic. But catechetical instruction was reserved for the clergy of the several sects, and was administered by them according to their own arrangements, and commonly on Sunday in the Protestant churches by the minister in his proper person. For this purpose, after the service in the Protestant churches, the children regularly came forward and ranged themselves outside the railing of the communion table, and were there instructed by the minister, standing inside; and, in the part of the country with which I was acquainted in early life, this was as regular as the church service itself. In like manner, in the Roman Catholic houses of worship, the children were assembled at convenient times, and ranged round the railing of the altar or on forms in the chapel, and there received catechetical instruction from their clergy. It was also common to hold what were called stations, at the most commodious house in places remote from the chapel, at which catechetical instruction formed part of the business. I do not think that any candid man will deny that the system of religious teaching thus practised, and thus personally administered by the clergy alone, but never in a school, had the desired effect. It had also the inestimable advantage of leaving the children free to mix in the secular schools, which were in no way whatever subject to the control of the clergy of any persuasion, and were not suspected of any design to tamper with their religious convictions. The effect of so mixing was, in the course of time, to mitigate sectarian antipathies, and to propagate friendly feelings in the rising generation of every creed towards each other. To this may be fairly, and I believe truly, attributed the disappearance of that dismal prejudice which suggested to the Roman Catholic of the last century the necessity for scrubbing the chair on which a Protestant visitor had sat. In justice to the Roman Catholic clergy, I must add, that I never knew or heard of one instance in which they directed their people to give even a preference to the school of a Roman Catholic master on the ground of religion.

Since the establishment of the National Schools (in which it was determined to combine religious with secular instruction), many and various devices have been resorted to for the purpose of allaying the apprehensions of Roman Catholic parents, and of removing their objections to these schools. To one of these (I believe the last device, and that now in use) I have before called attention—that of giving notice to the children that religious instruction is about to commence, and intimating that all who do not desire to receive it may leave the school.

I have before observed on the inevitable effect of this daily warning upon the young minds of the children, for whose protection it is avowedly given. I do not believe that this effect has ever been seriously and rationally considered. Those children come to the school—it must be assumed, and truly assumed—having, from their parents, or their clergy, and most probably from both, received a strict caution to fly from the school the moment the religious teaching (in which they are not to participate) is announced; and to fly as from something pestilential, and worse, from a thing inconsistent with salvation in the world to come. The poor children of each sect, when flying from the school, I repeat, must regard their schoolfellows who remain, as they must believe, one class to learn bigotry and superstition, and the other to learn heresy, whereby they are doomed to perdition.

No reflecting man, anxious for the moral and material condition of this country, can contemplate these results without pain and sorrow. I cannot too strongly repeat my belief that this daily-recurring ceremony cannot fail to sharpen the line which severs these two classes, and to blacken that sharp line with the gall of reciprocal feelings of mingled pity, contempt, hatred, and malice, and all uncharitableness. No temporal benefit that can possibly result from these schools is sufficient to countervail the mischiefs flowing from this source.

If all the inhabitants of the country professed the same creed, no rational man would question the utility and the expediency of combining spiritual with secular instruction in the public schools. In that case, it would be not only practicable, but easy. So far from generating dissension, it would tend to confirm and perpetuate uniformity and concord; and it would be suggested by every consideration of human happiness, both here and hereafter. The diversity of creeds, and the assumed inconsistency of the truth of each with the truth of the others, and the belief (common to them all) that truth is essential to salvation, totally alters the case, and makes it impossible, without doing mischief, to combine any measure of religious instruction with secular teaching, in a school frequented by children of different persuasions.

Many earnest men, both clergy and Protestant laymen, complain that, in the State system of education the reading of the Bible is prohibited; and the clergy who so complain plead this as a justification for refusing all co-operation in this system, alleging that to co-operate in it is to commit sin, in the true and religious sense of the term. With a strange perversion of truth, they assume that the reading of the Bible is prohibited, because it is not made obligatory on the children to read it. I find it difficult to believe that this is candid.

The obligation to read the Bible is insisted on chiefly for the instruction and the salvation of the Roman Catholic children. The moment an attempt is made to enforce this obligation all the Roman Catholic children fly from the school; and if there be no other school, and no other means of learning to read, these children must grow up to be illiterate men and women, to whom the Bible is a sealed up, and wholly unintelligible book, as much so as a Hebrew Bible to a man who knows no language but English. On the other hand, remove all colour of obligation to read the Bible, and also remove every shadow of reason for apprehending interference with religious convictions, and children will freely attend, and learn to read, and the Bible will no longer be a hieroglyphic to their eyes. Being able to read it, curiosity, or other motive, may, at some time of their lives, prompt them to exercise the power. Thus it is a perfectly demonstrated proposition, that those who, by insisting on Scripture reading, scare children from the schools, are the persons who, of all mankind, most effectually prevent these people from reading the Bible. They, in effect, take the same course in respect of those children which the slave owners took with their slaves, when they made it criminal in them to learn, and in freemen to teach them how to read.

If some system, wholly confined to secular instruction, cannot be made acceptable to Irish parents of all creeds; if a combination of religious instruction is held to be indispensable, then State schools are doomed, in Ireland, to be a national calamity, an enduring subject of angry and bitter controversy, and a perennial source of agitation and animosity, much more obstructive of progress, and moral and material improvement, than any probable amount of ignorance, consequent on the absence of State schools, could possibly be. When you contemplate the formation of a governing Board, in which all religious creeds, and all political parties, shall be duly represented, you may with perfect truth be told,

> "Pergis pugnantia secum
> Frontibus adversis componere."

With this observation, I take leave of this grievance of the National System of Education in Ireland, as one which does not admit of any remedy, if religious instruction must be combined with secular teaching.

CHAPTER IV.

LANDLORDS AND TENANTS.

Another subject of agitation is the relation of landlord and tenant. That this relation, as it exists, constitutes an Irish grievance, appears to have been assumed by nearly all the popular writers and speakers in England who profess ability, and assume the right to discuss the subject of Irish affairs. Various remedies are suggested for this assumed grievance, and urged, with more or less assurance, by those who propose them. One is called fixity of tenure, the meaning of which I cannot understand, unless it be, that once a man gets possession of land, as tenant, at a rent, he shall never after be disturbed, as long as he pays the rent. How such a tenure as this can be reconciled with any respect for the landlord's property in the land no person has yet demonstrated; and I confess my inability to understand. One consequence of such a law would be, that no landlord would in future let his land, unless upon such terms as would be a full compensation to him for parting for ever with his property, in consideration of the rent reserved. In short, every letting must, under such a law, be equivalent to a fee-farm grant, on the reservation of a fee-farm rent, as high as, in any possible event, any tenant could pay for the land, or the landlord hope to get. This would be its effect on future lettings; but how is such a law to be applied to the existing contracts of tenancy, multifarious as they are? This question imposes a task which no practical man has yet approached. The difficulty of it will soon present itself, when any one proceeds to frame a bill upon the subject sufficiently plausible to become the subject of discussion in Parliament. I think this notion of fixity of tenure may be therefore postponed for the present, if not dismissed from further discussion, as a mere vision—an *ignis fatuus*—very suitable to an agitator's purpose, being a distant light to dazzle the eyes of deluded pursuers, but which will ever recede as they advance, and leave them at last to deplore the lost labour of their pursuit.

Tenant right is not so visionary, or so difficult to understand, because it is said to have, and has, a real and long established existence in Ulster.

In the spring of 1847, I was counsel for the Dublin and Belfast Junction Railway Company on the inquisitions, in Ulster, for valuing the land required for the undertaking. Much discussion took place upon the subject of tenant right when set up as an interest in the land, for which the occupier claimed distinct compensation. Every tenant who had a terminable lease, or held from year to year, in addition to the value of the tenancy, set up a claim to so many years' purchase of the value of the land itself; and this he claimed, not only over and above and in addition to the value of his legal tenancy, but also without professing, in the least, to diminish the claim of the landlord for the full value of his reversion, expectant upon the actual tenancy, estimated according to its legal duration, irrespective of tenant right. It was admitted, on all hands, that the Company ought not to be forced to pay more than the value of the fee-simple, and that the landlord was entitled to the full value of his reversionary estate, diminished only by the value of the outstanding legal term, or tenancy from year to year, determinable at the end of any year, by service of a notice to quit. It was also admitted that the tenant was entitled to the full value of the legal tenancy. That these two estates—one in reversion, and the other in possession—comprehended and exhausted the entire fee-simple in the land was too obvious to be even plausibly denied. After much discussion, sometimes very angry, on the part of the tenants, the jurors were brought, in most cases, to ignore the tenant right, and to value the two estates in the land as in other places, but sometimes tacitly assuming the duration of the tenancy to be more permanent than it would be regarded in other parts of Ireland.

It was impossible to deny that tenant right had some meaning and practical effect, in several counties in Ulster; and what that precise meaning and effect was no one could explain, further than to assert that the tenant could get money for it. However, I learned very clearly the nature of it from a single case which had occurred to a respectable tenant (whom I happened to know), whose lease had expired a few years before. His landlord refused to renew the lease, or allow him to hold on as yearly tenant, and altogether repudiated the claim of tenant right, as groundless in point of law. The tenant was a respectable, and well-to-do man, in the rank of a gentleman, and being advised by counsel, that he had not a legal right to overhold the farm, he gave it up on the expiration of the lease. He had succeeded his father, who had been for many years the tenant in possession of this farm; and turning him out was a clear and strong repudiation of the favourite notion of tenant right. However, he left quite peaceably, and took another farm, in the same county, a few miles distant; settled with his family upon it, and thought no more of his tenant right. In six or eight months after so quitting, the landlord accidentally met him on the public road, and stopped him, to say that he was then ready to give him a new lease of his farm, at the old rent. The tenant answered that he had taken another farm, and had settled upon it, and could not come back: but added, that if the landlord would give him a new lease, and allow him to sell his interest under it, he would accept it, and be thankful. The landlord consented; and, within a month, the tenant sold the new interest under the lease for £500. This fact may be relied on. I had it directly from the tenant, a highly respectable man, whom I had known for many years, and whose veracity I could not in the least doubt. He told me that no one had made any offer for his farm; that he had learned, that the tenants on the estate had exhibited evident dissatisfaction to the landlord, and generally passed him, without any mark of respect; and to this he attributed the willingness to grant a new lease. There was no threat, or thought of violence of any kind, nor did the landlord at all apprehend it. The law of opinion alone operated upon him, and vindicated its power, when the common law was imbecile to protect the old tenant.

Such is the true foundation of what is called, in Ulster, tenant right. In that province, public opinion on this subject is strong and prevalent; and, whether for good or for evil, it asserts, and enforces this tenant right, not by agrarian violence, but by force of general disapprobation, which few are able to resist.

To the existence of this right, such as it is, the prosperity of Ulster is sometimes attributed. But the true cause of that prosperity is the energy, the thrift, the determination, and strong will, which prevail more in that province than elsewhere in Ireland; and tenant right is one of the effects of these moral qualities: prosperity is another; and this prosperity is much more the cause than the effect of tenant right.

It requires but little reflection to see that no such right as this could be given, or in like manner enforced, by any enactment of statute law, consistently with the essential rights of property. No attempt has ever been made, on behalf of northern tenants, to clothe this local custom, supported solely by public opinion, with the force of a legal obligation. It rests on, and flows from, mutual confidence between landlord and tenant, every violation of which is strongly and generally discountenanced by public disapprobation. It is not in the power of the legislature to create such confidence, or give force to such public opinion, where they do not spontaneously exist. They must, like many other moral feelings and duties, be left entirely dependent upon the sanction of praise and blame, which must ever operate powerfully on the conduct of men in civilized communities. Any attempt on the part of the legislature to transplant this principle of tenant right from the province to which it is indigenous into any other part of Ireland will, to a moral certainty, prove abortive.

Another defect is alleged to exist in the law of landlord and tenant, in Ireland, from which it is asserted that a national grievance flows; and that is the landlord's power, by evicting his tenant, to seize, unjustly, the tenant's improvements. An elaborate attempt has already been made to apply a legislative remedy to this assumed evil. In 1860, an Act was framed, with a manifest effort to devise a remedy, without inflicting an injustice, or violating the rights of property. That Act has now been eight years on the Statute Book: all the legal machinery for working it is in existence, and at hand. The Chairmen of the several counties have jurisdiction, where landlords object to proposed improvements by tenants, to entertain applications for securing to the tenant the value of contemplated improvements. Yet I believe no tenants have ever resorted to them, and the part of the Act relating to improvements by tenants, to the present hour, is simply a dead letter. Its only effect is to prove the futility, by legislation, of any attempt to force free men into speculative contracts to which they are not prompted by reciprocal interests. If a tenant holds a farm on a terminable lease, and has capital which he thinks may be advantageously expended on improving his farm, and if what he proposes to do be, in the opinion of his landlord, beneficial to the reversion, there are but few cases in which these parties have not the power and inclination to carry their common wishes into effect. If they disagree in opinion, then, and not till then, comes the necessity for a compulsory law, which cannot be enforced without an appeal to some tribunal.

The 23 & 24 Vic., c. 153, sets up this tribunal, and with much apparent care defines the steps by which the willing tenant can force the unwilling landlord into compliance with his design. No one of any experience in the law, either as a practitioner, or as a victim, can fail to see that this preliminary suit must be costly and intricate, and be also invested with a full measure of the uncertainty of the law. This Cerberus, with the three heads of intricacy, expense, and uncertainty, standing at the door of the temple of justice, has for eight years effectually scared all suitors from attempting to enter. With no short or inconsiderable experience, both as a tenant and a lawyer, I know no more desperate subject of legislation than this of compulsory security to tenants for the value of their improvements.

To a superficial view, it is obviously plausible, that a tenant who lays out his capital, and applies his labour and skill in building, draining, or other improvements on his farm, should be protected from eviction; and that public interests demand such protection for him. This demand is not new, and the absence of this protection was, more than two centuries ago, complained of, in England, in very nearly the same terms which are now, every day, used in Ireland. A small book was published, and dedicated to Cromwell, in the year 1653, by Walter Bligh, one of his captains. In this dedication, the author "takes the boldness to present some few of the very great discouragements to the ingenuous and active prosecution of the improvements of the nation. The first prejudice," he says, "is, that if a tenant be at never so great paines or cost for the improvement of his land, he doth thereby but occasion a greater rack-rent upon himself, or else invests his landlord into his cost and labour *gratis*, or, at least, lies at his landlord's mercy for requitall; which occasions a neglect of all good husbandry, to his own, the land, the landlord, and the

Commonwealth's suffering. Now this I humbly conceive may be removed, if there were a law enacted, by which every landlord should be obliged either to give him reasonable allowance for his clear improvement, or else suffer him, or his, to enjoy it so much longer as till he hath had a proportionable requitall." I know of no such enactment as by this very remarkable passage was suggested. The difficulty then existed which now exists, and which for ever must exist, in determining beforehand the complicated question—what is an improvement for which the landlord should be compelled to pay? This question must ever be the subject of a preliminary suit, where the parties differ. Where they agree, neither Act of Parliament, nor suit is necessary.

When the relation of landlord and tenant is said to be vicious, and productive of discontent in Ireland; when the law on this subject (substantially the same as it has been, and still is in England) is stigmatized as productive of injustice to tenants and of obstacles to improvement; and when exceptional legislation is demanded, applicable solely to Ireland, common sense suggests the inquiry, whether any general enactment would be operative on, and applicable to, all the different classes of tenants existing in the country.

The separate legislatures which existed in England and Ireland, to the end of the last century, created differences in the laws of the two countries, notwithstanding a very general practice of the Irish Parliament, to follow and adopt the changes in the law which were made, from time to time, in England; and this disposition to imitate especially prevailed in respect of the relations between landlord and tenant. Almost every enactment made in England, on this subject, from the time of Henry VII. (up to the tenth year of whose reign all the previous laws of England were adopted for Ireland), was soon after followed by an Irish Act in the same terms. The national codes, however, materially diverged, and the divergence became a subject of complaint. The last commission to inquire into the state of the law, in both countries, ended in a Report strongly recommending assimilation, as a salutary and necessary measure of law reform, demanded by the interests of both countries; and on this recommendation the new Chancery Act for Ireland was passed, in opposition to strong arguments, and grave doubts as to the utility of the change.

In the face of this Report and recent legislation, England is now called upon to create a new divergence of Irish from English law in the all-important code relating to the tenure of land. In yielding to this demand, England will exhibit a new instance of the inconsistency with which she has legislated for, and governed Ireland, and thereby created nine-tenths of the difficulties with which she is now embarrassed in her connexion with this country.

The great extent of the tillage land which, in Ireland, is held by poor people, in small farms of from one to five or six acres, is so conspicuous a feature in the agricultural aspect of the couutry, that it has not escaped the notice of the most ignorant and heedless of the English professional and amateur State Physicians, who think themselves qualified to dictate remedies for Irish disorders.

The estates of lunatics and idiots, the estates of infants, and estates involved in litigation, are taken into the management of the Court of Chancery. Of these estates there are at present 655 in the custody of that Court. An officer of the Court, called a Receiver, is appointed over each, whose duty it is to collect the rents, and attend to the management of the property, subject to the control of the Court, as an agent does to the estate of his principal. Of the estates thus circumstanced 452 have come into the custody of the Court since 1850, and are under my jurisdiction: 203 are under the other three Masters, having been in Chancery before 1850. On the 452 estates in my office, there are 18,287 tenants, paying rents amounting to £330,809. On the 203 estates in the other offices, there are 10,294 tenants, paying rents amounting to £163,248. This shows an average rent, payable by each tenant, of about £17 a year. These estates are situate in all the counties of Ireland, and it will not be far from the truth to assume, that they fairly represent the general condition of all the landed estates in the kingdom.

Amongst the 28,581 tenants on these properties, some pay £500, and upwards, per annum, and some less amounts in a gradually descending scale. Those who pay over £100 are but a small fraction of the total number; and those who pay over £20 are still a great minority. Upon one estate producing a rental of £13,193, there are 2493 tenants, being an average for each tenant of about £5 6*s.* a year. The majority of the tenants on this property pay less than £3 each.

The land held in these small quantities, through the whole of Ireland, is nearly all in tillage; for it is only by tilling it that these poor people can pay rent and live. The cabin in which the tenant lives is generally of the most wretched description, both in structure and in size. Commonly it is without a chimney, and without a window; the only aperture for admission of air, and escape of smoke being the door. Although a person accustomed to a ventilated house could hardly breathe in the smoke of these cabins, yet custom not only makes it tolerable, but makes the warmth of it agreeable to the inhabitants.

From the principal entrance to Rockingham, the demesne of Lord Lorton, in the county of Roscommon, there is a fine view of a mountain at the opposite side of an intervening lake. On the side of the mountain, and high land over the water, a number of cottages are in view, and form a conspicuous feature in the landscape. To improve their appearance, the late Lord Lorton constructed a fireplace in each, with a projecting chimney. Some time after this improvement, the tenants sent a deputation to his lordship, complaining of the cold, and stating that all the heat of the fire escaped by the chimney, along with the smoke; adding an earnest prayer, that they might be allowed to place a flag on the top of the chimney, and thereby confine both the smoke and the warmth.

I should not be surprised to find that one half, if not much more than half, the tilled land of Ireland is held by tenants of this description. I have already assigned what I believe to be the chief cause of this remarkable and and socially important fact, viz., the general impossibility of cultivating the land by hired labourers without loss.

The aversion from tillage of large landholders in Ireland is of long standing, and was the subject of much complaint in the last century.

In a letter, already adverted to, addressed to the then Lord Lieutenant, on the 24th Feb., 1727, Primate Boulter, on the subject of a bill then before Parliament, commented on this grievance in the following terms:—" I shall now acquant your Grace with the great want we are in of this bill; our present tillage falls very short of answering the demands of this nation, which occasions our importing corn from England, and other places; and, whilst our poor have bread to eat, we do not complain of this; but, by tilling so little, if our crop fails, or yields indifferently, our poor have not money to buy bread. This was the case in 1725, and last year; and, without a prodigious crop, will be more so this year. When I went my visitation last year, barley, in some inland places, sold for six shillings a bushel, to make the bread of; and oatmeal (which is the bread of the North) sold for twice or thrice the usual price; and we met all the roads full of whole families that had left their homes to beg abroad, since their neighbours had nothing to relieve them with. And as the winter subsistence of the poor is chiefly potatoes, this scarcity drove the poor to begin with their potatoes before they were full grown; so that they have lost half the benefit of them, and have spent their stock about two months sooner than usual, and oatmeal is, at this distance from harvest, in many parts of this kingdom, three times the customary price; so that this summer must be more fatal to us than the last, when, I fear, many hundreds perished by famine.

" Now, the occasion of this evil is, that many persons have hired large tracts of land, on to 3000 or 4000 acres and have stocked them with cattle, and have no other inhabitants on their lands than so many cottiers as are necessary to look after their sheep and black cattle; so that in some of the finest counties, in many places, there is neither house nor corn-field to be seen in ten or fifteen miles' travelling; and daily, in some counties, many gentlemen (as their leases fall into their hands) tie up their tenants from tillage; and this is one of the main causes why so many venture to go into foreign service at the hazard of their lives, if taken, because they can get no land to till at home."

The bill thus alluded to passed that Session into the Act 1 Geo. II., cap. 10, the 7th section of which is in these terms:—"For as much as several persons in this kingdom keep great quantities of land under stock to the great discouragement of tillage, and manifest prejudice of the poor of this kingdom; be it enacted, that, after the first day of November, 1729, all and every person and persons who shall keep in his actual possession, or occupation, any quantity of arable or pasture land, amounting to 100 acres, plantation measure, so as the same do not lie within five miles of Dublin, shall annually till, plough, and sow, with corn or grain, five acres at the least, plantation measure; and so proportionably for any greater quantity of any such arable or pasture land that he shall so possess, or occupy, notwithstanding any covenant to the contrary; from which said covenant, so far as same relates to the ploughing of said five acres, the said tenant is by the authority of this present Act discharged, and saved harmless. And every such occupier who shall neglect or refuse so to do, shall forfeit for every acre that shall not be tilled, ploughed, and sowed, according to the true intent and meaning hereof, 40*s*., to be recovered by civil bill."

The large holders of land being thus driven to till one-twentieth of what was arable, and not finding it profitable to do so by hired labourers, they let the five acres to poor yearly tenants, who tilled it with their own hands; and the land so let, in obedience to this Act, was called corn-acres, which has been corrupted into conacre, the name given in Ireland to this sort of tenure. I have no doubt that to this Act of Parliament—passed as a remedy for a then assumed Irish grievance—may be traced a vast number of the cottier holdings, the existence of which constitutes an Irish grievance of the present time, when they have become so numerous in Ireland.

To imagine that these poor people could devise and make permanent improvements on their paltry farms, and miserable hovels, and pursue a course of legal proceedings, by which to compel their landlords to pay for the unexhausted remains of these improvements, at the termination of the tenancy, is the visionary dream of men who have no practical knowledge whatever on the subject, and know less about the habits of the people for whom they would legislate than they do of the inhabitants of central Africa.

Above the cottier farmers here described, there are several grades of occupiers of land better entitled to the name of farmers; and in localities where the soil is peculiarly fit for corn crops, tillage is carried on to a considerable extent by tenants of more or less capital, and of various, and very widely different degrees of skill and intelligence, and with corresponding variety in the result of their operations.

The high prices of corn during the long war greatly increased the number of these; and promoted improvements in agriculture, of which but little notice is taken in the discussions on the state of Ireland; and which improvements have taken place, and are still advancing, not by any aid from the Legislature, but notwithstanding its sinister activity. To this class of farmers belong Scotchmen, who have come on farming speculation to this country, and, perhaps, a few also from England. About nine years ago an Englishman took a farm near mine, applied much industry and skill in the cultivation of crops for Dublin market; and after six or seven years' unavailing struggle against the cost of labour, gave it up, and returned to England. To the class of tenants here mentioned belong all who can, with any reason, be regarded as able to expend capital in the improvement of their lands. To these will be exclusively confined the operation of any enactment securing to the tenant the value of unexhausted improvements. Such of these as are well to do, and have capital to expend, are quietly attending to their business, and having nothing to do with the agitators who disturb the peace of society, no legislation for tenants, even should it confer some benefit on these, will have the effect of quieting traders in agitation.

There is another class of tenants, who hold large tracts of pasture lands, in some cases mountain land and light coarse pasture, on which money is made by breeding and rearing black cattle and sheep; in other cases rich grass lands, used for fattening cattle and sheep, purchased as stores, from the breeders. These cattle farmers are neither tillers, or improvers. They give very little employment, nor are they disposed to become employers. They are the modern representatives of those persons complained of by Primate Boulter, in the last century, who, by hiring large tracts of land, and stocking them with cattle, occasioned the mischief which produced the corn-acre Act. Many of the extensive tillage farmers, and of these cattle farmers, I have no doubt, are desirous of some enactment by which difficulties may be thrown in the way of landlords desirous to resume possession, or to raise the rents, at the termination of existing contracts; but if any one expects, that, by any such enactment, the country will be tranquillized; that agriculture will be improved, or that any other beneficial effect will be produced by it, or by any other legislative interference between these tenants and their landlords, he will certainly be disappointed. If in framing such new law, the rights of property shall be respected and sufficiently protected, no tenant will attempt to take advantage of its provisions, complicated as they must be, and certainly will be; and it will fall dead-born, like the former Acts, from the hands of the Legislature. If, as desired by the tenants, it shall confer the power of improving the landlord out of his estate, it will sharpen the ingenuity of one party to assail, and of the other to protect the property affected by it, and confer on the legal profession what will probably be the only benefits derivable from it. If it shall produce any effects, this will be one of them. It is also likely to be a peculiarly Irish law, and, according to a national principle before noticed, it will invert the rule of justice, by rewarding ingenuity and fraud, and by punishing simple honesty, if it happens to be deficient in ability to defend itself against crafty assailants.

CHAPTER V.

THE FORMER AND THE PRESENT CONDITION OF THE IRISH PEOPLE, AND ALLEGED CAUSES OF DISCONTENT.

It is assumed that Ireland is discontented, and that the poor and wretched condition of the people is one of the causes of their discontent. In this assumption another is involved, viz., that those who are discontented are the Irish nation, or the Irish people, whichever you please to call them. When it is thus assumed that those who are poor, destitute, and miserable, and therefore discontented, are the Irish people, no notice whatever is taken of the energetic, the industrious, the prosperous, but silent part of the community, who mind their business, and mind nothing else, unless when their attention is forced to, and their alarm excited by, the agitation which disturbs the peace of the country, provokes empirical legislation, and gives these also some just reason to be discontented. Yet this numerous, industrious, intelligent, but silent, and therefore ignored, body of the nation, are those who efficiently carry on the business of the country, and have, under all difficulties and discouragements, accomplished the improvements which are in all parts of Ireland obvious to the most careless observer, and to which I shall call attention, when I come to contrast the present with the past condition of the country ; when I come to state how the poor and labouring classes formerly lived, how they were fed, clad, housed, and protected, in former times, and how at present. Their modern life and condition are still seen and remembered: their ancient state is now but traditional, and not easily rescued from oblivion. History takes but little notice of the cottager, or his habits, food, raiment, wants, and woes. Battles are fought, victories achieved, and revolutions accomplished; these are recorded, and give notoriety, or reputation, to the nation, and interest to its history; but the starving multitudes, who co-existed with those events, perish unnoticed, and with them all memory of the sufferings which they endured, and the squalid misery in which they existed.

It is only from tradition that the habits and the domestic condition of the Irish people, in and previous to the last century, can be rescued from oblivion. It would be vain to seek in books for any adequate description of them. In Acts of Parliament, and in pamphlets, and ephemeral publications which are still extant, passages are to be found by which to corroborate tradition, or test its truth or accuracy. The accounts given by such writers as Arthur Young are delusive, and give a coloured, and, in important particulars, a false complexion to the state of society which they describe. A tourist comes with introductions to people in high life, who delight in showing him the happy circumstances which surround themselves, and the expensive works which they sometimes carry on for the improvement of their demesne lands. To compose an agreeable narrative of a pleasant tour is the author's object; it would run counter to his purpose, to mention the stupid operations, or squalid misery of cottiers and peasants, even if such objects attracted his attention.

From my earliest childhood I lived in constant and most intimate association with a man who was born in 1748, until his death in 1837, at the age of eighty-nine. He was of the middle class, and spent his long and laborious life in constant intercourse with the working people, of whom, for many years, he was an extensive employer. The agricultural operations of the country were, winter and summer, constantly under his view. Having lived to see great changes, he was fond of comparing things as they had been in his early memory with those which he saw in his old-age. His father was born in 1710, and died, at the age of eighty-four, in 1795. Thus many social habits, and many endemic calamities, not noticed by any historian, have traditionally descended, and are still fresh in living memory. In the annals of Ireland, as it was before the English Invasion, there is little to be found descriptive of the social and domestic habits of the people. So far as these can now be traced, by inference from what is known of their laws, and other authentic records, nothing can be discovered in them which a philanthropist could desire to see revived. No effects of laborious industry or agricultural skill can now be traced. No evidence of national union or national strength can be discovered; while the proofs of intestine discord, broils, and battles, and internecine feuds, are patent in every page of their authentic history. A disposition, and apparently native propensity, to continue these destructive quarrels, is one of the most obvious parts of their moral inheritance. Aversion from tillage, and partiality to cattle and to pastoral life, was also one of their most palpable characteristics, and so continues to the present hour. The aboriginal Irish followed the wandering habit of the Scythians, and continually sought new pastures for their cattle. Hence what Spencer observed of them, in the sixteenth century, that neither landlords would give, nor tenants take, land for any greater term than from year to year, or at will. From the reason which he gives for this, we can infer one of their social habits, viz., "that the landlords there used most shamefully to racke their tenants, laying upon them coigny and livery at pleasure, and exacting of them (besides his covenants) what he pleaseth." These exactions were countenanced, not by English Government or English laws, but formed a part of ancient Irish dealing of landlords with their tenants, and were protected by native Irish laws, until they were restrained by a statute in the 10 & 11 Charles I., c. 16, entitled "an Act for suppressing of cosherers and wanderers." This Act recites that these cosherers and wanderers were young gentlemen that had little or nothing to live on of their own, and, in the preamble, gives a graphic account of the way in which these gentlemen (who were no other than native Irish landlords, or, perhaps, their sons) sessed themselves, their followers, their horses, and their greyhounds, upon the poor inhabitants; sometimes exacting money from them, to spare them and their tenants, and to go elsewhere for their "caught and edraugh"—old Irish words for supper and breakfast. These cosherers and wanderers were the still existing specimens of native Irish gentlemen and landlords, whose homes were destitute of provisions or comforts (from the difficulties which existed in the conveyance of supplies from distant places), and who, therefore, made wandering visitations upon their tenants—analagous to the ancient progresses of the

English Sovereign and courtiers, whose approach, in the sister Island, was a calamity from which their subjects often fled, as from devouring locusts.

The Irish race of farmers are tenacious of the national pastoral habit to the present day, and it still exists, especially in the counties of Limerick, Tipperary, and Roscommon, where the richest pasture land in Ireland is to be found. The extensive grazing and dairy farms of these counties, and the habit of *hiring* them which is yet practised, are an evident relic of Irish nationality. There is, in the neighbourhood of my country place, within six miles of Dublin, a well-known individual, who very accurately represents the true aboriginal race of Ireland. His dress, an ample frieze surtout, is nearly allied to what Spencer describes as the Irish garb, in the reign of Elizabeth. He cannot read or write. He has, as I recollect, four sons, all grown: none of these can read or write. He holds very little land (and this but recently) by lease, or permanent contract of any kind. Yet he is commonly the owner of five or six thousand sheep and one or two hundred head of horn-cattle. These he buys at fairs, and pastures them upon lands which he hires for the summer half-year, or winter half-year, or for the whole year, just as he can get it, from extensive farmers who hold it on lease, or from gentlemen who find no profit in farming their demesnes, and get rid of risk and trouble by hiring the grazing of them to this man, who competes for it with the owners of Dublin dairy cows. He tills no land, gives no employment, lives in what an English farmer would call a den: his sons are dressed as he is himself, and have no ambition to be anything but what their forefathers have been since Noah's flood. To suggest improvement, in person or in condition, to these, is to speak on a subject they neither understand nor wish to study. They are a perfect specimen of the Irish farming class which existed when the English first came amongst them, and for many centuries after, and which still exists, but in a modified form. It is not many days since one of this class, as like one of the sons of my neighbour as a twin brother, appeared in my office, to bid for the grazing of a farm in the county of Limerick, for one year; and I accepted his offer of £400—one half of which he paid on getting the possession, and for the second half he was considered excellent security.

I had directly from my old friend, who was familiar with Ireland in the last century, a vivid description of the residence of one of this type, as he saw it about the year 1795, when, in the winter season, he went to it to buy a cow. The wall of the house was about six feet high, covered with a thatched roof. It was over fifty yards long, and wide enough to allow a passage between the tails of two rows of cows, tied with their heads to the walls inside. The door was at one end, and there was no other aperture in the walls or the roof. The visitor was informed, by a cow-boy, near the house, that his master was in bed, and that the stranger might go to him if he pleased. The door was open, and through this a fire was faintly visible at the other end of the house. The stranger entered, and made his way to the fire, by the long passage between the tails of the cows, through muck three or four inches deep. The owner lay in a rude bed, beside the topmost cow at that side, and within three feet of the tail of a cow at the top of the other row. He raised himself up, and expressed pleasure at seeing his customer, to whom he had sold cattle before at fairs. Though he was in bed, long after high noon, there was nothing amiss with him, except the chronic sloth which made bed the place most agreeable on a winter day. While the treaty for a cow proceeded, the beast, at whose heels the bed was, backed a little, and her bowels being free, she sent a volley, which fell on the coarse rug that covered the bed. An exclamation burst from the visitor; but the tranquil host quietly shook off as much as the rug was willing to part with, repeating an Irish proverb, which, in English, declares, that "there is luck in muck." His wife and her maid were enjoying the light and heat of the fire, at a distance of a few feet from the cows and the bed; and, with about fifty cows, made up the family of a man who had the reputation of a wealthy cattle farmer. When we hear so much lamentation over the loss of Irish nationality, this traditional description of one feature of it is surely worth preserving.

When false and exaggerated descriptions of Irish misery of the present time are forced upon public attention, with disastrous effect upon the temper of the people, and ruinous consequences to the reputation and the material advancement of the country, it cannot be useless or impertinent to call attention to that state of things, from which it is boldly and without a blush asserted, that the people have FALLEN into a hopeless and intolerable state of suffering and starvation.

Touching the former state of Ireland, although history is silent, there are some authentic records still in existence, which corroborate, but in no way depend on tradition.

Thus an Act of Parliament, 10 & 11 Chas. I., cap. 15,

passed in 1635, recites:—"Whereas, in many places of this kingdom, there hath been a long time used a barbarous custom of ploughing, harrowing, drawing, and working with horses, mares, and geldings, by the tail: and whereas also divers have and yet do use the like barbarous habit of pulling off the wool yearly from living sheep, instead of clipping or shearing them:" it then enacts a penalty to restrain these barbarous customs; yet, after the middle of the last century, the gentleman who lived to see the horses of 1837, saw the barbarous custom still used of *harrowing* by the tail, a century and a quarter after it was made penal to practise it.

The next Act of the same Session recites, that "whereas there is, in the remote parts of this kingdom of Ireland, commonly a great dearth of cattle yearly, which for most part happeneth by reason of ill husbandry and improvident care of the owners, that neither provide fodder nor stover for them in winter, nor houses to put them, in extremity of cold weather; but a natural lazy disposition possessing them that will not build barns, to house and thresh their corn in, or houses to keep their cattle from the violence of such weather, but better to enable them to be flitting from their lands, and to deceive His Majesty of such debts as they may be owing at any time, and their landlords of their rents, do for great part, instead of threshing, burn their corn in the straw, thereby consuming the straw, which might relieve their cattle in winter, and afford materials towards the covering or thatching their houses, and spoiling the corn, making it black, loathsome and filthy;" for preventing of which a penalty was enacted, with a proviso giving liberty for two years to burn six bartes, i. e. 120 sheaves, in consideration of the difficulty of suddenly changing an inveterate custom.

Although the burning of the corn was not continued to the time of my informant, the cattle were still starved, and were in, what was called, a lifting condition, during the months of February, March, and April of every year. His account was, that in the longest day's ride, every beast to be seen in the fields, in these months, (and very few were housed until towards the end of the last century), had a straw rope round its body, by which to set the poor animal on its legs, being, without help, unable to rise from starvation. This process of lifting was performed by five men, of whom two at each side laid hold of the rope, and the fifth took his hold by the tail. A proverbial expression, which I still remember, in Irish, is founded on the operation thus described; the English of which is, "let the owner go to the tail," that being the most disagreeable hold of the poor beast.

Such was the annually recurring condition of the cattle, in the spring months of the year. In June, July, and August, man's turn to starve came, as certainly as the cattle famine had come in spring. When the potatoes were done, as they were from the middle of June, the poor man was reduced to live on cabbage, simply boiled in water, and improved by a mixture of sour milk, from which the cream had been skimmed. Butter being the principal produce of the extensive grass farms; the skimmed milk was of little value, except for pigs and poor labourers, and on this nauceous diet they were reduced to live for more than two months of every summer. Its effect was to bring on diarrhœa, by which the poor population was more than decimated every year, and kept below two millions and a half, which it had not attained until 1765, a time long within the memory of my informant. Another proverbial expression relates to this state of things, viz.: "July and cabbage." I also remember a common saying in the county of Limerick, viz., "that the cows in Kerry knew Sunday. The origin of this proverb was, that in Kerry, during the famine months of summer, when the cows had recovered, and had fattened on the summer grass, it was customary with the starving owners to bleed them, on Sunday, and make a holyday meal of the blood, boiled with a mixture of sour milk, and seasoned with salt.

In a letter of Primate Boulter to the Duke of Newcastle, dated March 7, 1727, he wrote: "Since I came here, in the year 1725, there was almost a famine among the poor: last year, the dearness of corn was such, that thousands of families quitted their habitations to seek bread elsewhere, and many hundreds perished. This year the poor had consumed their potatoes, which is their winter subsistence, near two months sooner than ordinary, and are already, through the dearness of corn, in that want, that, in some places, they begin already (i. e. in March) to quit their habitations."

In a letter to the same Duke, dated November 23, 1728, he describes the melancholy state of things in the North of Ireland, from which above 4200 men, women, and children, had been shipped off for the West Indies within three years, and of these, 3100 in the then last summer. He adds, "that of these perhaps one in ten might be a man of substance, and might do well enough abroad, but the case of the rest is deplorable; the rest either hire themselves to those of substance for their passage, or contract with masters of ships for four years' servitude when they come thither, or if they make a shift to pay for their passage, will be under a necessity of selling themselves for servants for four years for their subsistence when they come there. The whole north is in a ferment at present, and people every day engaging one another to go next year to the West Indies. The humour has spread like a contagious distemper, and the people will hardly bear anybody that tries to cure them of their madness. The worst is that it affects only Protestants, and reigns chiefly in the north, which is the seat of our linen manufacture."

In a letter to Sir Robert Walpole, dated March 31, 1729, he wrote: "I cannot help mentioning on this occasion, that what with scarceness of corn in the north, and the loss of all credit there by the numbers that go, or talk of going to America, and with the disturbance in the south, this kingdom is at present in a deplorable condition."

These letters of Primate Boulter end in 1737, two years before he witnessed the famine, occasioned by the great frost of 1739–40, and which for two years continued to depopulate the country, and for the partial relief of which Primate Boulter's humanity expended his own portion of the Protestant Church revenues. Of the horrors of that famine I know of no record, except by tradition. The father of my informant was then thirty years of age. The scenes which he then witnessed made deep impressions upon him, and were a natural topic of conversation in his family. His descriptions have thus traditionally reached me through a perfectly authentic channel, and they agree with another tradition of those sufferings, to which I shall immediately call attention. He described famishing men, women, and children, during the two ensuing summers, wandering, like living skeletons, in the fields, and by the ditches, searching for sorrel, dandelion, cresses, and any other edible weeds, which they ravenously devoured, and died in hundreds and thousands, from the diarrhœa, brought on by such food. He described one village, in the county of Waterford, (the name of which I do not remember), in which the only human being who survived was an old man. The corresponding tradition, to which I have alluded, is contained in a letter from Mr. Eugene Curry, the late eminent Irish scholar, dated the 7th March, 1847, and addressed to the late Doctor Petrie, whose memory will long be honoured in Ireland. That letter was, during the famine which ensued the potato blight of 1846, published, in a pamphlet, with such notices of the plague of 1740 and 1741 as could be found in the ephemeral publications of that time. These cotemporary notices have been also collected and reprinted by Sir William Wilde in the Census of 1851, page 124.

Mr. Curry's letter, being an authentic description of one of the greatest national calamities that ever afflicted any country, is worth preserving. The plague of London, so graphically described by De Foe, who took it only from tradition, was a subject of inferior magnitude and interest, if compared with the depopulation of Ireland, in the middle of the last century. Mr. Curry's letter is as follows:—

March, 7, 1847.

"You will, I think, recollect that I have more than once since the commencement of the present most distressing season of famine and disease spoken to you, from traditionary recollection, of the dreadful famine and mortality which raged throughout Ireland, especially in the south and west, during the years 1740 and 1741. I well remember Ann Curry, who was sixteen years old in 1740, and who died in 1817. She was my father's cousin, and lived much in our house, and distinctly remembered the appalling circumstances of that fearful season.

"It was not usual, as I have often heard both my father and cousin say, for the farmers to dig their potatoes until about Christmas; and very few of the great farmers stored them at all for use. In 1739, the frost set in severely some days before Christmas, and totally destroyed all the potatoes that had been left in the ground. The frost was so great, and of so long continuance, that the people were not able to open the ground for the reception of the spring seed; and hence a great dearth of food, and a destructive mortality ensued. My grandfather was at this time living at Moveen, near Kilkee, in the west of the county of Clare, and, with his brother, farmed one thousand acres. When the famine and mortality were raging, in 1740 and 1741, his out-houses and barns were always full of the poor, and his constant business during these two seasons was to take care of those sick and dying creatures, and frequently to bury them himself, alone. The ordinary burial grounds were not capacions enough to receive the crowds that were dying around him; but there was a long unfrequented burying ground, called Killoasheen, on his own lands, and about two miles from his own house. In this place he got his workmen to dig deep and long trenches, in which he buried all that died in his neighbourhood, covering them often with his own hands; for such was the terror of the stoutest men, that they fled from the presence of the dying and the dead: not only did he aid in burying those who died in his own neighbourhood, but he went with his horse and slide (a cart without wheels, of which I remember to have seen some specimens) all over the parish, taking the dead and often putrid bodies out of the deserted houses, and out of the ditches, and heaping them on his slide, like so many sacks of corn, brought them to his own burying ground, and there cast them in as best he could, without any assistance, and, of course, without coffins.

"The general complaint of the people was fever and flux, and the mortality was not confined to the poor and starving alone, but it attacked and carried off great numbers of the comfortable farmers and gentlemen of the country.

"Tillage in the year 1740 was sadly deficient, owing, perhaps, as much to the despair of the people as to their actual sufferings; but, whatever the cause, the effect was the same, and the year 1741 was even worse than that which preceded it. Horses, cows, sheep, pigs, and poultry, all were struck by the plague, and perished; and the mortality of the people must have been increased by feeding on the diseased animals. There were, it is said, shoals of dead fish cast on shore, on which the people also fed, but it is not believed that such food was unwholesome.

"The next harvest was plentiful, and it was said that

cows being very scarce, a sheep produced as much milk that year as a cow would in ordinary seasons.

"The year 1741 was always mentioned as *bliadhain an air*, i. e. 'the year of the slaughter.'

"The district to which these recollections apply extends from Kilkee to Loop Head, and includes the Catholic parishes of Morgarta and Killballyowen, and, doubtless, there must have been many other acts of humanity and generosity, performed by individuals of whom I have never heard."

The frost which produced this national calamity commenced on Christmas Day, 1739, which corresponds with the 6th of January of the present style. The people of Ireland then numbered about 2,300,000; of these, according to a computation in the small pamphlet just referred to, extracted from a record which I have not seen, by Rutty and O'Connell, one-fifth of this population perished by starvation, and consequent pestilence, in 1740. According to another publication in 1742, called "The Groans of Ireland," it was computed that 400,000 perished—taking it that one person died for every house in the kingdom. An extract is given from a pamphlet published by the Rev. Philip Skelton, in 1741, in these words: "It was computed that as many people died of want, and disorders occasioned by it, during that time, as fell by the sword in the rebellion of 1641. Whole parishes were almost desolate; and the dead were eaten in the fields by dogs, for want of people to bury them."

Such was the ignorance of the people, that they were unable to devise any means of preserving the root on which they existed from destruction by the frost. They saved what served for seed, by stuffing potatoes into the bed ticks on which they slept, but all the rest was abandoned in despair.

When England is abused for the alleged misgovernment of Ireland, and when to such assumed misgovernment miseries are ascribed, which flow not from misgovernment, but from moral causes which no government has any power to remove, which must be left to the operation of time, and to the slow process of intellectual improvement, it cannot be impertinent to compare the consequences of the great frost of 1739–40 with what followed a very little, if anything, less intense frost in 1814. This last frost commenced on the 6th of January—the very anniversary of the former frost: it continued for four weeks, unabated. The Shannon, at Athlunkard, two miles above Limerick, was bridged with ice (where a stone bridge has since been erected)—a thing which nobody had ever seen or heard of before. I saw the ice, which, in vast sheets, floated down the river at the thaw, measured, and it was fourteen inches thick. In the middle of the streets in Dublin the snow was piled in a high bank, through which apertures like arches were made at the crossings. It was not completely thawed until the end of February.

In 1814 the population of Ireland was 5,937,856, according to the Census recorded in Thom. It is not an exaggeration to say that the potato crop of 1814 was ten times as large as that of 1739; yet no potatoes were destroyed by the frost of 1814, and no famine followed, because the people had acquired sufficient agricultural knowledge to protect them. This knowledge resulted not from any legislative remedies for ignorance, prescribed by State physicians, or suggested by patriot orators, but had emanated from particular points and localities, in which enterprising and energetic men had introduced improvements from abroad, or discovered by individual ingenuity and observation. Much of it, in the south of Ireland, flowed from a colony of German Protestants planted near Adare, in the county of Limerick, about that calamitous year, 1740. These men maintained their ground, and some of their descendants still maintain it, in slated houses, defended by well-armed owners against the assaults and the hatred of the natives who surrounded them; and who, in despite of their hatred, came, year by year, to imitate the good husbandry by which the strangers produced crops conspicuously better than their own. From this colony came the fact, that the best cultivated crops of potatoes and corn I ever saw in Ireland were to be seen in the county of Limerick, from Adare to Rathkeale, where these Germans had been located.

The Scotch plough and the Scotch cart made their first appearance in Ireland about the year 1808, or 1809; and when we are comparing the agricultural state of the kingdom, from which, it is trumpeted, we have *fallen*, with our present alleged condition, it is worthy of some labour to call attention to the implements which were so effectually superseded by those from Scotland, that it has been, for many years, impossible to find a specimen of the old implements in the length and breadth of the land. One of them would now be considered worthy of a place in a museum of agricultural curiosities.

The Irish plough was all wood, except the coulter and

the sock, and one narrow plate of iron rudely nailed on the sole of the plough, where the friction was greatest. What was called the board was a log of crab-tree, or some other hard timber, shaped with an axe to resemble one of the bows of a Dutch ship: the beam was short and quite straight: the handles were also straight, and were fixed in the sole at an angle of about 45 degrees. This implement, and the mode of using it, are pretty fairly described by Horatio Townsend in his Statistical Survey of the county of Cork, first edition, page 190, published in the year 1810, when he states that the Scotch plough was then very much used in the neighbourhood of Cork. He thus describes the then existing plough in all parts of Ireland.

"The common plough of this country is rude in its form and defective in its execution. The handles are short and thick, the beam low, and bending a little to the right hand. Instead of standing upright, and making a fair and handsome furrow, the coulter and sock are placed so obliquely as to oblige the ploughman to turn it to the left side, in such a manner as to keep the mould-board entirely out of the ground. The office of turning over the sod is therefore performed partly by the heel of the plough, and partly by the foot of the man, who is obliged to assist the operation by frequent kicks. Though they remove but little earth at the time, no part but the sock entering the soil, the draught is rendered difficult by the length of the chain. In ploughing old ground, an additional man is often required, to keep the plough in the ground, by leaning on the beam, as well as to free it from weeds and briars that collect upon it."

Three inches was the utmost depth at which the strength of two, and, in some counties, four horses, could draw this implement through the soil. To the eye of a modern farmer, a field turned by this plough would suggest the belief that a herd of swine had had their will of it.

The complement of men required to work this Irish phough, when least, was three, viz., one to lead the horses, one with a worn spade to be continually poking at the mould-board, to rid it of the clay which adhered to it, and the ploughman between the handles. To these, in stiff soil, or in lea land, should be added a fourth, with a wooden fork, to lean on the point of the beam, to keep the coulter in the ground; this man and he who kept the mould-board free from clay stood at opposite sides of the plough, and moved side foremost the whole day.

Arthur Young tells us, that, in the county of Clare, they yoked four horses all abreast to their plough, and there his description ends. I cannot believe that he saw the Clare plough at work, or he certainly would give a more ample description of the curious mode of using that machine. I have that description from a man who saw it at work every year from his childhood to the end of the last century. The four horses, all abreast, were guided by a man who held the two centre horses, one in each hand, and walked backward himself, like a rope-spinner, from morning till night. It frequently happened that he was tripped up by a clod, and thrown on his back, and owed his life to the readiness of the horses to stop, and to the well-known reluctance of that animal to set a foot on a fallen man. This *guide* made a fifth man necessary to complete the working staff of the Clare plough, because this man who guided, walking backward and hands engaged holding two horses, could not also drive ; and a man, with a whip in his hand, walked with the team, and whistled musically to please the horses. Such was the plough of Ireland, and the only plough to be seen for years after the beginning of my own memory : I never saw any other until after I left my first school. The Clare team I did not see, for I never was through that county until after it was superseded by the Scotch plough.

The Irish cart, called, in that country, a truckle, was in all respects a worthy rival of the Irish plough. It consisted of two clumsy shafts, about five feet asunder at the rere, and converging so as just to admit room for the horse at the points. These shafts were connected by transverse laths, morticed into them behind the horse, with a rail at each side, and a rail at the back, supported by upright rails on which they were mortised, and which were also mortised into the shafts. These enclosed the space in which the burthen, whatever it might be, was to be placed. The wheels were about two feet in diameter, and consisted of three segments of a circle of solid wood, about four inches thick, dowled together, and shaped into two equal circles, as accurately as a country carpenter could do. In the centre of each was a square mortice, into which the axle was inserted, which axle was about six feet of a natural tree, six inches in diameter, and of which the parts next to the wheels were made as round and as smooth as the carpenter could accomplish with a chisel, or a spoke-shave. It follows that the two wheels and axle revolved together, like those of a railway carriage, which made it important that the wheels should be made accurately the same size, a task to be only approximately performed by a hedge carpenter, without lathe, or callipers, or other proper tools for the purpose. To the lower sides of the shafts, at the point which was to rest on the axle, a plate of cast iron (called the bolster) was nailed, the down-side being concave, to fit the round axle, which was kept in contact with the bolster by two round iron loops, like the letter U, embracing the axle, and thrust up through the shafts, and there kept by nuts screwed on the points. The tire was not a hoop; it consisted of four or five separate pieces called streaks, nailed on the circumference of the wheels with large nails, having heads the size of walnuts, and projecting, the object of which was to save the tire from being too speedily worn. These lumps of iron were about six inches apart on the face of the wheel, and each as it touched the road became an impediment to be overcome by the horse. These nails were at last attacked by the Legislature, and treble toll exacted for them at turnpike gates—a law which records this specimen of mechanical skill. For the truckle thus constructed the common load was from 4 cwt. to 6 cwt., according to the ability of the horse. Eight cwt. was considered an extraordinary weight, and to be drawn only by an extraordinary horse. In a journey of any length, it was common to have the grease on the axle exhausted; and I have heard the screams of it at a quarter of a mile distance. This truckle, such as it was, had succeeded a still ruder vehicle, which moved on slides, without wheels, and is mentioned in Mr. Curry's letter.

From the state of the roads, and the defective approaches to habitations at a distance from roads, carriage or horse-back was very generally used ; and often used in a way highly characteristic of the nation. On my return from the Connaught circuit, I once paid a visit to Dr. Sandes, the then Bishop of Cashel, who had been my tutor in Trinity College. He asked me about what I had seen in Connaught. I told him I saw in Mayo what I had often heard of, but had never seen before, viz., the load suspended at one side of the horse, balanced by a stone of equal weight, at the other side. "Well," said he, "for twenty years of my early life, I saw, every year, several times during the butter season, fifty horses, each led by a man, and having a firkin of butter suspended at one side, and at the other side a stone to balance it, all leaving my father's townland of Sallow Glyn, in the county of Kerry, in a troop, for Cork, a journey of fifty Irish miles ; and it never occurred to them to leave twenty-five of the horses and the fifty stones at home."

These are a few specimens, and only a few, of the agricultural skill and social habits of the Irish people, not imported by the English intruders, but forming a part of the nationality which the British Legislature is called upon to restore to Ireland, in which this nationality flourished before an English foot was set upon the island.

If nationality means anything, it must mean an assemblage of those things which are peculiar to, and pervade one section of the human race, to which the name of nation is given : such as to inhabit a defined country: to speak a common language : to wear a peculiar dress: to relish certain kinds of food, cooked according to a pervading national taste: to live in houses, with or without windows or chimneys, or burrowed in the ground, like the Armenians described by Xenophon, &c. It would be well to call upon some eloquent Irish patriot to specify some time in the authentic history of Ireland, and to group the social habits peculiar to the Irish, and constituting, at that time, the nationality which he would now restore to the Irish people. If I mistake not, this would be an embarrassing requisition.

That a fertile country so inhabited as Ireland was, according to every tradition which exists of the aboriginal people, should attract invaders, no one can be surprised. That it was defenceless is conclusively proved by the success of Strongbow's descent, with a force almost as contemptible in modern eyes as the Fenian army which was encountered and put to flight by a few policemen, last year, within a mile of my country house.

The wars and rebellions; the cruelties, and oppressions which ensued; the spoliations, and seizures of property; the forfeitures of land by original owners; and the grants made to their invaders, were nothing different in kind, and were less in degree, than the wrongs of the same character suffered by every nation in Europe, during those centuries which followed the ruin of the Roman empire, and ended in the final settlement now established in the western continent of Europe.

The Britons were invaded, slaughtered, or enslaved, by the Saxons, except the few who escaped into Wales. The victorious Saxons were plundered, worried and tortured by the Danes, who intruded, and forced a tyrannical settlement amongst them. The united Saxons and Danes were, in their turn, subdued by the Normans, and despoiled of their lands, their goods, and their liberty.

A succession of wars, invasions, and cruelties, may be enumerated in every country in Europe, from the fourth to the seventeenth century. The present generation are no more answerable for those inflicted on Ireland than on any other nation. Justice no more demands that we should trace out the aboriginal Irish, and restore to them their language, their country, and what is called their nationality, than it prompts us to perform the same service towards the Britons, the Scots, and the Picts. The aboriginal Irish race is not as distinct, and as unmixed with the blood of the invaders, as the Britons, who now live happy, and contented in Wales. The ancient social happiness, civilization, and prosperity of Ireland, and its inhabitants, assumed by professing patriots, is purely mythical. The present condition of the people is grossly misrepresented; and their so-called degradation and penury unscrupulously exaggerated. What is alleged of their former prosperity, from which it is asserted they have been degraded, is certainly not recorded in any authentic history, anterior to the invasion by Strongbow, in the twelfth century. It will be vain to search for it, at any later period, before the present century. What their actual condition was from the earliest time to which it can now be traced back, with any truth, has been already described.

But suppose the Irish nation, before it was subdued by invaders, had been wealthy, civilized, and happy; and assuming that it was reduced by the violence and cruelty of conquerors, and of barbarous conquerors, in those turbulent times, from a state of the utmost felicity to the very depths of human misery (which was the case of all the Roman provinces in the fifth, sixth, and seventh centuries), does that constitute any right or title, at the present day, when peace has been long restored, and after the lapse of seven hundred years, to break up the settled order of things, and to take away from the present owners, even when known to be descended from original wrong-doers, the property and rights which they have inherited, in order to restore them to the descendants of those from whom they were taken, or for any other purpose whatever? Thus, to abrogate the pacifying effects of time, even in the case here assumed, would be but a repetition of cruelty and injustice, and must work intolerable mischief to civilized society, and be utterly destructive of security and social happiness.

In a great many cases, property and rights, as they now stand, have been honestly and peaceably acquired by the present owners, who derived nothing of them from their ancestors, and who have nothing, and claim nothing which was not purchased, or acquired by their own peaceful labour. In a great multitude of cases also, where property has been inherited, it was originally acquired by those from whom the title is derived, not by conquest, or violence, but by peaceful industry and thrift; and many who so acquired, and now possess it, are the descendants of those who had been conquered and despoiled; and many who would now claim it are descended from the spoliators.

If the aboriginal Irish were still a distinct race, wholly unmixed in blood with the posterity of their invaders (which they certainly are not), the cry of "Ireland for the Irish," now set up by the discontented and seditious, would, even in that case, be raised in opposition to the soundest and best established principles of peace and social order. It is a cry raised for no honest purpose, and has no other tendency than to excite, in the labouring poor, who must ever be the most numerous part of every nation, feelings of envy and hostility towards the rich and prosperous, on whose knowledge and guidance the safety of the poor themselves depends. In nine hundred and ninety-nine of every thousand cases, the Irish who are now poor and destitute are the descendants of ancestors who were from the earliest time to which they can be traced more destitute and wretched than any of the present generation.

Up to the invasion of the American continent by the European races, it had been in the undisputed possession of the Indian tribes. It was their country, in the fullest sense, by the clear title of immemorial possession; and had they the power to defend their country and their nationality, every principle of patriotism and justice would have warranted the use of that power. Wanting the power, they were conquered; they were slaughtered; they were enslaved, tortured, and driven from their native forests by force, and by fraud. They are still a pure and unmixed nation, wholly distinct from all the races who have expelled them. When some of these ruthless spoliators of the unoffending Indians cry "Ireland for the Irish," it seems strange that they should not see how much more strongly and clearly the same principle will demand the whole American continent for the Indians—an *argumentum ad absurdum* the force of which, I presume, no citizen of the States will deny, or question.

What justice would there be in taking from the present owners the lands which they and their forefathers, according to God's law, subdued, cleared, and cultivated; and replenished, in obedience to that law. To take from them the cities and the houses which they built; and all the other improvements which they made, with infinite toil, and skilful art; to turn all back into a wild and dreary forest, and deliver it back to the Indian tribes, for space to hunt in, and to live naked and exposed, or with no covering but the skins of their prey, and no shelter but the wigwam, according to their nationality; which consists in neglecting the faculties for association and political union which Providence had given them, and in disobedience to God's command to increase and multiply, and replenish the earth, and subdue it.

Three centuries ago Ireland was covered with forests, bogs, and morasses, and was as different from Ireland of the present day as the American wilderness was from the modern States. It had not been reclaimed from that disgraceful condition by the cattle farmers, who lived and slept with their cows and pigs in dark and noisome dens: whose nationality demanded desolate tracts of pasture land for their cattle, to the exclusion of civilized and industrious men. To demand Ireland for the descendants of this aboriginal race, and to claim a restoration of their nationality, is to insist that the country should be again turned into a howling wilderness.

Improvements of incalculable value have been made upon the surface of Ireland, within living memory, and in numberless instances by the present owners of the soil; those who talk of disturbing, or meddling with the rights of these owners, by legislation, must be forgetful of authentic history, heedless of the unalterable laws by which the universe is governed, and deaf to all the suggestions of reason and commen sense. Those who talk of invading this property, with pikes and guns in their hands, speak intelligibly, and the honest owners have no difficulty in determining what to do.

But when men armed with the power of legislation threaten to do justice to Ireland, by empirical enactments subversive of existing rights, devised for sectarian and party purposes, and conceded to turbulence and agitation, we cannot be surprised at the feelings of uneasiness and alarm which prevail in all the classes of Irish society who have anything to lose. Against this kind of invasion of their property and rights, honest, peaceful, and industrious men feel that they are defenceless.

No resolute reflecting man in Ireland has the least fear of danger from the Fenians. If we can imagine some hundreds of wolves, getting over from the forests of America, and craftily landing in different parts of England and Ireland, and there making their appearance in prowling packs, and stealthily attacking property and life, wherever they find them insufficiently guarded; and having made some successful snatches, then slinking into obscure holes and corners, and cunningly evading detection, those packs of mere wolves would excite the sort of alarm which at present exists in Ireland, at the appearance and doings of the Fenian packs, who have been so closely imitating the savage brutes which, two or three centuries ago, kept peaceful men on the alert to guard their flocks, their children, and their lives, from the prowlers of the forest. The Fenians differ from wolves in the faculty of human language, by which, when captured and convicted, they can make plausible speeches, and profess ardent love for the Irish people, whom they address, as the wolves in the fable addressed the sheep, when they would persuade them to expel their dogs, and to rely on the protection, and love, and patriotic kindness, of their professing friends, of whose services they were deprived by the dogs.

That these lurking spoliators will be speedily and effectually exterminated, no rational man has any doubt: that hunting them, capturing them, hanging, or caging them can ever be regarded, by civilized citizens of the United States, as any infringement of international law, is not to be seriously apprehended for a moment. If we could imagine anything so absurd as the interference of Congress with the right of England to punish and expel these marauders, we should be forced to the conclusion that America had determined to provoke, and to face, the hostility of all the civilized nations of the world. From the Fenians, therefore, or their abettors in America, no reasoning man apprehends any serious or lasting obstacle to the material prosperity of Ireland.

It is from a session of Parliament, devoted to the discussion and redress of the so-called grievances of the country, that obstacles to improvement, and danger to property and peace, are seriously to be feared. From this source we have had already many calamities inflicted upon Ireland, in the mistaken belief that the Legislature was acting the part of a physician, and administering a remedy for existing disorders.

It is not easy to imagine a stronger or more lucid instance, in proof of this assertion, than the Charter of the last century, so benevolently solicited, and so credulously granted, for the education, the improvement, and the spiritual salvation of the Irish. During ninety years, under the operation of this expensive remedy, 12·749 of the children admitted into the Charter Schools survived the treatment administered in those abodes of misery, desolation, and woe, and escaped from them, not to freedom, but still in bondage to mercenary masters, willing to undertake the training and management of starved, ragged, sullen, and dogged wretches, to whom their probation in those purgatories was an indelible disgrace, and the bitterest reproach that could be uttered. How many thousands of the hapless children, who entered these falsely called asylums, perished by the treatment and torture inflicted on them, before they attained the age of apprenticeship, there is no record, or means of now discovering. How many hundreds, or thousands, absconded from them in those ninety years, and to what final doom those demoralized and helpless fugitives were destined, without home, without kindred, without heart, or other feelings towards their fellow-men, than the savage inflictions which had scared them from the schools, must have engendered in their breasts, there are now no means of discovering. It is equally impossible to ascertain how many of the 12·749 apprentices absconded from the cruelty of ferocious masters, or how many of them escaped from bondage to die on the gallows; or how many of those who did not abscond, survived the training, during the years of bondage, to masters who had received them from no other motive than hope of profit from the labour which they could extort from these bounden slaves. It is ascertained that only one in every eleven of the apprentices completed his servitude and married Protestant!!

The infliction of those Charter Schools upon the country was meant to remedy the so-called grievance of devotion to the Roman Catholic religion. If those who would keep their Roman Catholic flocks within the fold by the fear of eternal punishment, as the consequence of leaving it, desired an illustration, by the judgments falling, even in this life, upon those who yielded to the temptations to leave that fold, they had, in all parts of Ireland, the poor, starved, tortured, sickly, and sullen proselytes, who were enduring an earthly purgatory in the Charter Schools, as examples, and truly terrifying examples, under the eyes of those who remained stedfast, and, who notwithstanding their rags, and their poverty, were still—according to the Rev. Mr. Lee's observation—healthy, vivacious, and intelligent children, free as the birds of the air, with the world before them, and unimpaired faculties to encounter it; with homes, however humble, to shelter them, affectionate kindred, to aid and to cheer them, and free from stigma or reproach of any kind. Taking the contrast, as described even by Mr. Lee, the panegyrist of the Charter Schools, what a barrier must these institutions have been to the accomplishment of the very purpose for which they were erected, and for ninety years, expensively and blindly maintained!!

The operation and obvious effect of these schools, and the cruelty of maintaining them, was exposed to the Irish Parliament, by Howard, in 1788, forty years before they were abolished, during which forty years there was no effectual attempt to reform them, or to mitigate their withering effect upon the established religion of the State. The clergy and laity of that State religion are now taunted and rebuked for being still a minority of the nation.

The same legislative power which was thus for ninety years exercised to make the propagation of the reformed religion impossible in this country, is now called upon to abolish the Established Church, because it is still confined to a minority of the people, and because it did not perform what the legislature itself had made impossible.

It is not alone the institution of the Charter Schools, and the manner of conducting them, but all the other State measures of the last three centuries, for suppressing the Roman Catholic religion, and propagating the Protestant faith in Ireland, although intended, and, no doubt, sincerely intended, to accomplish that object, were so taken, and so conducted, as to produce effects diametrically opposite to those aimed at and desired. The penal laws, by which the reformed religion was effectually propagated and the Romish religion suppressed in England, did not extend to Ireland, and no such laws were there enacted, until several years after the Revolution of 1688. The adoption, or rejection of the reformed religion was, in Ireland, left to the free choice of both the Irish and English races. Even the option of embracing it was not given to the Irish race; for very few of them understood the English language; and no one ever spoke to them, or preached to them in their own language, on the subject of religion, except their own priests. They were left entirely in the hands and under the instructions of these, who were all Irish, and hostile to the reformed religion, not only because they condemned it as a heresy, but because they and their flocks hated it as the creed of their English enemies. The very word which signified Protestant, also signified Englishman; there was no other Irish word for either, but Sassanagh, which to the present day means a Protestant, as well as an Englishman. After allowing free liberty to the Roman Catholic clergy for 140 years, in the Irish tongue (the most expressive spoken on earth) to abuse the Protestant religion, and to confirm the Irish in the old faith, two most absurd and cruel penal Acts were passed in 1695, followed by others, passed afterwards, at such times, and under such circumstances, and so administered, as to make the Roman Catholics of Ireland cling to the ancient faith, with proud and defiant tenacity. When these laws were found to be as imbecile, as they were cruel and absurd, they were relaxed; but, at every stage, tardily, and reluctantly relaxed. Having ignored, with stolid stupidity, the strongest arguments of reason, and rejected, with insult, the petitions of unjustly oppressed subjects, the same men relaxed the penal laws, when assailed by bold and seditious agitation. The governing power, which was strong as adamant against reason and justice, was yielding as a reed, when boldly assailed; demonstrating, that nothing would be conceded to prayers and petitions, however supported by every principle of justice, reason, and humanity, and that anything, and everything would be surrendered to turbulent agitation, and threats of physical force. For more than two years before 1792 the Roman Catholics refrained from agitation; and, by every demonstration of orderly and peaceable conduct, proved their title to relief. On the 8th and 13th February, 1792, they humbly petitioned for repeal of some of the most absurd of the tyrannical enactments of the penal code inflicted on them since the Revolution. The petitions were rejected scornfully and promptly, on the 20th February, by a majority of 203 to 25. The Catholics immediately began to form associations, and to agitate. A convention of delegates was formed, a bolder tone was assumed, and grew more minacious as the pressure of a French war emboldened them. The same Government, and the same Legislature by which the dutiful petitions had been rejected in February, with a majority of ten to one against them, before the end of the same year, gave a large measure of relief by the Act 32 Geo. III., c. 21; and being further pressed by agitation and threats of sedition, they, in 1793, passed the great relief Act which gave the Catholics the elective franchise, which Act begins with a recital that it was granted "from the peaceable and loyal demeanour of His Majesty's Popish or Roman Catholic subjects;" which preamble every Roman Catholic in the nation must have derided as a false and hypocritical pretence; they must have known, that it had been extorted from the fears of a quailing Government and Legislature, who had disregarded and insulted peaceable and loyal demeanour, when it really existed.

During the long struggle for perfect emancipation, a large, intelligent, and earnest section of Protestants (in which domination I include all who dissent from the Roman Catholic faith) heartily joined in every constitutional effort for the restoration of their fellow-subjects to the liberty which was their birth-right, and to which their title was clear, as soon as they ceased to fight for the domination of an intolerant hierarchy. The feelings of the liberal Protestants were, from time to time, eloquently expressed by many of their able representatives in Parliament. When, at last, justice appeared to have triumphed, by legitimate means, and was, by one

House, conceded to constitutional entreaty, the salutary and sedative effect of the wise concession was not only defeated, but, by a fatal resolution of the other House, was turned into a maddening stimulus to the agitation and violence which experience had proved to be the only means of succeeding. These means were promptly resorted to; and these means succeeded in 1829, four years after concession to constitutional petitions, and convincing argument had been refused. In 1830, the Reformers of England, profiting by the lesson thus given, determined to adopt threats, in place of arguments, to support their petitions for reform. Then it was that the clubs and coffee-houses of London heard of armed thousands prepared to march upon them from Birmingham, and other places. The men who had answered clear proof of existing abuses by a bald denial, and conclusive arguments for the necessity of reformation, by a peremptory refusal of all reform, speedily yielded, and the Reform Act was passed in 1832. No reasoning man can be surprised, that agitation and minacious vapouring about physical force have become the established method of supporting every demand upon the attention of the Legislature.

The country is now at a crisis, in all essential particulars, similar to that which was passed through, by the wrong road of concession, in 1829. On the method of dealing with it, whether by conservative firmness, or yielding timidity, must depend the future peace and progress of Ireland.

The Fenians, despicable as they are, have threatened to overturn, by force of arms, the long-established and well-fortified throne of England. Alarmed at this threat, and yielding to the mischievous atrocities, and absurd audacity of these imbecile and vicious conspirators, timid politicians countenance proposals to give up the Protestant Church of Ireland, as a sop to pacify the clamour which alarms them. The party in office have declared their reluctance to sacrifice this institution; some of them have avowed their resolution to uphold it; and thus what appears to be a favourable opportunity is presented of raising an issue upon which the party in opposition may achieve a victory, and, by manœuvre, take the place of the present Ministry—upon a pretext of doing justice to Ireland.

Unhappy Ireland is made the battle-field of this party strife. Victory being the sole object of the leaders, civil rights, and religious and municipal institutions are no more to be spared, when they come as obstacles in the way of a skilful manœuvre, than corn fields, gardens, houses, or churches, when the general of an army sees them obstructing a junction of forces, or any other military movement. The artillery is commanded to batter down, and level the church and the house; the pioneers are ordered to prostrate the fences of the corn field and the garden; to fell and devastate, and sweep away the erections of industry and skill, and have no regard to anything but the free passage of the moving column in its march to victory.

When the thing to be thus prostrated is the State Church of a sister kingdom, by solemn compact firmly, and, as was for 300 years believed, indissolubly united, for weal or for woe, with the Crown, and with its powerful ally, the Church of England: when an institution established for the religious instruction and worship of

700,000 Christians is the thing to be abolished, after surviving the warring elements of 300 years; and when the property set apart and granted for support of this religious Establishment is to be confiscated, some consideration is obviously due to its history, and to the political and social purposes for which it was established, and firmly united to the Throne.

On the principles which led to, and which justified the Reformation in the sixteenth century, and made England a Protestant nation, and which also led to, and justified the Revolution of 1688, the State Church of Ireland rests, and as long as those principles are respected by the English people, the bond of union between this Church and the throne of the United Kingdom should be inviolably maintained. This bond is now assailed by the Roman Catholic Hierarchy, as a grievance to them, and to their congregations. Certain members of rank and position in the Roman Catholic laity have made a declaration, that they feel the existence of this State Church to be a grievance, but beyond the bare assertion of this sentiment, they give no reasons for so feeling. When the title of the Roman Catholic hierarchy and laity of the present time to complain of the State Church of Ireland as a grievance is to be estimated, the part which the Roman Catholic hierarchy and laity of 1688 took in the contests of that time, and the doctrinal differences which led to the Reformation, and the Revolution, should never be forgotten. In estimating the title of the same parties to the fullest measure of toleration, and to the most perfect social equality, there should be entire oblivion of by-gone wars and controversies, and differences of creed should be ignored.

Whether the Protestant religion is a heresy, and its doctrines heteredox, and whether the Roman Catholic religion is the only true religion, and its doctrines alone are orthodox, are theological questions, with which I have no intention to meddle, and which are distinct from, and have nothing to do with the purely secular question, whether the Established Church of Ireland is to be maintained, as a protection to liberty, or abolished, as a social grievance. When I state the difference, operative upon social rights, between the doctrine of the Protestant Church, and the doctrine of the Roman Catholic Church, I am expressing no opinion on the question, which of them is theologically right or wrong.

There is no necessity for erudition, or extensive reading, to discover what that operative difference is—the school-boys' Catechism of each Church makes it conspicuously visible. In the Roman Catholic Catechism it is dogmatically, and, *ex cathedra*, laid down, as doctrine necessary to salvation, "that true Christians are to be found only in the true Church"—"that the true Church is the holy Catholic Church"—"that there is no other true Church besides the holy Catholic Church, because there is but one Lord, one faith, one baptism, one God and Father of all, so there is but one true Church" —"that every body is obliged to be of the true Church —and that no one can be saved out of it"—"that the Pope is the visible head of the Church, and is Christ's Vicar on earth, and supreme head of the Church"— "that one of the advantages enjoyed in the true Church, is the forgiveness of sins," and that this means, "that Christ left to the Pastors of His Church the power of *forgiving* sins;" "that when any one falls into mortal sin (the greatest of all misfortunes), he must repent sincerely, and go to confession, as soon as possible, that he may recover God's friendship, and be always prepared to die"—"that souls in purgatory can be relieved by our prayers—and that it is by the authority of the Church, which is the pillar and ground of truth, that we can know with certainty what God has taught."

If all mankind be obliged to be of the true Church, it is but an easy step to the conclusion, that the clergy have a right to enforce that obligation; and they, in plain and positive terms, assert that they have been appointed by Divine Providence to guard this faith, and that they are answerable to God for the souls of men. The obligation to be of this true Church, or of any other than the Church of their own choice, Protestants of the Church of England deny. Against the assumption of divine right, to guard the faith of men on earth, and of responsibility to God for human souls, those of the reformed religion protest. They further repudiate the obligation to go to confession; and they do not believe that the pastor has the power of forgiving sins, upon condition of repentance, or on any other terms whatever. They also deny, and wholly disbelieve, that the souls of the dead can be relieved from purgatory by the prayers of the living, or even by the masses of the clergy; and they thus dry up the greatest sources of priestly power on earth, and priestly dominion over the minds and religious fears of their congregations.

In the Catechism of the Church of England, there is not one word intolerant of any other creed; not one word upon which a claim to priestly power could be founded; not one word to countenance an assertion that the pastor has any colour of right to enforce, otherwise than by reason and persuasion, the obligation of belonging to his Church, or that any such obligation exists, independently of free choice, prompted by reason.

When I thus simply, and without commentary, state the catechetical teaching of the Roman Catholic hierarchy, I do not say that their teaching is theologically wrong. When I state that the Protestant hierarchy eschew such teaching, I do not say that they are theologically right. When I assert that Protestants repudiate the Roman Catholic Catechism, and the asserted dogma that all are obliged to belong to that Church, I only state a fact; I do not deny to the Roman Catholic clergy the liberty minaciously to say that Protestants do this at their own peril; I only say that they do it, and feel no apprehension of God's anger, when thus using the faculties of reason which God has given them; and that, as one of them, I do it; and, for myself, I add, that when I cease to have free liberty to do it, I hope I may cease to live.

When James the Second ascended the throne, having previously renounced the Protestant religion, and declared himself a member of the Romish Church, and acknowledged its doctrines and catechetical dogmas, his title to the crown was still admitted by his Protestant subjects, notwithstanding his apostacy. It soon became manifest, that a union between the temporal Sovereign and the Papal clergy was incompatible with toleration of any but what they dogmatically asserted to be the only true religion; and that the open violation of the laws which Protestants had enacted for their protection against the ferocious persecutions inflicted on them when the same union had taken place before, in the reign of

Mary, would soon come to a repetition of the same inflictions. The nation soon discovered that when the secular Sovereign had submitted to the spiritual jurisdiction of those who claimed it by appointment from Divine Providence, the organized and armed force placed under his command would be prostituted to enforce the obligation of belonging to the only true Church, as then was, and as now is explicitly imposed upon all by the authority of that Church, and emphatically expressed in its Catechism. When, by the just rage of his subjects, this tyrannical bigot was forced to fly, he took shelter under the French king, who was engaged in the congenial work of persecuting his own Protestant subjects, of whom, by revoking the edict of Nantz, he had expatriated 50,000.

By the aid of that most powerful of England's enemies, James was enabled to try the question between himself and his English and Scotch subjects by force of arms. For that great trial he selected Ireland as his battle-field.

If the estimate of Sir William Petty, made in 1672, be correct, there were, in Ireland, at that time, and probably also at the time of the Revolution, about 100,000 legal Protestants and Conformists; about the same number of Presbyterians, Independents, Anabaptists, and Quakers, of the English race, and 100,000 Scotts Presbyterians. All the rest of the population, about 800,000 in number, were Roman Catholics, like James himself, and ready, as he believed, to fight his battle.*

Having safely landed in Ireland, he marshalled his forces, French and Irish, and proceeded to trample down the Protestants, who appeared to be no match for his superior numbers. How this brave minority stood at bay —how they baffled him, at Derry and other places—how

* See note at the end of the volume.

they rallied round his successor, and gained the victory, I hope will never be forgotten by the English people, or by any one who values civil liberty, no matter what may be his country, his party, or his creed. That was not a battle to determine theological differences; it was a contest for freedom of speech, freedom of action, freedom of thought, freedom of conscience, and protection against the ferocious bigots, who, by the rack and the gibbet, had driven the most loyal and duty-loving subjects on earth to expel their hereditary and lawful Sovereign. It became, also, a contest between England and France, for the Sovereignty, and the possession of Ireland. When that mortal strife was ended, and when the victory was won by those who fought for, and who vindicated, the rights and the liberties of the human race against those who would trample them down; and when the government of Ireland came to be settled, according to the principles of civil liberty and religious toleration, by the elected King of the United Kingdom and his Protestant subjects, to whom were that King and those Protestants to entrust the care and defence of the kingdom which they had rescued from the most powerful enemy that England ever had? The Pope and the Papal hierarchy, to a man, were on the side of Louis and his cruel and bigoted tool. The Protestants of Ireland, to a man, were marshalled on the side of England, and fought and bled for the English cause, and for maintaining their political and social union with the English people. When William and his Protestant subjects had to select a State Church for Ireland, what other could they choose than that on which the hundred thousand loyal and faithful Protestants then depended, and on which 700,000 loyal and tolerant Protestants now depend, for worship and for spiritual instruction? The property set apart for the maintenance of religion was then, and had been, for more than a century before, in the possession of the Irish Reformed Church, and was not at the disposal of the Crown: was any part of it to be taken from that Church, and given to support a hierarchy who had just been defeated in their efforts to dethrone the new King? The Crown and the Legislature, long previously, had allocated that property to support a Church, whose doctrines were not only consistent with, but powerfully ancillary to, the progress of freedom and toleration in the civilized world. To whom was that property to be secured, other than the hundred thousand loyal subjects, for whose religious uses, and the maintenance of whose worship, it had been appropriated, and vested in their clergy, more than a century before, and by whose aid and faithful and loyal services it had been just rescued from the grasp of the King's enemies, and the enemies of British liberty, and of the English nation.

It is a mistake to assume that the Church property was granted to the Protestant clergy, in the sense that property is granted to individual subjects. It was granted to them, in the same sense, and upon the same trusts, that the church buildings, and churchyards were granted to them, and legally vested in them, for the use and benefit of the Protestant people of Ireland, in the maintenance of their religion, and for affording them the means of worship, according to their religious opinions, and conscientious convictions.

When this property, at the Revolution, was thus appropriated and left for the maintenance of an independent clergy, and to support the Protestant religion in Ireland, there were of Church of England Protestants only 100,000, men, women, and children, which to the entire residue of the people bore the ratio of one to ten, and, to the Irish Roman Catholics, the ratio of one to eight. The descendants of those Protestants, and those who belong to their body at the present day, at the last census numbered nearly 700,000; therefore they now bear to the rest of the people the ratio of one to seven, and to the Roman Catholics, one to six and a half. Had the property then appropriated to maintain religious worship for 100,000 persons remained unaltered by modern commutation and adjustment, it would now be, as the Protestant people are, about seven times what it was at the Revolution. The English Sovereign, and English Lords and Commons, are now called upon to act with marvellous inconsistency, when they are solicited to take away from 700,000 people what remains of the property that was granted to serve the same uses, in respect of 100,000, the total number who existed at the time of the grant. They are called on to do this act of injustice, and to inflict this forfeiture, in order to obliterate what is termed a memorial of conquest. Rationally considered, that was not a conquest and victory of Protestants over Roman Catholics, or of English over Irish; it was a victory of freemen over those who had conspired, and laboured, and fought unsuccessfully to enslave the people of the three kingdoms. The disabilities, and the oppressions which ensued to the Roman Catholics, were the consequence of their adherence to, and the aid which they gave, and still appeared willing to give, to those who would have used the victory with tenfold cruelty, had it fallen to them. As the descendants of those misguided Roman Catholics of the 17th century exhibited a resolution to sever their temporal and political union with the enemies of English liberty, and the organized opponents of universal toleration, those disabilities were gradually lessened, and finally have been entirely removed, and for forty years those oppressions have wholly ceased. A principle has triumphed, and not a nation or a party. Toleration and civil liberty are the victors: persecution and oppression have been vanquished: and the result is, that Protestants and Roman Catholics, Presbyterians and Dissenters, are equally partakers of the liberty, freedom of conscience, and municipal rights, which have been successfully asserted and established for the benefit of all; but they are partakers of these rights and liberties under a Protestant Sovereign, who must be a member of the Reformed Church of England, and who, in honour and conscience, is pledged to hold and believe the creed and doctrines of that Church; and who is bound in duty, to all subjects of every persuasion, to maintain and uphold it, as the State Church, and as the spiritual guide and instructor of that portion of the people who have embraced a creed which recognizes the right of private judgment, and imposes no shackles upon freedom of thought and liberty of conscience. By this characteristic, and fundamental principle of their religion, the Protestants of the Reformed Church of England are qualified, and, by inclination as well as doctrine, disposed, to allow to others, and to protect and defend for all others, whatever may be their creeds, the same liberty of conscience which every Protestant claims for himself. Whatever acts of persecution, in derogation of this, the proper characteristic of their creed, may be truly imputed to them, during the struggle for the liberty which they claimed, it cannot be denied that universal toleration, and a full and unequivocal concession to others of the liberty of conscience, which they claim and enjoy for themselves, is now the established and ruling principle of their government. To maintain and protect this liberty for themselves, and their posterity: to maintain and protect it for all other sects, of whatever persuasion they may be, and to what spiritual authority soever they may please to submit, it is essentially necessary that those who accept and hold this tolerant and liberal faith (be they many or be they few) shall be the governing body, and shall have in their hands the full power of protecting to every British subject the just and rational liberty which, as a free-man, he is entitled to enjoy, without regard to his religious convictions.

The governing power thus assumed, and thus conceded to Protestants, after it was by a revolution taken out of the hands of the Roman Catholic king, is rather imposed as a duty than acknowledged as a disparaging privilege. The possession and exercise of this governing power is no more a badge of conquest, or of social inequality on the people of other persuasions, than the rank and power of the sovereign, or of the nobility, or of the magistrates, is a badge of social inequality or inferiority on the subordinate classes of society, for whose peace and protection those gradations of power and rank have been instituted.

Many sensible and earnest men believe that, by taking away the endowments of the Protestant Church of Ireland, and by severing the union of that Church with the Crown, they will be doing nothing more than reducing the Irish Protestants to a level with their fellow-subjects of other creeds; and that, by so doing, they will promote peace and tranquillity in the country. That these views are sincerely and honestly entertained by many respectable and patriotic men, I have not the least doubt. That the effects of the contemplated measure will be entirely different from those intended, and so expected, and that bitter disappointment will be the result, I am equally convinced.

Before this empirical measure is adopted—before a step is taken which never can be peaceably retracted, and before that body of the Irish people to whom nine-tenths of the national improvement is due, shall be deprived of the means of religious worship, as by this measure they will be, some more attentive consideration of the past ought to be applied, than as yet appears to have been bestowed by any who have discussed this complicated and hazardous experiment.

When it is alleged that the Church of Ireland has failed to perform its mission, because the majority of the Irish people are still Roman Catholics, and because only a minority belong to the Protestant Church—and when this is assigned as a sufficient reason for now severing the connexion between this Church and the State, and for taking away its endowment, and establishing in Ireland the voluntary system—truth, and justice, political honesty, and regard for national good faith, demand, an historical examination of the facts on which this partisan statement is founded, and a cautious scrutiny should be made of the measures suggested, and founded upon it.

Those who in Ireland embraced the reformed religion,

when it was established in the reign of Elizabeth, were English settlers, or descended from such settlers, and who spoke the English language. The aboriginal Irish were nearly all Roman Catholics, spoke no English, and knew nothing of the reformed religion; for they did not understand the language of those who professed it, and who were deputed to teach its doctrines. It is now asserted that the Protestant Clergy were then sent to Ireland, and that with those already in Ireland, they were charged with a mission to convert the Irish people to the reformed faith, and to propagate that faith amongst them. This mission, it is assumed, was sent by the English sovereign, and English government. It is certain that those who were sent or employed upon it were selected by that government, and appointed by that sovereign, and that they were subject to the control, and ruled by the appointees and deputies, of the English sovereign, and English ministers.

The Protestant clergy of Ireland, in the year 1868, are taunted with the failure of this mission; and told that because it failed they must be severed from all connexion with the State; that after the present vested interests are provided for, the future Protestant clergy must depend, for maintenance, on the voluntary contributions of those whom they can retain in, or convert to their faith. The 700,000 Protestants of the present time are told, that this State measure works no injustice to them, that it only reduces them to an equality with their Roman Catholic, and Presbyterian fellow-subjects, by leaving them to support their own clergy; and that, therefore, no wrong is done to them by confiscating the property which for fully three hundred years they have enjoyed, for the support of the clergy whose religious doctrine they approve, whose instructions they receive and value, and whose diligence in the performance of their duties, and sincerity in their convictions, calumny itself cannot deny, or throw a doubt on, for at least two generations.

As to the failure of the mission, suggested to the English Legislature, and promulgated to the English people, as an asserted fact, and as a justification for thus dealing with 700,000 of the most intelligent, most energetic, most industrious, and to the English nation and Government the most loyal part of the Irish people, the least informed of the 700,000 may be prompted to ask, why did that mission fail? How did the English Government of Elizabeth and subsequent Governments act in aid and furtherance of that mission? What missioners did the Governments send, to merit the respect and reverence of the then existing Protestants of Ireland, and to preach gospel truth to the Irish Roman Catholics? Let Spenser, an Englishman—a learned man—a man of genius—a man of high moral character, and a contemporary, answer the question. His answer is as follows:—
" First—there are no such sufficient ministers sent over as might be presented to any bishop for any living, but the most part of such English as come over thither of themselves are either unlearned or men of some bad note, for which they have forsaken England, so as the bishop to whom they shall be presented may justly reject them, as incapable and insufficient. Secondly—the bishop himself is, perhaps, an Irishman, who being made judge by that law (viz., a statute previously referred to) of the sufficiency of the ministers, may, at his own will, dislike of the Englishman, as unworthy, in his opinion, and admit

of any Irish whom he shall think more for his turn. And if he shall at the instance of any Englishman of countenance there, whom he will not displease, accept of any such English minister as shall be tendered unto him, yet he will underhand carry such a hard hand over him, or by his officers, wring him so sore, that he will soon make him weary of his poor living. Lastly—the benefices themselves are so mean and of such small profits, in these Irish countries, through the ill husbandry of the Irish people which do inhabit them, that they will not yield any competent maintenance for any honest minister to live upon; scarcely to buy him a gown. And were all this redressed (as haply it might be), yet what good should any English minister do amongst them, by teaching or preaching to them, which either cannot understand him, or will not hear him? Or what comfort of life shall he have where his parishioners are so insatiable, so intractable, so ill-affected to him, as they usually be to all the English; or, finally, how dare almost any honest minister, that are peaceable civil men, commit his safety to the hands of such neighbours as the boldest captains dare scarcely dwell by."

To a previous question, whether he found any particular abuses in religion in Ireland, besides that of being Popish, Spenser answered: "Yes, verily; for whatever disorders you see in the Church of England, you may find there many more, namely, gross simony, greedy covetousness, fleshly incontinence, careless sloth, and generally all disordered life, in the common clergyman. And besides all these, they have their particular enormities; for all Irish priests who now enjoy the Church livings, they are, in a manner, mere laymen, saving that they have taken Holy Orders, but otherwise they do go and live like laymen, follow all kinds of husbandry, and other worldly affairs, as other Irishmen do. They neither read Scriptures, nor preach to the people, nor administer the Communion; but Baptism they do, for they christen yet after the Popish fashion, only they take the tithe and offerings, and gather what fruit else they may of their livings, the which they convert as badly, and some of them (they say) pay as due tributes and shares of their livings to their bishops (I speak of those which are Irish) as they receive them duly."

To the question, "But is that suffered amongst them? It is wonder but that the governors do redress such shameful abuses," Spenser answers: "How can they, since they know them not? for the Irish bishops have their clergy in such awe and subjection under them that they dare not complain of them, so as they may do to them what they please; for they, knowing their own unworthiness and incapacity, and that they are, therefore, still removeable at their bishop's will, yield what pleaseth him, and he taketh what he listeth. Yea, and some of them, whose dioceses are in remote parts, somewhat out of the world's eye, do not at all bestow the benefices, which are in their own donation, upon any, but keep them in their own hands, and set their own servants and horseboys to take up the tithes and fruits of them, with the which some of them purchase great lands, and build fair castles upon the same. Of which abuse, if any question be moved, they have a very seemly colour and excuse, that they have no worthy ministers to bestow them upon, but keep them so bestowed for any such sufficient person as any shall bring unto them."

Such was the mission, and such were the missionaries,

sent and intrusted by the English Government, in the sixteenth century, to propagate the reformed religion in Ireland! No one can be surprised at the result, as described by Primate Boulter 150 years after Spenser wrote this description of it. The character of the missionaries appears, during that long interval, to have been steadily kept up to the original standard of unworthiness, and it must have been truly deplorable to justify Swift's sarcasm, accounting for the vile character of the English who came over to fill the Irish benefices, in his time (and he was a contemporary of Primate Boulter's), viz., that they were the highwaymen who had robbed the true and reverend missionaries on Hounslow Heath, on their journey towards Ireland, and, personating their victims, came to this country, with the vestments and credentials so robbed by them, and procured admission to the Irish Church livings.

If it had been the deliberate aim and purpose of the English Government to disgust the Protestant laity of Ireland with the reformed religion, and to make the ministers of it odious in their sight; if it had been their design to leave the Irish people in total ignorance of the reformed religion, by sending preachers who could not speak or understand the Irish language, to confirm the Irish people in their adherence to the Romish creed, and to deter them from listening to the missionaries, even if they could understand their English tongue, could they have done anything more effectual to accomplish these ends than what they did, as described by Spenser and Swift? I should, perhaps, except what they did in 1733, to convert the children of the Roman Catholics, as already detailed, in compliance with Primate Boulter's petition for the Charter Schools, "when, instead of converting the adults, the missionary clergy were daily losing many of their meaner people, who went off to Popery."

We have now arrived at a conspicuous application of the rule of justice, inverted as it too commonly is, when what is called justice is administered in Ireland. To the unworthy clergy of the sixteenth, seventeenth, and eighteenth centuries (who in truth were mere aliens in respect of the Irish people), of whom such a character comes down to us from their cotemporaries, the State and Crown allied themselves with an affectionate will. In contempt of the Protestant laity, their congregations were insulted by the imposition upon them of those alien fugitives and dunces, and mere laymen in the garb of pastors. In support of these unworthy ministers, the property (clothed, as it was, with a sacred trust, that it should be applied for the benefit of the laity, in attracting, and worthily supporting competent, pious, diligent, and devoted men for the offices of religion, and for the edification of the people) was for two centuries misapplied, in its entirety, and given by the English Government, with good will, to men, who, if they be not maligned, deserved deprivation and punishment, rather than reward. Now, when, for more than half a century, comprehending two generations, the native Irish clergy of the Protestant Church in Ireland have been exemplary, in all essential attributes; extorting, even from their avowed enemies, unqualified approbation and praise; this same trust property, having been for more than half a century duly and properly applied, according to the trust, in the support of ministers who have faithfully and zealously performed their duties, the Government and the Legislature are roused from their lethargy, and as if doing wrong when doing justice, they are suddenly called upon to despoil the Church, whose dignity and character have been for over fifty years, and now are, well supported by these meritorious ministers, and to repudiate this Church, and sever its union with the Crown; and to declare that the provision is extravagantly too large for supporting the clergy of 700,000 people, being only a fraction of what was for two centuries allowed for the support of clergy who shamefully neglected their duties, confined as they were to the religious wants of 100,000. The Government and Legislature who, for 250 years, allowed the temporalities of the Church, in all their integrity, to be enjoyed by the alien clergy, whose congregations were but one-eighth of the Roman Catholic population, are now threatened with sedition if they do not take away those temporalities (modified and diminished as they have been) from the native clergy, whose congregations have multiplied absolutely seven-fold, and have also relatively increased to little less than a sixth; which increase in the congregations has taken place under the ministration and pastoral care of the clergy who are to be so deprived. Thus the unworthy pastors of the few, in the sixteenth, seventeenth, and eighteenth centuries, by whose defaults the mission failed, were extravagantly rewarded, and honoured by strict union with the Crown; and the meritorious clergy, by whose piety, learning, and diligence 700,000 of the most intelligent and respectable classes are edified, are to be spoliated and punished, and discarded from all connexion with the Crown, as if performance of duty was a crime!!! The English people, who profess peculiar love for justice and fair play, are worried, and agitated, and entreated thus monstrously to invert the rule of justice in dealing with 700,000 of their Irish fellow-subjects, who, and whose ancestors, have been the most loyal and faithful supporters of British rule in Ireland. If the ratio of the Roman Catholics to the Protestants still remained as it was at the Revolution, this would still be foul injustice, and no sophistry of a party leader, or of his expectant followers, can conceal the enormity of this unprovoked manœuvre for recovery of power and place. How the infliction of this unmitigated injustice on 700,000 perfectly peaceable and orderly subjects of this country, at the instigation of agitators, can promote harmony and peace, no one can possibly comprehend who knows anything of Ireland.

The Protestants who gained the victory over persecution in the 17th century, the memory and vestiges of which the Roman Catholic hierarchy now complain of, and insist upon obliterating—the same Protestants who enacted the penal laws, and for more than a century kept the Roman Catholics under oppressive disabilities, were allowed to enjoy their Church, with all its endowments, and its rank as the State Church, not only unmolested, and without question, but their right and title so to do were repeatedly, and most solemnly acknowledged by the leaders of the Roman Catholic people, both laymen and clergy, when supplicating relief from penal laws. The Protestants of 1829, who successfully laboured to emancipate their fellow-subjects, and who still survive to rejoice in that measure of justice; the younger Protestants of the present generation, who freely recognize the right of their Roman Catholic countrymen to perfect social equality, are to be despoiled of the endowment which supports their Church Establishment, are to see that establishment degraded, and its future ministers thrown upon the voluntary support of their congregations by the agitation, and at the bidding, of the Romish hierarchy, who owe their power so to agitate for infliction of this injustice to the liberality and aid of those upon whom they would inflict it. Here again is the rule of justice inverted, with the addition of ingratitude, to make that inversion still more detestable.

One of the securities which Protestants have devised for the freedom of thought, and the right of private judgment, which they claim according to conscience, and according to reason, is the State provision made for support of their clergy, independent of their congregations; thus taking away from those clergy the motive for seeking and discovering (as Lord Macaulay says the Jesuits did) "the precise point to which intellectual culture can be carried without the risk of intellectual emancipation." This independent provision makes it unnecessary for the Protestant clergy to teach such a Catechism as that from which I have made some quotations. They have no interest in the creation of religious terrors, or the assumption of supernatural authority, for the purpose of making their flocks subservient to their domination. They have, by this provision, been exempted from any motive to preach to their congregations subservience to themselves, admission of their heavenly title to earthly power or obedience, except to God, and to the lawful authority of their temporal sovereign. To take away from a clergy so constituted the provision thus made for them, and to reduce them to the eleemosynary support of their congregations, is to annihilate the independence which forms the essential difference between them and the clergy against whose machinations for power Protestants have thought it necessary to guard. So to despoil the clergy is not to place them on an equality with other clergy, who stand upon a totally different foundation; who for ages, being dependent on the influence which they could establish over the human mind, have taken the proper means of propagating that influence, and making it effectual; a course of conduct absolutely forbidden to the Protestant clergy.

This theory of reducing the clergy of the Church of England to equality with the clergy of other sects, is nothing but the theory of abolishing altogether, in this country, the religion and the worship of this section of the people. Into what other sects these Protestants and their posterity will be distributed, or what new creeds and forms of worship will spring from the ruins of this liberal, enlightened, and tolerant religion, time alone can disclose; but that any such congregations as now resort to the Protestant churches can continue to assemble for any considerable time, after the divorce of the Church from the Throne, and the confiscation of its endowment, or that any such ministers as they now reverence can be there to meet them, is morally impossible. Whether for good or for evil, these congregations will be scattered, and there will be no successors of the independent ministers who now address their reason, and all who may not be willing, or, from existing convictions, may not be able, without hypocrisy, to assent to the dictation of some dogmatical, or some terrifying creed, will no longer have churches open to them, where they may sincerely and devoutly worship God, and yet enjoy some latitude of private judgment.

If any of the advocates of this experiment sincerely believe that to confiscate the property set apart for maintenance of the religion, and the clergy of 700,000 intelligent, independent, and energetic members of the community in Ireland, will have a pacifying effect, either upon the agitators, at whose instigation this act of political turpitude, and social wrong, is to be perpetrated, or upon those who shall suffer the injustice, they will soon discover how erroneously they have calculated. It cannot alleviate any real grievance that Ireland is subject to. The alleged existence of social or religious inequality, for redress of which it is demanded, is purely fictitious, and nothing but a pretence for agitation. The measure itself will be a grievous infliction on that class, by whose intelligence, industry, and steadfast love of order, the interests of the country have been advanced, in spite of the misconduct and turbulence of other classes, and of the mischievous legislation provoked by them.

The new-born agitation of the Romish hierarchy, and those of their congregations who join in it, for destruction of the Established Church, and the confiscation of its property, is a remarkable, and not a tardy, corroboration, by accomplishment, of those prophetic arguments formerly used in opposition to Emancipation, which the liberal Protestant advocates of that measure were accustomed to treat, and to ridicule, as the visionary dreams of prejudice and bigotry.

If the Romish hierarchy claimed the ecclesiastical property, in assertion of the title which they had to it before the Reformation, that claim might be urged, without confessing a design to destroy the Protestant Church, and persecute the Protestant religion. But when they disclaim all title to the property, and quarrel with nothing but the enjoyment of it by the Protestant clergy, and urge this enjoyment as their grievance, they make it evident that demolition of the Church is their purpose and object; and the ulterior design of becoming the dominant hierarchy is too transparent to escape the most careless observer. The enjoyment by Protestant clergymen of the rent-charges, which must continue to be paid, can be no more a grievance to the Roman Catholic clergy than the enjoyment of similar rent-charges by lay impropriators. They allege that, because their congregations are more numerous than those of the Protestant clergy, they are better entitled to a State provision than those to whom the law gives it; and that they feel insulted at the spectacle of a wealthy and less deserving Church thus, by an unjust preference, kept before their eyes; and the preference thus enjoyed by what they call less deserving pastors is the grievance which they complain of. This grievance, upon this, which is their own plain and simple statement of it, is nothing more or less than envy, and comes within the strict definition of that unamiable passion given by Locke, and his definition of it presents it in a less odious form than that to be found in any English dictionary. Locke defines it as "uneasiness of mind, caused by the consideration of a good we desire to obtain by one we think should not have had it before us." Johnson defines Envy in these words: "Pain felt and malignity conceived at the sight of excellence or happiness." The excellence of the existing Protestant clergy of Ireland is confessed, and the confession of it is mixed with the complaints which emanate from the envy, hatred, and malice of their assailants.

The *odium ecclesiasticum*, and rage for power, can alone account for the bitterness with which the Romish hierarchy complain of the preference given by a Protestant Sovereign and a Protestant nation to the clergy of that portion of the Irish people who have embraced the religion of that Sovereign, and the religion which that nation, by a fundamental law of its constitution, has solemnly adopted as the State religion of England and Ireland, and as the sole religion which it is constitutionally lawful for the Sovereign to embrace.

According to their own assertions, the Romish hierarchy lose nothing by the liberality, or, if they so call it, the extravagance of the provision made for the Protestant clergy out of the national property; they not only disavow any design to claim any part of that property, but they protest, that, if offered to them, they would not accept it. No one, therefore, can possibly understand how they are damnified or aggrived by the application of it to the support of the Protestant worship, upon any other principle, than that toleration of that worship is a grievance to them, and no rational man can believe them, when they deny the burning thirst of power to persecute that worship by which they are themselves tormented.

The union of the Protestant Church with the Crown is another part of the same grievance. This union is an honour and a happiness of the Protestant clergy which gives pain to their assailants, i. e. which their assailants envy; but when this grievance is complained of by the Romish clergy, they cannot, and do not, assert or pretend that by the adoption of the Protestant Church, as the State Church in Ireland, the Crown has unjustly excluded them from an alliance to which they can make the faintest shadow of a pretension. Nothing could possibly be more absurd, than to suppose, or to imagine, that a Protestant Sovereign could accept an union with a Church which repudiates the ecclesiastical authority of that Sovereign, and acknowledges an alien as its head; which dogmatically teaches, and, by the most solemn and explicit denunciation of eternal perdition, enforces upon the minds of millions who owe allegiance to that Sovereign, the belief, that there is no salvation for that Sovereign, or for the great majority of that Sovereign's subjects. That the propagation of such a doctrine amongst the people who owe allegiance to the Crown is, or ever was, permitted by a monarch and a government which itself repudiates such a ferocious doctrine, and denies the truth of it, was, and is, carrying toleration very far; and it is difficult to see how it can be pushed a step farther, without becoming persecution of other creeds. In Ireland, it is carried not merely to this extreme of giving full and free scope and liberty to the Romish hierarchy to teach this doctrine (horrible as it obviously is) to the people of their own persuasion, but 4,000 schools are maintained for them, at the expense of the State, and placed immediately, and exclusively under their patronage, guidance, and control, in which schools, they have license to teach their catechism, in which this is stated as a fundamental article of their religion. The 4,000 schools are not only thus supported by a Protestant government, out of a treasury replenished by taxes levied from a Protestant people, by this doctrine doomed to eternal perdition; but by the unequal, and overwhelming competition of these schools, all other schools, in 4,000 extensive localities, are driven out of existence, and the Protestant children in these 4,000 localities are reduced to the dilemma of remaining illiterate, or of attending for instruction at these schools, so subjected to the patronage, the management, and the control of Roman Catholic priests, who, in plain and unequivocal terms, assert that they have been, by divine Providence, appointed to guard and propagate the Catholic faith; of which one dogma is, that no soul can be saved except in communion with their Church, and that these priests are answerable to God for the souls of the human race, and therefore bound, as they will answer at the final judgment, to convert these children, and save their souls from the perdition to which, by their dogma, the parents of these children are doomed.

The Government and the Legislature, who have instituted these schools; who have placed them in the hands of the Roman Catholic clergy; who have made this arrangement, so favourable to the propagation of Romanism, and so insurmountably obstructive of Protestant teaching, and blasting to the Protestant faith, are called upon, in the name of toleration, and of religious equality, to go still farther, and to divorce the Protestant Church from the Protestant Crown, to take away its endowment, and to strip its clergy of all support, except what their congregations may volunteer to give them, and to enact that the Protestant Church in Ireland, as a State Church, shall cease to exist; because it has failed to convert the Irish people, whose old convictions have been thus thoroughly protected by all the power of the Government, and by the enactments of the Legislature itself.

Alien Church has been adopted as an abusive name for expressing a contrast with what is assumed to be the Church of the people, and the native Church of Ireland; and this invented name is used to cry down the State Church. This so-called alien Church consists exclusively of British and Irish clergy, and nearly all native Irish. Its acknowledged head is the English Sovereign of the United Kingdom; its ritual is entirely regulated by the Legislature of the same United Kingdom. It acknowledges no subjection to any foreign power, civil or ecclesiastical; its worship, and prayers, and all its ceremonies are conducted in the vernacular language of its congregations. To these congregations, or to the Irish people, there is nothing whatever of an alien character connected with this Church.

The so-called Church of the people, on the contrary, repudiates the jurisdiction of the national Sovereign; and acknowledges an alien potentate as its head; its Church service is in Latin; its discipline and ceremonies are regulated by its alien head; and its clergy are appointed by him, and from him derive their authority. Their disputes are all subject to his decision; and they travel to Rome to have these disputes heard and decided there. The regulation of penance for sins; of indulgences; of holydays, of fasts, and of ecclesiastical government, is all in the hands of this alien potentate; and it is with difficulty, and reluctance, that this so-called Church of the people submits even to the municipal laws and authorities of the country in which it exists; thus exhibiting every essential attribute of an alien Church. Again, by inverting the rule of justice, the name of alien, odious as it is meant to be, is transferred from the institution to which it properly belongs to the native establishment, which is in all respects national, and has nothing alien in its constitution or practice.

It is said that the Romish Church is the Church of the people, and this implies an assertion that the Protestant Church is not the Church of the people; and implies also that the Roman Catholics are the people of Ireland, and that the Protestants are not. To test the truth and accuracy of all these assertions, it is necessary to divide, and analyze the whole population of Ireland, that the title to the name of "the people" may be justly estimated.

At the census of 1861 there were 4,505,265 Roman Catholics, and 1,289,206 Protestants; the Roman Catholics being to the Protestants in nearly the ratio of 7 to 2. In the whole population there were 1,973,382 who could neither read nor write; a large proportion of these (probably nine-tenths of them) belong to the Roman Catholic population. Taking into account the rank, the property, the education, and knowledge of the Protestant two-sevenths, if the sects are to be estimated according to the consideration due to property, and to knowledge (which Lord Bacon says is power), and to civilization as well as numbers, it is a mere hyperbole to say, that the Roman Catholic faith is the religion of the people of Ireland.

If an independent provision cannot be made for the clergy of the three great sects into which the people are divided, this impossibility makes it the more necessary to make such provision for at least one of these sects, and to unite this one to the Sovereign. This has been done in both England and Ireland, and the utility of it in promoting and maintaining universal toleration and peace is perfectly obvious. The clergy of the State religion, being provided for, have no temporal motives to polemical anger towards other sects. They have no interest in restraining their congregations from the free exercise of reason and private judgment; their doctrines will therefore rest more upon Scripture, according to a logical and careful interpretation, than upon dogmatical authority. Not being dependent upon the number or the liberality of their votaries, they are not prompted to any unseemly efforts to gain proselytes, or to turbulent contests with other sects. Their union with the Sovereign, and the constitutional obligation to fill the throne by a monarch of their persuasion, is a perfect security against that worst of social calamities, a bigoted king, in the hands of a dogmatical hierarchy. The temporal power of the Sovereign, under the spiritual guidance of an independent clergy, is in no danger of being abused for the cruel purpose of religious persecution, and will be duly applied to restrain other sects from violence towards each other, should they be disposed to use it.

In such an enlightened community as that of the British Islands, it may be hoped that there will always be a sufficient number to see, and to appreciate the value of an independent Church, thus allied to the temporal Sovereign, as a security for universal toleration and liberty of conscience. Whether that number be a majority, or a minority of the population is immaterial, so long as it has the power, and the will to be an efficient peacemaker. The more numerous and the more powerful sects are, who form themselves upon the voluntary principle, and embrace doctrines, preached by dependent clergy, the greater is the necessity for a State religion, and an independent hierarchy, united to the Throne, and affording to tolerant men the means of religious worship conducted without unnecessary restraint upon private judgment, and flowing from, and founded on, a rational interpretation of Holy Writ, not dogmatically forced upon doubting or dissenting hearers, but offered for assent resulting from conviction, produced by logical argument and reason.

This view is confirmed by every page of the history of Europe, from the reign of Constantine to the present day. The religious equality contended for by the manœuvering and pretending Whigs means nothing more or less than license to all religious sects to worry each other, and freely indulge that envy and malignity with which the prosperity and happiness of one may affect the others. This phantom called religious equality has been adopted as a watchword by the spurious Whigs, now out of office, in derision and contempt of the principles by which the constitutional party who effected the Revolution; who framed the Bill of Rights; who achieved the Habeas Corpus Act; and who raised all the other bulwarks of British liberty, were guided and actuated. As a test of this pretended equality, let a question be put to the Roman Catholic hierarchy, whether the Protestant clergy can be, by any earthly power, raised to an equality with those who assert that they have been themselves appointed by Divine Providence as the guardians of what they allege to be the only true religion; and as the custodees of all human souls, for whose safety they profess responsibility to God. No one can doubt that these assertors of divine right would answer this question by a negative. Those who repudiated this enslaving pretension to divine right of princes and of priests, were persuaded that an alliance between the Crown and the Church which made no such pretension, was essential to the dignity, the legitimate authority, and to the very existence of that liberal Church. To admit the necessity for this union in England, and to deny it in Ireland, is contradictory and absurd. The necessity for it, in Ireland, is ten-fold greater than in England, for the most obvious reason. In England the Roman Catholics are few, compared with the Protestants, and other sects who are opposed to them. In England there has been, and there is but one language, common to all sects, whose consequent intercourse is, therefore, likely to soften the effects of that uncharitable doctrine of exclusive salvation, and to raise some humane doubt of its truth in the minds of those to whom it is propounded ; and thus, in some degree, to moderate the power of the clergy over their minds. In Ireland, there were, in 1861, 163,275 persons who could speak no language but Irish, and more than double that number ten years before. These were, therefore, disabled from social conversation with Protestants, very few of whom speak Irish at all. In Ireland also the Roman Catholics are a majority, and their clergy all the more powerful. I cannot better illustrate the effect of this intolerant doctrine on the minds of the Irish than by relating two anecdotes, the truth of which may be relied on.

The priest of my native parish was sitting with one of his flock, the wife of a shopkeeper in the village, while she was engaged in roasting a goose for dinner. The good woman, who had a full measure of the milk of human kindness in her nature, when the conversation turned on the hope of salvation, anxiously inquired of her pastor, whether for such good Protestants as Mrs. ——— (for whom she had an ardent friendship) there was no chance of salvation. The reverend father answered her question in clear terms, with an explanatory illustration. Laying his hands on the andirons, by which the spit was supported, he drew the goose to a greater distance from the fire, saying: "Don't you know that there may be degrees of torment in the other world; and that what I have now done may be done for Mrs. ———, on account of her good works; but as to salvation, she has no chance." The good-natured woman, in the hope of converting her friend, related to her the opinion and the illustration of her pastor, and from that friend I have the story.

The gentleman from whom I derive my traditional knowledge of Ireland gave to two of his farm labourers about a rood each, for potato ground, in a pasture field which he was about to break for tillage. He allowed them as much manure as they pleased from his farm yard, and they planted their potatoes in the fashion called lazy-bed. He ploughed his own part, in the proper and skilful manner, early in winter, and had it in good order in spring, and put in his seed in drills, between which the ground was carefully dug during the summer, and weeds destroyed. I was present, in October, when these two men were digging out their master's potatoes, and one said to the other: "Ned, that's a fine crop; isn't it well with the Protestants in this world?" "It is so," said Ned; "but how will it be with them in the other world?" I was a small boy, and my presence was no restraint on them, and perhaps they thought I did not understand them, for they spoke in Irish. I perfectly understood them, and their observations made a deep impression upon my mind. It never occurred to them to ascribe the good crop of their master to his good husbandry, or their own scanty crop to their lazy-bed method of tilling it.

One of the real grievances of Ireland, and one from which many great calamities have fallen upon the country, is that those who legislate for it know less about the moral condition and temper of the people than they do about the races in Central Africa, of whom some reliable information is derived from travellers. It is a sad fact, and to the Irish nation a degrading fact, that when any of its representatives in Parliament asserts anything about Ireland, he is promptly contradicted by some Irish member of the opposing party, from which it happens that the most respectable Irishmen in the House think it prudent to be silent, and to forbear from asserting anything themselves, or questioning anything alleged by others. The result is, that Englishmen legislate for this unhappy country either in ignorance, in anger, or in disgust; and we cannot be surprised at the inconsistency, the instability, and often the cruelty of the enactments inflicted upon Ireland.

I have before detailed the effects of the Charter School remedy for Popery, adopted in ignorance of the disorder then called Popery, under which the Irish were assumed to labour as it really existed here, or of the constitution and temper of the people to whom the remedy was to be applied. It is therefore not surprising that the remedy produced effects exactly opposite to those intended, and yet this absurd remedy, even after the absurdity, and the cruelty of it were exposed, continued to be obstinately administered for ninety years, until it made the disease incurable. In the middle of the present century, we have had another remedial Act of the Legislature, passed in anger towards the landlords, an important class of the Irish people, the real effects of which have been strangely ignored, and the imaginary effects marvellously assumed, as a principal cause of an improvement in the condition of the country which subsequently took place, and was produced by other causes, notwithstanding the ruin inflicted upon thousands by the application of the remedial law.

For the first time, a poor-law was enacted for Ireland in the year 1838, against the opinions of many men well qualified to judge of its probable effects. During seven years which immediately followed this new enactment the population was at its maximum, being considerably over eight millions. In these years, the harvests were good, and the condition of the people corresponded. In the years 1842 and 1843, those notorious monster meetings took place on the subject of repealing the Act of Union, and people have said that Ireland was rampant during those years, and I do not remember any time in which want or destitution was less talked of. Workhouses were built on a scale much more than sufficient to accommodate all who claimed relief, and there was not much, if any, complaint of the newly imposed burthen.

Unexpectedly, in the harvest of 1845, a disease appeared which threatened destruction of the potato. Sir Robert Peel was then in office, and, to provide for the apprehended deficiency in the food of the people, he secretly arranged with the house of Baring and Co. for the purchase of maize and other grain, to supply the expected want. It happened, fortunately, that the potato crop of that year, 1845, was unusually abundant, that the disease did not affect it until it was fully matured, and that more than an average produce of other years remained unaffected; that, therefore, the distress was partial and trifling, by which the precautionary measures became, to a great extent, inoperative. The success with which Sir Robert Peel had concealed his provident adoption of Joseph's advice to Pharaoh surprised his successors, when, for the first time, on coming into office, they discovered it from a minute in the Treasury. The wisdom of this secrecy was soon illustrated by the new Government, in the manner which will be immediately explained. It got some faint praise from his successors; but full justice has never been done, and never will be done, to the provident ability of the great statesman whose precautions proved more than adequate to the occasion.

In the beginning of August, 1846, before the potato was mature, an universal blight fell upon it, by which it was all but entirely destroyed. It was immediately manifest, that the food upon which many millions of people depended for life was blasted, and suddenly annihilated. The calamity had then really come, which had been only threatened the year before.

In August, 1846, there was a large quantity of the corn of the previous year still on hands, both at home and abroad; and the new corn harvest being abundant, the prices were moderate and the demand was dull. There was no mistake or doubt as to the approaching famine, and its magnitude was evident and appalling.

Had Baring and Co., and other like agents, been secretly instructed to buy up maize and other grain, and the operations repeated which were disclosed by the Treasury minute of the previous year, and which that minute ought to have suggested, some millions of lives might have been saved. But that was not to be. A different course was adopted, and a sadly different effect was produced. Upon the plausible principle of not interfering with ordinary operations of trade, the Government announced, in Parliament, their intention not to interfere with the regular trade by which Indian corn and other grain could be brought into the country; and the trade, upon their economical principles, was to be left at liberty, both wholesale and retail, free from interference of Government. This announcement immediately excited a disposition to speculate in grain. The demand, which was previously dull, was sensibly quickened; prices began to rise, and the assurance that the market would not be affected by Government operations gave confidence to buyers. Large purchases were made on speculation, at constantly advancing prices, both at home and abroad; and great numbers of floating cargoes were bound for British ports, and changed owners ten or twelve times during the winter and spring, but were still tenaciously held for a rise, and kept out of consumption. The prices at which these were speculatively bought continually advanced, and, in the month of May, 1847, became nearly double what they had been the previous August, September, and October. Many British and Irish merchants bought these at prices extravagantly over the value, in the hope of getting still more. The general result will clearly appear from the case of one merchant, a client of mine, who, in the winter of 1846–7, became the owner of corn cargoes of such number and magnitude, that if he had accepted the prices pressed upon him in April and May, 1847, he would have realized a profit of £70,000. He held for still higher offers, until the market turned in June, fell in July, and rapidly tumbled as an abundant harvest became manifest. He still held, hoping a recovery, and in the end of October he became a bankrupt. The effect of the speculation, excited by the published determination of the Government not to do anything to affect the markets, was to transfer a large amount of Irish capital to foreign growers, and foreign merchants, to keep corn out of consumption, while the famine raged, and to multiply the expense of keeping the people alive in the poor-houses.

It required great care and skill, and very difficult and able arrangements to conceal from the public the active operations of Sir Robert Peel in 1845, and he did most effectually conceal them, and bought largely without exciting or disturbing the markets. The Government of 1846 had no operations to conceal, and to avoid doing mischief, they had only to be silent. They were, however, tempted to earn the cheers of speculators, which ended in bitter lamentations and disaster to the people.

As a substitute for Sir Robert Peel's remedy, which his rivals and successors in office boastingly declined to adopt, certain works were devised upon public roads in all parts of Ireland, for the purpose of giving employment, at ten pence a day, to the people. The announcement of these works, and the Government scheme of employment, impressed the starving class with a belief that their support was to be permanently provided for by the Government; and they abandoned all ordinary operations and exertions of their own for earning support. They crowded on the public works in such multitudes, that it became impossible to devise for them any useful operations. They were set upon the roads to cut down hills, and fill hollows, where scarcely a hill or a hollow existed, and public traffic was interrupted, and highways seriously injured. Labourers left ordinary employments for some public work, and for no better wages, solely because the public work was in fact no work, but a farcical excuse for getting a day's wages. The demoralizing effects of those works upon the Irish labourers continued for many years after the country recovered from the famine.

The old and decrepit, the women and children, and the surplus multitudes for whom no employment could be devised, crowded all the poor-houses to overflowing, and the people entered those dreadful abodes never to return. They died there daily by hundreds; and, in effect, the poor-law became but an expensive mode of destroying them.

A maxim was adopted that the Irish land should support the Irish paupers, whose existence and whose destitution were imputed to the landlords. The poor-law gave active operation to this assumed rule of justice, and in all the Unions the poor-rate became a crushing tax. In some it amounted to 20*s.*, in others to 25*s.*, and even to 30*s.* on every pound of the valuation, and thus turned many estates into a burthen on the owner, in place of being his support. Such was the condition of landowners, and their tenants, in the year 1849, when the Legislature proceeded to enact a remedy for the calamity by which Ireland was overwhelmed. Land having in many cases become a burthen, and in many others of no present value; large tracts in some localities abandoned and made desolate; the cabins ruined, and the tenants dead or in the poor-house. The best estates in the country were depreciated to less than half their former value. The rents swallowed by the poor-rate, which was enormously increased by the price of corn factitiously kept up by the speculators. The tax was paramount to all other charges, and scarcely sufficient means to meet it could be raised by the famine-stricken agricultural population. Under these sad circumstances some State physician prescribed a remedy called the "Act further to faciliate the Sale and Transfer of Incumbered Estates in Ireland," which received the Royal assent on the 28th July 1849, when the famine and the poor-law had got full time to produce their worst effects. The short operation of that enactment was to enable the first incumbrancer, or any other who believed that the estate would fetch a price large enough to reach the payment of his own demand, by a summary proceeding, in a new court, instituted for the purpose, to force a speedy sale of the estate, regardless of the creditors whose demands half price could not reach, and regardless of the owner, whose equity of redemption under existing circumstances was worth nothing.

The advantage thus presented to the owners of early incumbrances was too obvious, and too tempting not to be seized, and, in addition to the previously existing causes of depreciation, the market for land became suddenly glutted; and to increase the chance of getting bidders, every creditor, except the petitioner who was forcing the sale, was at free liberty to bid, like any other person, and even the petitioner by leave of the court (which was easily procured) might become the purchaser, and the purchasing creditor was to have credit for his demand as against the price. By this new process, estates were sold to the amount of many millions, during the years 1849, 1850, 1851, and 1852, for less than half their value, and less than half the prices which the same estates would bring, had the sale been deferred to the end of 1863. Some of the most ancient and respected families in the country, whose estates were not incumbered to much more than half their value, were sold out, and beggared; thousands of creditors whose demands would be paid, if the sale had not been accelerated, were not reached, and lost the money which they had lent upon what was ample security at the time it was lent, and would again have become sufficient security, had the property not been ruined by the poor-law, and sold in that ruined condition, in a glutted market, under an enactment devised for the professed purpose of improving the condition of Ireland. The law's delay, which, in ordinary circumstances, is a grievance and a vexation, would have had a salutary and a just effect in those calamitous times. There was no justice in exonerating the early incumbrancers from all participation in the effects of the visitation which had come upon the country, and every feeling of humanity, and every principle of equity, demanded temporary indulgence from them. There was cruel injustice in turning a destructive visitation of Providence into an advantage to them, which they could not have had, if the law had been left as it stood when they made their contracts and took their securities; and as it still stands in England.

The administration of the crushing poor-law was effectually taken out of the hands of the guardians who were elected by the ratepayers, and committed to certain officials, whose powers were largely extended by two Acts passed in June and July, 1847, and who, having no interest in the chargeable property, had no motive to a jealous scrutiny of claims for relief, nor to vigilance in controlling expenditure. By this system, the rents of the land were sequestered for support of a starving population, who had abandoned all intention of earning their bread by labour, and who had fallen into the fatal mistake of believing that the Government was able and willing to provide for them.

The effect of forcing a peremptory sale of property, so circumstanced and so affected, will be best understood by considering a single case, which is nothing but an instance out of a multitude, and is by no means as grievous as many others which took place between 1849 and 1854.

An extensive estate in the West of Ireland, by the death of the owner, came into the possession of his son, who had recently completed his collegiate education. The family stood in the first rank of the gentry in their county, and had long been highly respected. The estate had been incumbered, but not to an amount equal to half its value. The young proprietor determined to sell as much as would pay off the charges, and had received offers which he did not think adequate to the value; and was holding on for better prices. For one portion, which he was desirous to sell, he was offered £15,000; for another division he was offered £10,000. He still held out for better prices. His creditors having confidence in their securities, he was under no obligation to sell his property for less than its value; and the prospects of the country were as bright as they had ever been before, when, in the first week of August, 1846, an unforeseen calamity annihilated the food of one-half the population of Ireland. The blight which destroyed the potato crop was an event of a single night, and the morning sun made the destruction evident to every eye. There was no room for doubt: there was no shadow of hope: dismay was the universal feeling of all classes, high and low. All thoughts of purchasing land instantly vanished, and every pending treaty was broken off. Those upon whom this calamity fell may be divided into two classes, viz., those who could afford to lose their potato crop of that year, and be only by so much the less prosperous; and those to whom the loss brought penury and want. The remedy devised for the destitute were the useless works, by which every effort to help themselves was paralyzed. It was soon discovered, that no Government has power to feed a nation that will not work. This truth was not known, or was not attended to, until experience made it fatally evident. The people relied on the Government to provide work and wages for them, and came in such multitudes, that the Government became bewildered and dismayed, and took shelter in the State maxim, that the land of Ireland must support the poor of Ireland, and this led to the cruel Act for Sale of Incumbered Estates. This Act got the Royal assent in July, 1849, and gave a summary power to the first mortgagee, and to every creditor who believed that a price could be got sufficient to reach his own demand, to force a sale, without regard to the inadequacy of the price, in respect of subsequent incumbrances, or in respect of the owner's hope of a surplus. If no stranger would bid the amount due to the first mortgagee, or other petitioning creditor, the new law entitled him to bid himself, and to become owner of the estate, leaving nothing for any subsequent creditor; nothing for the owner of the equity of redemption. This new law removed the expenses, the delay, and the uncertainty of a suit in Chancery, in which all who had an interest in the property should be parties, with a right to have their several equities justly attended to; one of which would certainly have been to forbear from selling at a sacrifice ruinous to all except the foremost creditor. No court of equity would have shut its eyes to the visitation of Providence by which the owner of the property had been disabled from paying the demand, or keeping down the interest. No court of equity would have despaired of a return of better times. Every principle of justice, and every sentiment of humanity would, under such circumstances, be a full warrant and justification for the law's delay. What happened in the case to which I am alluding, and what happened in, I know not how many hundred other cases, not only similar, but greatly more crushing to the parties than that to which, for a mere example, I am referring, could not possibly have happened, had there been no exceptional legislation for Ireland. The first mortgagee promptly availed himself of this *remedial* Act, and the *whole* estate was sold, under its provisions, before the end of 1850. The lot for which £15,000 had been refused was peremptorily sold for a trifle over £6,000. The lot for which £10,000 had been offered and refused was sold for £4,000. The rents payable by the tenants were all moderate rents. The highest prices obtained amounted only to twelve years' purchase of these rents, and many lots realized no more than seven years' purchase. The first mortgagee is now the owner of the family mansion, and a large part of the family property. The puisne creditors were left unpaid. The owner was cast pennyless upon the world; and such was the effect of one of the State remedies for one of the heaviest afflictions with which Providence had ever visited any country.

The ruined owner of this estate, fortunately for himself, was young, and had got a learned education. He turned his attention at once to the Church, was ordained; and the small benefice of the parish in which his hereditary mansion stands, subsequently became vacant. The bishop of the diocese, unsolicited, collated to it the ejected owner of the large estate in which the parish lies; where for twelve or thirteen years he has lived, and is passing rich on £115 a year, beloved and respected by every Protestant, and every Roman Catholic, rich and poor, within many miles of his humble manse; presenting an edifying example of submission to the will of Him whose mercy tempers the wind to the shorn lamb.

The remuneration given to this educated gentleman for performing the duties of a parish, and answering the demands of charity in what is frequently a famine-stricken locality, suggests attention to the true and actual magnitude of the endowment of the Church Establishment in Ireland, which has been exaggerated by those who declaim against its existence; the declamation being founded almost entirely on two grounds—viz., the large incomes of bishops, and the small congregations of some incumbents. There are, in Ireland, 1611 of these incumbents, and the net income of each is stated in Thom's Directory. In some parishes the yearly amount is under £20. In 357 it is under £100. In 351 it is under £200. In 435 it is under £300. In 238 it does not exceed £400. In 100 it does not exceed £500. In 62 the income does not exceed £600. Only 18 have incomes exceeding £700. The same number have incomes not exceeding £800. But 15 have incomes exceeding £900. Nine have incomes not over £1000. Only four have £1100 ; and the same number have £1200 ; and this is the largest income enjoyed by any parish minister in Ireland.

Most of the rectors who have the large incomes are obliged to support curates in chapels of ease, and to assist also in the parish church, and in the other duties in large and populous parishes, of which there are many in Ireland, and the Protestant congregations of which are numerous. All notice of these is suppressed in the declamations of assailants. There are many parishes, in which the congregations are so large, and the duties so onerous, and yet the income of the rector so small, that the parishioners support a curate, and, in some cases, more than one, to assist in ministering to the religious wants of the Protestant parishioners ; being too onerous to be discharged by the incumbent alone.

The Protestant rector of a parish must support the rank of a gentleman. That he shall have a family is not only allowed, but expected; and that he shall maintain them with decency in his proper rank is imperative upon him. The curates also must keep their place as gentlemen upon stipends which seldom exceed the wages now paid to carpenters and bricklayers, and other skilled labourers, in Dublin, and other cities in Ireland. Both rectors and curates must be in constant view of, and in close contact with, the poor and the destitute, who, as well Roman Catholic as Protestant, come to their doors with claims upon charity not to be answered by an accusation that they have embraced a different creed. I shall ever retain the deep and painful impression made on me by an artless, but graphic description given to me of the daily scene which, during the famine years, was exhibited at the parlour windows of a Protestant clergyman in the neighbourhood of Skibbereen, in the county of Cork. When this clergyman, his wife, five or six children, and his aged sister (from whom I had the sad account) sat at breakfast, or at dinner, a crowd of living skeletons stood craving at the windows; and the family, by feelings which could not be resisted, were compelled to act as if they were on board a disabled ship at sea, and to divide their morsel of food, retaining for themselves only the famine allowance, which they distributed to the craving crowd. This poor man's income was but £75 a year, and he had nothing else to live on, and support his family. His brother was vicar of the parish in which I was born, the income of which was, and is, about £150 a year. Of this income, during the famine years, the poor-rate took away one-half. In 1849, the wife of this clergyman, leading her son, about six years old, by the hand, entered my study in Dublin, and gave me a harrowing account of their sufferings, during those awful times. She had a hope that I might use some influence, as an old friend, for their relief; but she mistook my position, I was addicted to no party; I had no influence; and I was unable to help them.

These clergymen are bound to constant residence in their parishes, however remote, and however poor. During the frequently recurring summer famines, when landlords and impropriators can enjoy their incomes far away from spectacles of starved and destitute fellow-creatures, the Protestant clergy, their wives, and their daughters, have constantly to behold them, to listen to their supplications for a morsel of food, and to deplore the inadequacy of the means in their power to relieve them. The Roman Catholic clergyman, who is known to be dependent on the voluntary contributions of his flock, and has not a family, is not so obviously, and so painfully exposed to inportunities of the destitute as the Protestant rector and his family.

The present incumbents will suffer nothing from the manœuvre by which the Protestant clerical order is to be abolished, to which these useful men belong; when they die out, and disappear, the Protestants, whether many or few, will be without the means of worship in numberless remote localities; and in those places the religion must also die out. This is the effect desired and expected by the rival hierarchy, and, according to their Catechism, it is an effect which they may glory in producing for the salvation of souls. The 700,000 Protestants, who repudiate this Catechism; who believe that rational liberty, emancipation of the human mind, and religious worship, according to human reason and according to conscience, are bound up with, and must stand or fall with the independent clergy of the Protestant State Church, will be the principal, but not the only sufferers, by the abolition of that Church—that the Roman Catholic laity, and especially the poor and ignorant part of them, will lose a protecting shield, I have no doubt, and many intelligent Roman Catholics are of this opinion. But what shall be the precise nature, or what may be the extent of the suffering resulting from this party manœuvre, or when it will begin to be felt, I cannot foresee, nor can any other man. I have great faith in the power of a sensible, intelligent, and earnest people, to find some means to mitigate and to prevent the bad consequences of mischievous legislation ; and to evade, and turn aside the operation of pernicious State measures. This country has recovered from the destructive remedies for its disorders which for centuries have been prescribed by State physicians, and administered by officials. That it survived and recovered is mainly due to the constitutional vigour and energy of those Protestant sects, both of the English and Presbyterian creeds, against whom the present manœuvre is directed. I trust that some solution of the difficulty into which the proposed measure will bring the nation may be discovered, which will be consistent with the prosperity and happiness, and, above all things, with the peace of the country. That portion of the Irish people, before referred to, who are not known to the English nation, who are ignored by the legislators ; who are disregarded by the agitators, or regarded with envy and hatred, will suffer the first and most immediate effects of the attack upon their worship. It will affect the other Protestants, who belong not to the Church of England, less directly, but not less certainly. These two classes of Protestants make nearly one-third of the whole people ; but to them the great bulk of the landed and personal property of the country belongs. This property they possess and enjoy in the sight and presence of the Roman Catholic population, who are mingled with them, more than double their number in the whole island, and in some localities twenty to one. If the abusively termed wealthy clergy of the State Church be an insulting spectacle, kept in view of the Roman Catholic clergy, who are assumed to be poor, in order to support the argument that the wealth of others is an insulting grievance to them—if tender regard for religious and social equality demand confiscation of the property, the enjoyment of which by its owners is an insult to those who have not any similar provision; if this be sound argument, and if any such motive in truth or sincerity exists, it becomes difficult to understand why the Roman Catholic laity should not feel insulted at the spectacle of a wealthy minority of Protestants, kept continually before their eyes, poor and wretched as nine-tenths of these Roman Catholic people are ; and why they should not have as just reason to call for an abatement of this insulting grievance, by confiscation of the property thus insultingly enjoyed in their view by a few Protestants, as the Roman Catholic hierarchy have to demand the confiscation of the Church endowment for the same reason. Most of the Roman Catholic laity are *really* poor, and the majority of them often almost destitute. Scarcely one of them is exempt from the grievance of beholding the insulting spectacle of some Protestant rolling in his carriage, and otherwise enjoying enormous wealth, as compared with his own penury: the clergy of these poor people are *not* poor, and to say they are is an audacious misrepresentation. The spectacle of a wealthy Protestant minister, as compared with the poorest Roman Catholic curate in Ireland, is rare, if any such exists at all; and yet the existence of such spectacle extensively is assumed, as the justification for confiscating the endowment of the State Church. This property was granted by the Crown to the several incumbents and their successors, in exercise of the same prerogative which empowered the Crown to grant any other property to the grantee and his heirs. If the Roman Catholics claimed this property for their clergy, as successors to those who were the owners before the Reformation, such claim would raise a pure question of title. If they claimed for their clergy an equivalent provision out of some other property or fund, this would raise only a question of compensation for public services, and performance of religious duties to a large section of the people. But when they assail the endowment of the Protestant Church, as a grievance to themselves, merely because their own clergy are not endowed; when their clergy assert that the wealth of the Protestant Church is an insulting spectacle in their eyes, and therefore a grievance, the foundation of the complaint is socialism. Every class in the community has the same right to complain, on the same grounds, of the superior wealth of any other class, and every individual to complain of the superior wealth of his neighbour. The sentiment which excites to this complaint is the passion of envy, in its plainest form, and without the least disguise. To exercise the legislative power, as now proposed by a manœuvreing political party, is to prostitute that power for the gratification of a malignant passion in one hierarchy towards another, in violation of vested proprietary rights, and in contempt of that moral restraint which is the only protection British subjects have against the otherwise unlimited power of the three Estates.

The proprietary rights which the Legislature is called on so to violate are vested legally in the clergy, but beneficially for the Irish Protestants of the Church of England and Ireland. The property which is so vested, and which the Legislature is called on to confiscate, was granted for the support of their religion and worship. If that religion and worship have become blasphemous, or in any other way socially intolerable, it may be proper, or necessary to exercise the legislative power in abolishing the religion, and in prohibiting the worship; and the dupes of such a depraved persuasion may thus forfeit their right to the property originally granted for support of a true religion. By such a forfeiture the property would revert to the Crown; and might be legally, and properly granted to other uses. This is what took place at the Reformation. If the Roman Catholic religion has become, in the opinion of the Legislature, the only true religion, as by its Catechism it is asserted to be; if all men be obliged (in the words of that Catechism) to be of that only true religion, and if it be the duty of the temporal Government to enforce that obligation, and to persecute the clergy, and the laity of every other persuasion, then we have arrived at a second Reformation, and the endowment of the condemned Church may be legally confiscated. This was the counter Reformation which took place on the accession of Mary. This counter Reformation inflicted not only a forfeiture of property on the Church of Edward VI., but a cruel forfeiture of life upon the clergy and the laity of that Church.

James II. was proceeding to accomplish a Reformation

analogous to Mary's. He began in Scotland with the Presbyterians, pretending that he tortured them with the boot and the thumbscrew, because they refused to join the Episcopalian Church of England, which he himself detested, and he proceeded in England at the same time by prosecuting the bishops of that Church, because they refused, at his command, to violate the law in favour of those who embraced his own creed.

The Romish hierarchy who persuaded Mary, that it was "an act of faith" to light the fires, and burn Protestants in Smithfield; who persuaded James to adopt the course by which he lost his throne, are still the same hierarchy, by succession; organized under the same head, teaching the same Catechism, claiming the same direct authority from Divine Providence to guard the deposit of the Catholic faith on earth, and assuming the same responsibility to God for the souls of their flocks.

He must be a superficial observer of passing events who does not see, that this hierarchy are availing themselves of the toleration granted by a Protestant Government, to regain their lost power in England—that they occupy Ireland as the base of their polemical operations—that the Irish branch of the State Church of the United Kingdom is an outwork of that ecclesiastical fortification, by which the liberty of these countries, both civil and religious, is protected—that the same artillery with which they are now battering this outwork is quite as applicable to the demolition of the principal fortress, as soon as they shall have cleared their way to it. Since Emancipation has been achieved, and perfect civil and religious liberty established, this island has been an available base of operations to the Roman Catholic hierarchy for accomplishing their future designs. In it they very soon opened their trenches unobserved; and all their approaches have been made slowly, insidiously, cautiously, and skilfully; until they believe that a favourable moment for unmasking their battery has been presented by the present unexpected position of the contending parties in England. Now we hear the cry that the "hour is come, and the man is come," and the Irish Church must fall, outwork though it obviously is of the great fortification of English liberty. When, with James II. on the throne, it was supposed that the hour was come, and the man was come for a counter Reformation, England was saved, by a rash attack upon its Established Church, in the prosecution of the seven bishops. Whether the present assault upon the Irish Church will produce a similar reaction, I am unable to foresee; but I have no difficulty in seeing the necessity for it.

In the last century, and in the Irish Parliament, the landlords, by an iniquitous resolution of the Commons, exonerated the pasture lands of Ireland from the burthen of the Church, and threw the whole weight of it upon the tilled land. It has already been shown how this tilled land formed but a small part of the whole, and how it was held and cultivated by the poor labouring cottiers. These were obliged to give to the Protestant minister one-tenth of their crops, or else to buy this tenth at the clergyman's price. It followed that the farmer who spent most manure and labour, and applied most skill in the cultivation of his land, paid, or was, for that reason, bound to pay, a larger amount to the minister. This sort of impost necessarily became odious, and the clergy were forced into a practice of setting the whole tithe of the parish to men called proctors, whose profit depended on the rigour with which they enforced payment from the farmers. It frequently happened that the price demanded for the tithe was such that the farmer preferred paying it in kind; and nothing could be more vexatious than the process of severing it from his own part of the produce. While this system continued, the Protestant Church was a heavy grievance, and the pressure of it was borne chiefly by the tillage farmers, the great majority of whom were poor cottiers and Roman Catholics. The discontent created by it was then loud, violent, and universal throughout the country, and the Legislature was forced into a measure of adjustment, by which the cultivators of the soil were effectually exonerated; by which the unjust exemption of grass land was reformed, and by which the liability of the landlord was substituted for that of the tenant, and a large abatement made as a consideration for undertaking that liability. This adjustment is now fully thirty years in operation, and it is no longer true that the Church is a cause of popular discontent, nor is there any just reason why it should be.

One of the difficulties by which this empirical measure of confiscation is pressed is the absence of all, even colourable, claims upon the confiscated property, and the variety, if not conflict, of opinion as to the uses to which it should be applied. No two of the abolitionists have agreed upon this important point, nor have they even seriously discussed it. For 300 years it has been appropriated to defray the expenses of religious worship for those who embrace the creed, by the law and constitution of the country, not only sanctioned as the national creed, but imperatively enjoined upon the Sovereign, as the only creed which it is lawful for the Sovereign who fills the throne of this realm to profess. No other party has, or pretends to have, any colour of right to this property. It is difficult to understand upon what principle of justice, or of benevolent legislation, an endowment and a right can be taken away, after 300 years' acquiescence in the enjoyment of it, and in the absence of claim to it by any other party. That the existing generation to whom it has descended are only 700,000 in number seems a very bad reason for confiscating the property, for so long a time applied in providing churches and clergy for this section of the Queen's subjects. These subjects and their ancestors, for 300 years, have been exempt from the charge of supporting public worship, and of administering religious instruction, according to the doctrine and form of worship adopted by the State, and used in all the churches of England and Ireland to which Protestants resort. This doctrine is publicly, and constantly, and by legal authority, pronounced to be the doctrine of the "true religion established amongst us." It is difficult to understand how the Legislature can now justly reduce these 700,000 subjects to the dilemma of shutting up their churches, and dispensing with the services of clergy, or else bear the newly-imposed burthen of defraying the expense of supporting these churches and clergy themselves. Five millions of other subjects live in the same island with these 700,000, but do not resort to the same churches, and do not submit to the religious teaching of the same clergy; and, therefore, derive no benefit from the property by law set apart for support of the churches and worship of the smaller number. The five millions do not pretend that they have any right to the property thus enjoyed for centuries by their fellow-subjects. The absence of all right to claim it themselves increases the difficulty of comprehending what right they can have to insist upon the confiscation of it, in derogation of the rights of their fellow-subjects. Suppose a tract of land intervening between a village and a church, over which the owner, 300 years ago, or thirty years ago, suffered such of the inhabitants as resorted to that church to make a short passage to it over his land, and for thirty years did not interrupt them, this use would make their right of way indefeasible. If, during all the same time, a Roman Catholic chapel stood also at the other side of the same land, but the Roman Catholics, for some reason, did not cross the land, but resorted to the chapel by the longer public road, and, therefore, acquired no right of way to their chapel: no one can understand how these facts would warrant a complaint on the part of the Roman Catholics, founded on the assertion that they felt aggrieved at the enjoyment of the short cut by their Protestant neighbours; that the constant view of their Protestant neighbours exercising this right of way had become an insult to their feelings, ten times more numerous, as they find they are, than the favoured Protestants. The owner of the land, if willing, could not redress this grievance by stopping the way, after thirty years of acquiescence: (just as the owner of a chargeable estate is disabled from refusing to pay the rent-charge). If, under these circumstances, the Roman Catholics preferred a petition to the Legislature, to have redress of this grievance, by abolition of this offensive right of way (made offensive only by the passion of envy), it is impossible to imagine that the unquestionable *power* of the Legislature would be exercised in such a case. If the right was founded on an express grant by a partial and prejudiced Protestant owner, for the benefit of those of his own persuasion; and if he expressly had refused to give a similar liberty to those of any other creed, this might account for the privilege enjoyed by one class, and for the exclusion of the other, but it would not alter their rights. For right of way if we substitute rent-charge issuing out of the land, and for thirty years applied to defray the expenses of worship for the benefit of Protestants, it seems impossible to see how the principles of justice, which govern one of these cases, can be differently applied to the other. That a Protestant Sovereign, in disposing of property according to his lawful and constitutional prerogative, had a right to prefer the clergy of his own Church to those of any other, and to grant property for the support of that Church, in exoneration of the laity of that Church, and to support an independent clergy, according to his clear constitutional right to dispose of that property, and, at the same time, to decline making any such grant for support of any other Church, seems as plain a truth as any that can be conceived. The same Sovereign, at the same time, granted exactly similar property (vested in him by the same events, and on precisely the same title), not for the support of any Church, but to laymen; thereby diverting it from the uses to which it had been originally destined: no one can understand upon what ground of reason or justice this grant to a layman can stand good, and be considered irrevocable, if the grant for the proper religious use is to be avoided. It may be even said that the grant, to a layman, of ecclesiastical property should not stand, because it was improvident and illegal; and even long enjoyment may be answered by the maxim, *nullum tempus;* much may be plausibly urged against the impropriators' title, of which not a word would be applicable to the title of the Church. The poor and multitudinous neighbours of the wealthy impropriator may, with as much reason, complain of the insulting spectacle, constantly in their view, of his luxurious enjoyment of the property so given to him, as the Roman Catholic clergy or laity now complain of the Protestant bishop's enjoyment, in their view, of his large income; not to mention that this latter complaint is, by the present agitation, and without a blush, extended to the humble incumbent of the poorest benefice in Ireland, as well as to the bishop.

When toleration has been conceded to the extent of allowing the Roman Catholic clergy to teach, "that true Christians are to be found only in the true Church: that the holy Catholic Church is this true Church; and that there is no other true Church: that all are obliged to be of this true Church, for that no one can be saved out of it:" does it not behove Protestants, and especially the Protestant Sovereign, who are insulted by such doctrine as this, to provide teachers for themselves and their children, to strengthen their minds, and to fortify their reason against the terrors of such a denunciation?

The propositions here stated are copied from "THE MOST REVEREND DR. JAMES BUTLER'S CATECHISM; REVISED, ENLARGED, APPROVED, AND RECOMMENDED BY THE FOUR R. C. ARCHBISHOPS OF IRELAND

AS A GENERAL CATECHISM FOR THE KINGDOM." Published in Dublin by James Duffy, 15, Wellington Quay, and 22, Paternoster Row, London, in the year 1866, and sold for three half-pence.

I should like to ask the two Chief Judges, and the seven puisne Judges, placed by our gracious Sovereign on the Irish Bench of Justice, did they learn this Catechism? Do they believe it to be true? If they do, what do they suppose to be the sentiments of their Protestant brother judges, who sit beside them, and who pray for that Sovereign, under the style and title of their most gracious and religious Sovereign, as at least every Protestant subject in the realm most sincerely and affectionately believes her to be? Do they believe that her confiding faith, her unaffected piety, her exemplary virtues, both public and private, her anxiety for the happiness here, and hereafter, of all her subjects, manifested by every act of her life, do yet not entitle her to the name of a true Christian, and are to be unavailing for her salvation, as this Catechism, *ex cathedra*, declares they must be? Is this Sovereign (who is, by positive contract with all her subjects, firmly bound not to be of this so called only true Church) to be prohibited from maintaining a Church and a clergy in Ireland to administer to her and her Protestant subjects, and to her Protestant viceroy, some rational and comforting antidote against the terrors of this doctrine, tolerated as it is; taught as it is; and preached as it is to millions of her subjects? The men who teach, and who preach this doctrine—the men who learn it, and hear it preached (in shameless abuse of a toleration unparalleled in the rest of Europe), complain that they are insulted by the support given to the Church and the clergy of those who are denounced and anathematized by it. Insulting, as it is to all Protestants, to propagate this doctrine amongst their neighbours, whom they are, by their own Christian faith, bound to love as they do themselves, the complaint thus made against the Church and the clergy of these Protestants, is still more insulting than the doctrine so propagated, for it must assume that they are devoid of understanding, and self-respect, when it is expected that they will listen patiently, not to say favourably, to such a complaint; and that they will abolish their own Church, and despoil their own clergy in deference to it.

When the Church revenue was levied in the shape of tithe, and was really a grievance, the discontent which it created amongst those so aggrieved was just; was violent and universal, and produced battle and bloodshed. It was wholly unlike the groundless, the palpably factitious discontent now exhibited by the Roman Catholic hierarchy; and, in deference to them, asserted also by some laymen, and expressed by a meagre resolution, underwritten by a long string of Roman Catholic peers and gentlemen, whose assertion that they feel aggrieved, no impartial rational man can see any adequate reason for.

When it is said that there are abuses in the Church, and particularly in the application and distribution of the temporalities, this raises a question entirely different from that of confiscation and abolition. The temporalities were granted for securing religious worship, and religious instruction, by a clergy not dependent on voluntary support, and according to the articles of the reformed faith, for the benefit of the laity who embraced that faith, and still hold it. To correct any misapplication, or abuse of the temporalities granted for this purpose, is entirely consistent with the grant, and in no way derogatory from the letter or the spirit of that grant. The commission for inquiring into, and reporting the condition of the Church, with a view of legislating for the correction of abuses, if any be found to exist, or of improving the arrangements by which the due application of the property may be enforced, and by which the effectual execution of the public trust may be secured, is not only consistent with, but conducive to the maintenance of the Church Establishment. There is, therefore, no logical force in the inference, suggested by way of *argumentum ad hominem*, that this commission is an admission, that the Irish Church cannot stand on its present foundation.

I have sincerely expressed in these pages the feelings and the views which I entertain on this subject, as an Irish Protestant. No one can truly say, that I ever felt, or ever expressed, an illiberal sentiment towards Roman Catholics, or towards the members of any other religious persuasion, or that I ever regarded persecution in any form, or in any degree, on account of religious convictions, with any other feeling than unqualified condemnation. If the other Protestants of Ireland view the assault upon their religious establishment in the same light, and with the same sentiments that I entertain, and have here expressed upon the subject, it is difficult to understand how the proposed measures can promote tranquillity in this country, or how they can be carried into effect without inflicting a bitter sense of injustice and insecurity, upon the minds of the large and important class of the people affected by them. The Roman Catholic hierarchy, by the terrors of the Catechism which they teach, have established a power of raising a revenue greatly exceeding that of the Protestant Church. The use of such means is forbidden, and made impracticable to the Protestant clergy; therefore to take away from them the provision made for them by the constitution and the law, is not to level and make equal, but to destroy the possibility of any approximation to equality with the rival hierarchy.

If this scheme of abolition be carried into execution, I cannot see what answer can be given to an Irish Protestant thus addressing the English Government, the English Sovereign, and the English Legislature:—

"Looking at the whole course of your conduct towards Ireland, and at all the proceedings adopted by you for the professed purpose of propagating the reformed religion in that country, I cannot believe that you sincerely intended to do what you so professed. For 140 years after your adoption, in England, of the reformed religion, you allowed the Irish people to remain in total ignorance of the principles of that religion, knowing that they did not understand the language of the clergy whom you sent to preach its doctrines in Ireland. During all that time, you left them under the instructions and influence of the clergy who spoke their own language, and who, by your permission and sufferance, taught the doctrines which you pretended to condemn; and who stigmatized the reformed religion as a damnable heresy, which it was certain perdition to embrace, or listen to. The clergymen whom you sent to live, and preach the reformed religion amongst them, although they could not speak intelligibly to the Irish people, could yet, by their course of life, exhibit the moral effects of the religion which they professed, and came to preach. They did exhibit such gross vices, and such dissolute habits, as to be a disgrace to their country, and a scandal to their profession.

"The maintenance which you designed for these unworthy clergymen you so arranged, as to be a crushing, and a galling tax upon those who could derive no benefit in return, while you suffered the Protestant portion of the people to evade the burthen by a proceeding which was no better than a conspiracy; thus exciting contempt for the reformed religion, detestation of the clergy, and hatred of the laity. In order to exhibit your pretended zeal for the conversion of this race, after you so allowed them for five generations to be confirmed in their convictions, you enacted pains and penalties against them, so absurdly cruel, that they could not be inflicted upon people guilty of no other crime than rejecting doctrines propounded to them in a language which they could not understand, and by teachers whom they hated and despised. Finding your penal laws ineffectual, you next, under pretence of teaching your language, and your religion to the infant children of these people, instituted nurseries, and chartered schools; and having got possession of a multitude of these children, you dealt with them so cruelly, and depraved them so shockingly, in these schools, as to make the children objects of pity and scorn, and the schools objects of raging detestation to the people. When this institution had been for fifty years exercising its withering effect upon the reformed religion, and furnishing to the Roman Catholic clergy a terrifying demonstration of God's anger against those who had deserted their creed, the abuses and atrocities practised in them were detected, and brought under your attention by

Howard; but his remonstrance produced no useful effect; and they were continued, unreformed, and unmitigated, for a further term of forty years, during which time the unworthy race of Protestant clergy appointed by you had gradually died out, or had been effectually banished, by the growing force of moral and religious sentiment in the Protestant laity, and were succeeded by earnest and pious ministers, the opposite, in all respects, of their unworthy predecessors. When, at the end of ninety years, the charter-school scandal was so exposed by the candid commissioners appointed by yourselves, that you could no longer maintain it, in the face of their report, you set up a new institution, the first effect of which was to ruin three-fourths of the independent schools of the country, to which children of all creeds were freely resorting, and in which they associated, and thereby mitigated, and were rapidly forgetting, their pre-existing antipathies. Those independent schools, by confining their attention to their proper business, and by refraining from all interference with religious convictions, or religious teaching, obtained the confidence of all sects, and provoked the jealousy or alarm of none. By your departure from this salutary principle, the schools which you substituted have become merely denominational; are a subject of strife, and angry sectarian controversy; and, with your permission, and by your acts, four thousand of them have fallen into the hands, and are subjected to the control of the clergy whose doctrines, for centuries, you pretended to condemn. Now that you, by the courses which you so pursued, have placed this hierarchy, which you formerly pretended to persecute, in a position of power and influence which, by that course of proceeding, you made it impossible for the Protestant clergy to attain; when the Protestant laity, notwithstanding all the difficulties which you have raised against them, have multiplied seven-fold, and notwithstanding your machinations, bear now a greater ratio than they formerly did to the Roman Catholics; when the Protestant clergy, for at least two generations, have been exemplary, and efficient teachers of a humane and liberal creed, breathing nothing but peace on earth, and good-will to all mankind; when the language in which they teach has become universal, and the language which they knew not has died away, and when some hope may be rationally entertained that the perfect toleration, which the Legislature granted, and a Protestant Government has established, would eventually produce universal tranquillity, you are now addressed by that hierarchy, which you pretended to condemn, but which, by your measures, you exalted, and called upon to abolish our Church; to confiscate its endowment; and to tell us that our clergy, like those of other sects, must, in future, depend upon voluntary support; knowing, as you must know, that a clergy, independent of voluntary support, is of the essence of the Church to which we belong."

If it were not incredible that a scheme of hypocritical treachery could be conceived, and persistently carried on for three hundred years, the Protestants of Ireland might be tempted to believe, that the English policy towards Ireland, in respect of religion, flowed from a resolution to prevent the Reformed faith from taking root in Ireland; and from a firm purpose to enable the Romish Hierarchy, as expressed by their bishops, to preserve and guard the deposit of the Roman Catholic faith in Ireland, until the storm raised by its abuses and intolerant cruelties had blown over, and from Ireland, as from a convenient base of polemical operations, to propagate and re-establish the Popish religion in England, by insidious agencies, and congenial ceremonies and practices, ingeniously devised for the purpose.

Although it is clearly impossible that any such design could have been formed, and treacherously acted on by a succession of rulers for three hundred years, yet the measures adopted were entirely, although, no doubt, accidentally, consonant with such a design; and the present position of affairs in the two Islands is exactly what it would be, if such a scheme had been craftily formed, and successfully carried into execution.

The pretext for taking this last step of abolishing the Church (which must have the effect of establishing, and giving a crushing ascendancy to, the Romish religion in Ireland, and of trampling upon the constitutional religion of the State), is the assumed tranquillizing effect of a pretended equality of religious rights. The constitution and laws, as they stand at present, concede equally to all subjects, the right to embrace any creed they please; the right to worship God in any form which conscience may dictate or approve; the right to preach to others, within the limits of decency, and even beyond those limits, the doctrines which they themselves embrace; the right to seek, and to obtain, wealth, titles, and office, without restriction on the ground of creed—with the exception of the throne, and the few offices which ought not to be filled by any who are not of the religion to which the Sovereign is bound. To such an extreme is this concession of religious liberty and equality carried, that the Romish hierarchy, as of right, are allowed to teach and to preach, and to publish and circulate, and by all the arts of persuasion, and threats of perdition, to propagate the doctrine of exclusive salvation; uncharitable, as it obviously is, towards the vast majority of the human race, and towards a large majority of British subjects, and their Sovereign. Holding this doctrine, and openly professing to teach, and effectually teaching and inculcating this doctrine; repudiating, also, the spiritual authority of the Sovereign; and nominees, as they are, of an alien power; it is not possible to conceive a *union* between them and the Sovereign, who is denounced by, but who is bound by the Constitution to repudiate, their intolerant doctrine. Being thus disqualified themselves from a State union with a Protestant throne, what right can they possibly have to say that they will not tolerate a union between the Sovereign who fills that throne and the Church of which that Sovereign is the head, and to which that Sovereign, by belief and conviction, belongs, and must belong? No property is set apart, and no State provision is made, for support of the Romish hierarchy, independently of their flocks; and they have publicly announced their resolution not to accept any such provision, if offered to them; thus absolutely prohibiting their own congregations from having an independent clergy, even should those congregations desire it. The Protestant congregations, upon very intelligible social principles, think it expedient, if not absolutely necessary, to make an independent provision for their own clergy, and they have done so, by a legal and absolute grant of property, adequate for that purpose. What imaginable right can the Romish hierarchy have, to say that they will not tolerate this provision for the Protestant Church? Had the property granted by the Crown, at the Reformation, to support the clergy of the reformed Church, not been so granted, no one can doubt that the same property would have been granted to lay members of that reformed Church, or to some other uses in which neither the Romish clergy nor laity would have any participation. Had it been so granted away from the reformed Church, it would now be enjoyed by Protestant owners, or their representatives or vendees, for private uses, as a large amount of the ecclesiastical property which fell to the Crown at the Reformation is now enjoyed, by virtue of grants made of it to private persons. A portion of the ecclesiastical property of the country was, however, granted for support of the reformed Church and clergy, in exoneration of the Protestant laity from the obligation of supporting their own clergy, and in conformity with that social principle which Protestants think a sound and rational precaution for the protection of liberty. To the present day, this property enures to the same uses for which it was so granted, and these are no other than uses beneficial to the Protestant laity of this country, and to which benefit every one of the 700,000 Protestants of Ireland has as clear and as indefeasible a right and title, as any of them, or any other British subject, has, or could have, to any property whatever.

By the theory of the Constitution, the Legislature has the power to confiscate this property, without any other than a moral obligation to assign a reason for so doing. This theoretical power extends over all other property, as clearly as it does over this. It extends not only over the property, but over the life, of every British subject; and it has been exercised, and, in savage times, brutally exercised, in taking away human life.

Had no property been granted by the Crown for support of an independent Protestant clergy; and had the Protestant laity (believing an independent clergy essential to freedom of conscience) by common contribution, at the Reformation, or at any subsequent time, purchased and conveyed to the Incumbents and their successors, adequate property for that purpose, the enjoyment of it now by the Protestant Church would palpably be the same grievance to the Romish Hierarchy, and laity, as they now complain of, and the Legislature would have the same power, and the same motive to remove that insulting grievance, as it now has to remove that which is alleged to exist. If the property which now supports the Protestant Church of Ireland be confiscated, by an act of legislative power—if the Protestant laity of Ireland, still believing that an independent clergy is an institution essential for the preservation of emancipated intellect, and civil liberty, should determine to purchase back this very property when brought to sale, or property equivalent with what is now to be confiscated, and grant, irrevocably, this newly purchased property to the several Protestant Incumbents, and their successors, in precisely the same amounts as they now enjoy, the Protestants would, by this proceeding, continue the same insulting spectacle of a richly endowed Church in the view of the so called poor clergy of the Irish people; and the right to complain of this, as a grievance, would be revived, and be just as good, or more properly speaking, just as bad a right, and not one jot worse than the present right to call for a legislative act of confiscation. The clergy of the State Church would not have to the property so purchased, and so conferred on them, any better title than they now have to the property vested in them (for no other or better title can be conferred, according to the British constitution). It would be a title to enure to them and their successors, not for ever, according to the terms of the grant, but only until the hour should come, and the men should come, when, and to whom, this Roman Catholic grievance should again offer a tempting opportunity of getting back to office, by a manœuvre supported by an eloquent denunciation of refractory Protestants, who had the audacity to counteract the tranquillizing policy of liberal leaders, by thus insisting upon having an independent Church and clergy, enjoying an endowment offensive, and insulting to Roman Catholic prelates and peers, whilst preaching a religion embraced only by a small minority of the people, and in opposition to the creed of the multitude. All the arguments which are now used for confiscating the present endowment of the Church would be equally applicable to such revived endowment. The Roman Catholic Hierarchy would be as intolerant of that revived endowment as they are of the present. They never can, and they never will endure a State Church, or an endowed ministry, in any form—such a Church cannot co-exist with their own, without being a restraint upon them. To remove this restraint is to surrender freedom of conscience, and to deny the means of public worship to those who would secure to themselves, and to others the enjoyment of this invaluable right. To say that the spectacle of a Protestant Church enjoying an endowment, and united with the Throne, is insulting to the Romish Hierarchy, is a flimsy pretence, and a perfectly transparent veil to cover their real design, and the true nature of their hostility to the Protestant Church and clergy. That Church and that independent clergy are an impediment, and an obstacle to the Romish clergy in the attainment of despotic power, to the full extent of their ambition, over the minds of their own congregations. This is the grievance which they feel, and bitterly feel, and nothing but abolition of the Protestant religion can ever remove this grievance. The claim of equality is absurd. They have more than equality already; and the excess which they have is that which prompts their attack on the Protestant Church, when invited to it by a party impatient for office, and having no legitimate grounds of opposition to the existing Government.

The Roman Catholic clergy depend upon the voluntary contributions of their flocks for the temporal goods of this life; and their flocks, by their teaching, depend upon them for the eternal blessings of the life to come. The clergy are satisfied with the results of these reciprocal dependencies, and declare that they will not accept a provision secured by the State. Protestants of the Church of England do not believe that any blessings in the life to come in any degree depend upon the will of their clergy. They expect from their clergy rational instruction in the articles of religion; and they depend on them for a sound, and it must also be an intelligible interpretation of Holy Writ, tested by individual perusal, and consideration of that writ itself, and by the free use and exercise of private judgment. The article of purgatory, the utility of prayers, or masses for the dead—the obligation of confessing sins to the clergy—the belief that the clergy can forgive these sins, are all rejected by Protestants. The belief in these articles is the chief source of the power which the Roman Catholic clergy have over the minds of their congregations. Protestants reject, and repudiate these articles, because they can find no warrant for them in the Scriptures, and they regard them as socially mischievous. The admission of these articles by Roman Catholics, the repudiation of them by Protestants, constitutes the essential difference between the two sects. The admission of them gives the clergy a power over their congregations, which renders an independent provision unnecessary. The rejection of such doctrines makes an independent provision absolutely essential to the existence of the Protestant clergy.

Those who embraced this reformed faith about three hundred years ago, being influenced by what they believed to be great abuses of clerical power over the human mind, which it was their intention and desire to correct, and, for the future, to prevent, determined to make a provision for the temporal wants of the clergy, independent of their flocks; and by this to remove all inducement to regain that influence which had been so cruelly abused during the dark ages, by their predecessors.

By the Reformation itself, property to a large amount became vested in the Crown, whose prerogative it was to determine the uses to which this property should in future be applied; and in the lawful exercise of that prerogative, the Crown out of this property granted the independent provision for maintenance of the clergy which was thought essential for their support. Once made, the Crown had no power to revoke this grant, and the property became absolutely vested in the incumbents, and their successors, as compensation for public services, which they became bound to perform for the benefit of the Protestant laity. The right therefore to this property is not the simple right of individual owners; it is a complex right, partly vested in the incumbent, and partly vested in his congregation. The clergyman's right to enjoy the property is no better, or clearer, than the right of every member of his congregation to have the religious duties of the parish efficiently performed by a competent, qualified incumbent; and the performance of these duties is a condition precedent to the right of the incumbent to enjoy the property. To confiscate this property, and sell it (which is the simple meaning of the more rhetorical phrase to capitalize it), and out of the price to pay to the incumbent the value of his life interest, ignoring the rights of the congregation, is plain and simple, and undisguised spoliation of their rights. To cover this spoliation by a pretext of reducing them to a level with other sects, who have no such rights, is palpable communism, and nothing else; and the same pretext will equally excuse the spoliation of any individual's property, in order to reduce him to a level with his poorer neighbour. If 700,000 energetic and intelligent Protestants have no protection against this abuse of the theoretical omnipotence of the three estates, it is hard to conceive how individuals can feel secure in the enjoyment of their rights and property.

I have demonstrated that the same power, by which the present endowment of the Church is confiscated, is equally potent to confiscate any new endowment, though provided by the Protestant laity, at their own expense. It follows that this legislative act of confiscation is a legislative declaration that no endowed Church will be tolerated in Ireland. That no clergy independent of their flocks will be tolerated. That no congregations will be tolerated, who shall not be brought together by the preaching and persuasion of clergy dependent on them for their bread, and able to overcome the strong motives by which the clergy of a different creed may be able to influence and make proselytes of them. The evils flowing from such contests darken the history of every country in which they have existed.

Young gentlemen now enter the universities, and, at great expense of time, of labour, and of money, qualify themselves for the ministry, and for the high and dignified duty of instructing a congregation claiming and possessing the right of exercising private judgment unfettered by dogmas repudiated by men of emancipated intellect. The expectation of being ordained to the ministry of such congregations, and of being promoted to one of the independent benefices, and of rising to one of the dignities of an endowed Church, calls forth a very different class of men from those evoked by the voluntary system. It remains to be considered whether any men of this stamp will spend years of life, and of laborious study, on the chance of being able to collect a congregation willing to pay for their services, but under no legal obligation to do so. This is to make a total change in the class and character of candidates for Holy Orders, and wholly to alter the relations between Protestants of the Church of England and their clergy—to abrogate the leading principles of the reformed religion, by destroying all means of preserving their purity from the corruptions necessarily incidental to the voluntary system.

By the peculiar circumstances in which the Roman Catholic Hierarchy have exercised their powers in Ireland, as before historically related, they have acquired advantages and powers over the minds of their congregations, which other clergy, and especially the Protestant clergy of the English reformed Church, can have no possible chance of attaining. The proposed reduction of them to what is called equality with the Romish Hierarchy is nothing short of destroying the equality which exists, and prostrating them, and their congregations to be trampled out of existence, and what the rising generation, and the immediate posterity of the present Protestant congregations will become, no living man can foresee, if this change shall be made. Those who opposed emancipation argued, that any power conferred on Roman Catholics must pass into the hands of their clergy, and would be, by the clergy, used for intolerant purposes. Liberal Protestants derided this argument, but to allay the fears of those who relied on it (many of them with with perfect sincerity) the oaths and pledges were devised, which were embodied in the Emancipation Act; and the chief object of these pledges was to protect the Protestant Church. The present attack upon this Church must recall the memories of those who were opposed to each other on that great question, and who still survive, to many a passionate assertion and denial of the danger of Catholic emancipation to the Protestant religion in these countries. If the Church of Ireland be now disendowed, and cease to exist as a State Church; then the Protestants who before, and up to the passing of the

Emancipation Act, had the whole legislative power in their own hands, will, by an abuse of the perfect toleration which they voluntarily extended to all other creeds, become themselves the only proscribed sect, to whom no toleration is to be given ; and their Church the only Church whose existence is pronounced to be illegal.

Those who in 1800 consented to an union of the Irish Crown with the English Crown—of the Irish Church (clergy and laity) with the English Church—of the Irish House of Lords with the English House of Lords—and of the Irish Commons with the English Commons, were all Protestants of the reformed Church of England. However corrupt the motives were of some of those who so consented, it is perfectly certain that many of them were impelled by honest and sincere conviction that the union was a beneficial, if not an essential measure for the prosperity of both the nations. It is equally certain, that, however they condemn the corruption of those who consented, not from conviction, but from selfish motives, the Protestants of the present day (and I include all denominations of Protestants) are unanimous in believing that the Union is absolutely necessary to the well-being of both countries, and that it should be indissoluble. That some of the higher classes of Roman Catholics agree in this opinion may be assumed; but the Roman Catholic Hierarchy have explicitly declared determined hostility to it. No one can doubt that the millions (of whose subservience to the dictation of their clergy every election is a proof) agree with them in hostility to the Union. The Fenian conspirators also agree with them ; but confess a design to go farther than the Romish Hierarchy profess a desire to go. This Fenian conspiracy has alarmed the public mind of England; and this fact is obvious to every one. The alarm in Ireland is trifling, and local, and nothing is apprehended from the Fenian conspiracy, beyond a repetition of stealthy acts of outrage upon undefended property or life. The Romish clergy, and their dependent associates in agitation, have taken advantage of the alarm created in England by the novel commission of atrocities by a few of the Fenian conspirators there; and, for sinister purposes, they exaggerate the discontent in Ireland extravagantly beyond the truth. By constantly harping on the grievances of former times, as if they still existed, they have struck the conscience of the English nation, and have excited resentment against the living for wrongs committed centuries ago upon generations which have long since passed away. Since 1829 many acts of great injustice to living Protestants have been done, in order to recompense living Roman Catholics for the penalties and disabilities imposed on those who are in the grave for more than a century, and with whom the living candidates for preferment have no other connexion than their communion with the Church of Rome. In the absence of all other grievances, the clergy especially attack the Union; and the Irish Church. The party who are out of office perceive that the public mind of England has been wrought into anxiety to do some act of justice towards Ireland, by which to stop the agitation, and by which to preserve the union, which nobody thinks of sacrificing to any amount of clamour. The Irish Church is a conspicuous object. Next to a repeal of the Union, the fall of this Church, impediment as it is in the way of the Romish Hierarchy towards clerical despotism, is the thing most desired by them. Irish discontent, both real and pretended, and even the treasonable conspiracy of the Fenians, are falsely attributed to the existence of this Establishment. The English public, by constant repetition of this unscrupulous assertion, have been misled into the belief, that the abolition of this institution will appease discontent, and tranquillize Ireland. That the Ministry now in office are not of this opinion, and therefore determined to uphold the Church, is a fact known to the Opposition, as also the fact that a majority of the House of Commons, some from one motive, and some from another, are ready to sacrifice the Irish Church, and to throw it as a sop to the malcontents, believing that it is a prey eagerly pursued by them all, whether professing loyalty to England, or declaring open war against it. Here is presented a tempting opportunity of defeating the Ministry on a resolution that the Irish Church ought to be cast to the dogs. The public were last year amused by a witty picture, founded on the story of the Swiss mother, who, with her children, driving in the forest, was pursued by howling wolves, and, to save herself, threw over her offspring, one by one, to delay the pack. All parties laughed at the humorous application of this dismal story to the abandonment of some favourite clauses in a reform bill, and the sacrifice provoked no censure or disapprobation from any. The heads of the Ministry were in no danger of being cloven, as that of the unfeeling mother was, by one of the indignant crowd to whom she related the cruel device by which she had saved her worthless life. Whether the Irish Church (with its 700,000 worshippers, intelligent, energetic, and attached as they are to that tolerant and rational institution, and having the sympathy, as they have, of an equal number of other

Protestants, who are not blind to the prospect, that they may be the next sop for the wolves) can be thus cast to its pursuers with a tranquillizing result, is an experiment yet to be tried, and tried at the risk of consequences to which men in the eager pursuit of office are very likely to be blind.

The English Government in 1800, acting with the sanction and authority of the English people, courted a union with Ireland, then represented by an exclusively Protestant Parliament. The means by which those who then represented the Irish people were induced to form this Union, whether justifiable or not, were the means selected and used by the English Government. It lies not, therefore, in the power of the English Government or people to say that the contract can be vitiated by the fraud which they themselves practised, if any such fraud existed. The long negotiations, the warm debates, and the great care at both sides which took place in settling the terms of this Union, all conclusively prove that the Union was a compact between two parties competent to make a binding contract. No solemnity necessary to its validity was omitted. The terms of it were stereotyped and placed upon the statute books of both nations, and remain there an indelible record, which to the end of time cannot be effaced. The Irish Church was then, as it is now, an endowed Church ministered by a clergy with a provision independent of their congregations. The Protestant people of Ireland then prized, as they now prize, this independence of their clergy, as the most valuable attribute of the Church. The English people then enjoyed, and they now enjoy, the benefits of a Church whose clergy are, in like manner, supported.

One article of the Union was that these two Churches, which were then separate and distinct, should thenceforth be united. No language could be stronger or more explicit than that used to express this article of the Union, then consented to by the representatives of the Irish people, viz., "That it be the fifth Article of the Union, that the Church of England and Ireland be united into one Protestant Episcopal Church, to be called the United Church of England and Ireland, and that the doctrine, worship, discipline, and government of the said United Church shall be, and shall remain in full force for ever, as the same are now by law established for the Church of England; and that the continuance and preservation of the said united Church, as the Established Church of England and Ireland, shall be deemed and taken to be an essential and fundamental part of the Union."

The Protestants of Ireland were one of the high contracting parties to this national compact. Their consent was absolutely necessary, and there could have been no such compact without their consent. They still exist as a perfectly distinct and definite body, enjoying the benefits of the united Church with which their own previously separate and distinct Church should be united, upon the terms that it should so remain united for ever, in order to preserve the doctrine, the worship, the discipline, and the government of both Churches under the name of the united Church; and as a security for the union of the Churches it is by the fifth article most solemnly declared that the Union of the kingdoms shall rest upon it as a foundation (for this is the meaning of its being a fundamental part of the Union), and that the union of the

Churches shall be, and for ever, essential to the union of the Kingdoms; that is, no union of the Churches, then no union of the Kingdoms. Upon these explicit terms, and upon these alone, the Protestants of Ireland consented that the Legislature of Ireland (the whole power of which then belonged to themselves) should be merged in the Legislature of the United Kingdom. The day after the compact was completed, and solemnly placed on record, all the powers, which now at the end of sixty eight years belong to the united Legislature, then and immediately belonged to it. The united Legislature has not now one shadow of right to violate any article of the Union which it had not the day after those articles were agreed to and recorded. It then had the same *power* also to violate those articles which it now has. Suppose in 1800, and immediately after the English King, Lords and Commons had induced the Irish Protestants, thus to merge their own Legislature, and to trust to the honour and good faith of the great English nation, that nation proceeded to do what it is now solicited to do, can it be doubted that everlasting infamy amongst the nations of the earth would be the price at which England would then have purchased the benefit or the advantage, or whatever else they may call it, of violating this fifth article of their compact with the Protestants of Ireland. The Protestants of Ireland had then, by the laws of the land, the whole power of the Irish nation; and that power was, by representation, placed in the two Houses of Parliament, which, by the compact of the Union, were dissolved. It is by asserting that the whole power of the Irish nation was so vested in the Protestant houses of the Irish Parliament, that England can sustain the legal validity of the Union. If England, the day after the Act of Union was made perfect, had, by an Act of the united Legislature, violated the fifth article, and enacted that the Church of Ireland should not only be no longer united to the Church of England, but that it should no longer exist as a State Church, that it should no longer possess an endowment, that the property which had been legally and for ever granted to its clergy for their support, independently of their congregations, should be confiscated and revested in the Crown for some other undefined uses—that the Protestant congregations, for whose religious wants and worship this property had been so granted to their clergy, must bestir themselves, and consider how their clergy were to be in future maintained, if they chose to have clergy at all; or if they chose to have religious worship at all; can it be in the least doubted that the two houses of the Irish Parliament would have been, by this shameless violation of a fundamental and an essential article of the Union compact, *ipso facto*, revived and restored to all their pre-existing rights and powers? can it be doubted that if they had the power they would also have the unquestionable right to appeal to that last resort for the redress of national wrongs.

If such would have been the consequences of violating this fundamental article of the Union compact the day after it was made, is there any warrant of reason or justice for now violating it, after being acquiesced in, and acted on, for sixty-eight years? The high contracting parties (as such parties call themselves) are still in full and distinct existence, and the Irish party has done no act to forfeit, or vary, its right to insist on the faithful observance of the fundamental and essential articles of the Union compact. That compact, so far from being invalidated, or in the least weakened, by time, is, in all sense and reason, to be considered as corroborated by time. The unquestioned enjoyment of the Church endowment, continued for sixty-eight years, in addition to more than two hundred years before, adds incalculable force to the stipulation in the Union compact, by which the title to this property was declared to be for ever inviolable.

The sophism by which the confiscation of the Church endowment, and the severance of the Irish Church from the Crown, are concluded to be within the legitimate powers of the United Parliament, may be thus fairly stated. No Act of one Parliament can bind future Parliaments, or take away from them the power of repeal. The Act of Union is an Act of Parliament, and, therefore, cannot take away from the present Parliament the right to repeal it. The fallacy of this syllogism is in the minor premiss. The Act of Union is not an Act of Parliament in the sense which would support the conclusion. It was not an Act of one Parliament; it was a national compact made between two Parliaments, of two distinct nations. It was a compact made upon valuable considerations, reciprocally passing from each nation to the other. If both these Parliaments were still in existence, they would have the power, by common consent of both, to rescind the compact which they had made, upon the principle that the same power which makes a compact may also unmake it; and this is the principle upon which one Parliament can repeal the Acts of a previous Parliament; because it has the same power, and the same authority, as the Parliament had which made the Act. The Union compact was not an Act of the United Parliament, which had no existence at the time that compact was made. The United Parliament derives its existence from the Union compact; and it has no legitimate power to alter any of the articles of that compact, except what the contracting Parliaments concurred in giving it, and expressed in the record by which the common will and intention of both was perpetuated, and the benefits of the contract for ever secured to the several parties to it. So far from conferring on the future United Parliament any power to rescind or alter any terms of their mutual agreement, they both concurred in the most explicit and solemn declaration that no such power should exist. The assumption of such a power, in violation of this express prohibition, is so clear and palpable an usurpation, that I find it as impossible to prove it as to prove any other self-evident proposition. I have suggested, by way of test, the question, whether it was competent to the newly created Parliament of the United Kingdom, on the first day of its existence, to violate all the essential and fundamental terms of the compact which had brought itself into existence, and by which it was solemnly bound to forbear from so violating one iota of those terms? If it could not lawfully do so on the first day, it lies on those who assert that it can lawfully do it now, to point out the time when, and the means by which, it acquired this lawful power.

The English people are annoyed and irritated by Irish agitation and discontent. They are alarmed by Fenian atrocities committed even in England, and by bold and constantly repeated assertions they have been persuaded that the severance and disendowment of the Irish Church will produce the peace and quiet which they are desirous to have. Are peace and quiet, more than any other benefits, to be purchased at the expense of national faith and honourable performance of contract? If it be right, and lawful, and honest for the English people to purchase peace and quiet by abolishing the religion, by confiscating the property, and by trampling upon the vested rights of 700,000 Irish Protestants, no one can see why the same reasoning may not make it right, and lawful, and honest to kill these Protestants, that England may be no longer troubled by the controversies between them and the Roman Catholic priests.

If perfect tranquillity were the certain effect of the wrong now threatened to the Protestants of Ireland, this result would not justify the infliction of that wrong. Those who expect tranquillity from a measure which inflicts not only injury but insult upon a numerous and sensitive body of the nation, must assume that the people so treated are devoid of self-respect and exempt from human passions and frailties.

But it is difficult to account for the existence of such a notion, as that tranquillity in Ireland can possibly be the effect of abolishing the Church. The Roman Catholic clergy have given express notice, that, although they approve of this measure, and will condescend to accept it, as part payment of what they claim for Ireland, yet that they have no intention of resting satisfied with it, and that nothing short of repealing the Union will tranquillize them, or those of the Irish people over whom they have the power of agitation. That abolition of the Church can have the least effect in breaking up the

Fenian conspiracy no one has been so absurd as to assert. The great body even of the Roman Catholic people are taking no part in the outcry against the Church. Although a number of Roman Catholic peers and gentlemen were stirred up to sign a meagre resolution that they considered the Church to be a grievance, they apologized for this step towards agitation by declaring that they were stimulated to it by an assertion which had been made by some parties that they did not consider it a grievance. The abolition of the Church will therefore give cause of exultation to the Romish clergy (and they are already exulting). It will be received with dignified approbation by the peers and gentlemen who signed the resolution. The general body of the Catholic people will look upon it as a triumph of their clergy, and it will wonderfully increase their readiness to join these leaders in further agitation for that undefined blessing called justice for Ireland. These are the several classes upon which it is desired to produce a tranquillizing effect. The Protestants of all denominations were already perfectly tranquil, and nothing more was required but to leave them quietly attentive to the business of life, of which, in Ireland, they are the principal conductors. The agitation carried on by the Romish clergy consists in speeches, pastoral addresses, and other compositions put into print, and sent to England and elsewhere, to make ignorant foreigners think that Ireland is in a state of insurrection, to which it is goaded by oppression and misgovernment. The sound and intelligent portion of the Irish people, by whose labour and devotion to their several duties the country has advanced, and is advancing in spite of all impediments, look with indignation on the effect upon foreigners and people in England of these scandalous publications, and with the utmost contempt upon their effect at home. They know that the power of these agitators for any other mischief than that of slandering the nation abroad is despicable. They never apprehended any serious injury from it at home, until this attack upon the Protestant Church has suddenly alarmed them. Now they are agitated, necessarily agitated; and this agitation is the first taste which England gets of the tranquillity which the disendowment of the Church is quite certain to produce. The agitation which the threat to destroy the Church has produced is not founded upon, or caused by ambition, or the desire of power, civil or ecclesiastical, or of any speculative benefits. It springs from alarm for their altars and their hearths. The feeling of resentment and indignation universally existing in the minds of all Protestants who have not sold their birthright to the Romish Hierarchy for a mess of potage, or a seat in Parliament, is, as yet, a suppressed and silent feeling, with few exceptions. Nine-tenths of the people affected with it have the most unconquerable dislike to participation in public demonstrations; any such demonstrations will, therefore, be an inadequate measure of the discontent which this attack upon their religion and worship will certainly produce. That this pretended remedy for agitation in Ireland will stimulate and increase that which before existed, I have no doubt: that it will drive the hitherto most peaceable and orderly part of the people to agitate for, and in defence of their invaded rights, is already manifest; but what may be the duration, the extent, and exact character of this reluctant agitation, or the ultimate consequences of rousing this peaceful, but determined and earnest body of men, I do not venture to conjecture, and I do not believe it possible to foresee.

If the Protestants of England, Scotland, and Ireland clearly see and correctly estimate the inevitable tendency, and certain effects of demolishing the Church of Ireland, in the way proposed, they have before them a plain course by which to prevent the calamitous consequences of a rash proceeding, hastily adopted for party purposes, and entered upon for the recovery of place, without regard to ulterior consequences. The first success of this manœuvre, which alarms the Protestants, affords them the most obvious means of defeating it. Had the design of destroying the Protestant Church been concealed, until a new House of Commons should be elected, 330 determined enemies of that Church would have gone to the pole undetected, and would have seats in the new Parliament, with ample time and opportunity of accomplishing their purpose. Now their designs are known, and if the same men shall be returned to the reformed House by the Protestant constituencies of England, the conclusion will be inevitable, that the Protestants of England are determined to crush the Protestants of Ireland, and to deprive them of the means of worship, according to conscience, and according to the reformed religion of England and Ireland. This will demonstrate that an entire revolution has taken place in the religious feelings and convictions of the English nation, and the event must be accepted, for good or for evil.

When James the Second, and the Popish clergy of that time, were plotting against the Protestants of England, they committed a mistake, and rashly exposed their designs, and thereby afforded to their intended victims an opportunity of defeating them. Had the seven bishops been convicted, and had the Protestants of England accepted and applauded the conviction, as they are now called on to applaud the ruin of the Irish Church, no one can doubt that the horrors of Mary's reign would have been renewed; and the reformed religion must have been stamped out by persecution, or preserved by civil war of a character much more sanguinary than that by which the Revolution was accomplished. The English people, however, perceived, and pursued the safe and sensible course—the bishops were acquitted; and the acquittal was hailed with such a storm of enthusiasm as to terrify the conspirators, and to scare their unhappy bigot into exile. It might be truly said of them, "*quos deus vult perdere prius dementat.*" Had the English people been so demented as to reject the right and adopt the wrong course at that crisis of their affairs, the same observation would have become applicable to *them*, and triumph would have been on the side of the bigots. But fortunately for the cause of civil liberty, the people were not demented; the bigots were; and an age of persecution was avoided. Whether the events shall prove that the assailants of the Church, in the present Parliament, are demented, in rashly pressing their crude, and, for every practical purpose, abortive resolutions, and thereby segregating, and conveniently for those who would preserve their rights and liberties, marking the enemies of those rights and liberties; or whether the electors of England and Ireland shall prove to be the demented parties, cannot be known until after the first elections under the Reform Act. That the present position of the country is analagous to its position in the reign of James II. is plain enough to any one who knows Ireland now, and who has even a moderate amount of historic information of that critical time when the seven bishops were acquitted, and English liberty established.

The Reform Bill for England having occupied the last Session of Parliament, there was a general anticipation that the present Session would be principally devoted to the discussion and redress of Irish grievances. The law of landlord and tenant, the system of national education, the want of a Roman Catholic University, and the existence of a Protestant State Church appeared to be the chief topics of complaint, and were made the subject of publications by which to create in the public mind a desire for extensive innovations. The English people derive their notions of the State of Ireland from such publications, from newspapers, and from reported speeches in Parliament. It is difficult entirely to disbelieve what appears in print, especially when the writer gives his name. English readers have no means of detecting misrepresentations of Ireland, many of which pass without contradiction ; and even when contradicted, it is often difficult to see at which side the truth lies. Special legislation for Ireland, when called for by one party, is generally opposed by another ; and English legislators are embarrassed by the contradictory statements which they constantly hear from men whose veracity ought to be unquestionable. The Irish members, who are about one-sixth of the House of Commons, are divided into three distinct parties, viz., a Conservative party, a Whig party, and a Roman Catholic party. The two first represent the Protestant interest, which is therefore divided, and becomes a neutral quantity in the contests between the two great English parties. The members of the third party are dependent for their seats on the Roman Catholic clergy, and must vote together upon every question in which these are interested. Thus united, they are a compacted body, and are not addicted to either Whigs or Tories. Evenly divided as these two great parties frequently are, the representatives of the Romish clergy can sometimes determine the fate of a ministry. No other constituency in the country at all resembles that which consists solely of the Romish hierarchy. All others are more or less divided; very much less attentive to the votes of their representatives; and more oblivious of occasional backslidings, even when they observe them. No one dependent for his seat on this clerical constituency can, in one iota, swerve from his allegiance to them, and have any hope of being again elected. This united and decisive body of members are therefore of vital importance to the party who can attach them, andt his can be done only by unqualified subservience to the views and designs of the Romish hierarchy. This hierarchy is an organization, distinguished from all others that ever existed in the world. The members of it are multitudinous in every part of the globe: they are by celebacy separated from the rest of the human race: the power of the order is the title of each individual to consideration and rank in society: to propagate that power is, therefore, the chief object of personal ambition. Centered as this power is in an absolute head, elected from the body, and chosen for his ability and devotion to the order, it can be wielded with almost irresistible force, and must ever be formidable to those who deny its authority. To subdue the minds of men, and secure absolute dominion over them, is the great aim and purpose of the organization, and the means used are always skilfully adapted to the end, and modified according to the season and the circumstances. This body has perpetual succession, and must last to the end of time ; the tenor of its existence is uniform, and its functions and character unchangeable : no future object is, therefore, so memote—no means of attaining it so dilatory, as to damp its ambition, or to slacken its exertion. When activity is dangerous, or useless, patience and affected indifference come easy to it, and "abide the time" is then its maxim.

England is the greatest nation which has freed itself from the thraldom of this formidable power ; its emancipation was effected by a complication and extraordinary combination of causes, some of which, for ages, operated as a traditional stimulus to vigilance in guarding the freedom that was obtained ; and the cry of "No Popery," now so frequently derided, was a traditional watchword which to many generations had an important significance. When this watchword means hostility, ill will, or harm of any kind to Roman Catholic fellow-subjects, it is a vicious and wicked suggestion : in this wicked sense it was the cry of a maniac in the last century, and produced some lamentable, although only momentary effects. When it expresses aversion and hostility to priest-power, it is a true and salutary exhortation to vigilance in the preservation of civil and religious liberty; and it is the traditional exponent of fears which were the effect of the savage persecutions inflicted upon the people by that power, when it had the arm of the secular Sovereign under its command.

The Church of England is the great bulwark and fortification of the national mind, and its reasoning guard and shield against the machinations of the Romish hierarchy. The prostration of that Church will be the sure and certain admission of the never dying, and ever vigilant enemy of human liberty. This was the opinion of the great men who laid the firm foundations of English freedom, at the Revolution, and then confirmed the union between the Crown and the Church. The cry of "the Church is in danger" is a traditional watchword derived from that opinion. Let that watchword not be derided, when the spurious Whigs of the present day call upon the English nation to tear down an outwork, and a most important and firmly attached member of that great guardian of religious liberty and freedom of conscience, which the true Whig party of the seventeenth century erected and transmitted, I hope, with sufficient stability to withstand the assaults of their unworthy successors of the nineteenth century. Alarm for the safety of the Church is sneered at by its enemies, and their sneers must import either that no danger exists, and that the alarm is, therefore, groundless and ridiculous; or that the Church is an institution obviously useless, and that anxiety for the preservation of it is, therefore, puerile and absurd. Before this attack upon the Irish Church, none of its derisive enemies ever dared to insinuate that his derision imported that the Church was an useless, or an unnecessary institution; and his sneers at the alarm of its supporters were, therefore, founded on an implied assertion that the notion of danger was a childish delusion. When the alarm is for the safety of the English Church, this will still be the explanation of the sneers. But anxiety for the safety of the Irish Church is now, and for the first time, derided on the express assertion that the Irish Church is not only useless but mischievous, and so obviously monstrous an establishment that all anxiety for its preservation is ridiculous, and efforts to uphold it absurd. If the friends of the English Church say it is in danger, when the Irish Church is assailed, their alarm is derided, still upon the assumption that it is obviously groundless; and the abolitionists indignantly protest, that, while they are demolishing the Irish institution, they feel the most profound reverence and respect for that of England. These are the protestations of men whose former professions of unalterable respect for the Irish Church are still ringing in our ears, while they are openly assailing its existence.

When these same men were seeking to be exonerated from the oaths by which they were required to deny all designs against the Church, their argument was that the oaths were useless, because no such designs existed—that the oaths were offensive and insulting, because they imputed the propensity to such designs, and threw doubt upon the honourable adherence of emancipated Catholics to the promises upon which emancipation was granted. They have scarcely been relieved from the pressure of these oaths, be that pressure more or less, when they do the very thing which those who took the oaths swore they would not do. The speeches which they now make against the existence of the Church are a striking demonstration of the hypocrisy of their reasoning for abolition of the protecting oaths.

If the people of England can be blind to the danger

which now besets them in this factitious crisis, the calculations of the Romish hierarchy may justly be considered as well founded; and a counter-reformation, whether for good or for evil, may be rationally apprehended as a coming event, which those who most dread it must be prepared to accept.

That certain constituencies in Ireland are now under the absolute control of the Roman Catholic clergy, and must return the nominees of these clergy, is a conspicuous fact which there has been no effort to conceal. That these nominees are now in alliance with the Whigs who are struggling for office is equally clear. In the House of Commons there are some who are equally hostile to both the English and Irish Churches, and also to the Romish Church. These are willing to attack the objects of their hostility in detail, and therefore have no objection to begin with the Irish Church, and consider the abolition of that as a step in advance towards an attack on the English Church. Although they detest Popery, they do not appreciate the State Church as a protection against it. In this political article they differ from the supporters of the Church. They enjoy the toleration extended to all Dissenters, but they give no credit or thanks for it to the Protestants, or to their Church. There are others in the House who are tired and disgusted with Irish agitation, and feel also some alarm at the audacity of the Fenians who have had the boldness to commit some atrocities in England. Although these are attached to the English Church, and would not join in any attack upon it, they have been by the calumnies on the Irish Institution brought to believe that it is a mission which has failed; that it is a Church without a congregation; that it is alien to, and an insult to the Irish people (thus assuming that the Roman Catholics are the Irish people); that in good conscience England owes some signal act of justice to Ireland, in compensation for past misrule; and that no act of justice will cost her less trouble, or less expense than the demolition of the Irish State Church. On the principle that what men wish they easily believe, they have been persuaded, that the sacrifice of the Church will tranquillize Ireland; and with these feelings and views they join in the assault, and swell the majority against the Irish Church. The least true knowledge of Ireland—a bare view of the congregations which assemble in the Irish churches—the least acquaintance with the real causes of agitation and discontent in Ireland would be sufficient to dispel the delusions of this section of the majority, and to convince them of the gross injustice, and the absolute futility of sacrificing this religious establishment as a means of appeasing an agitation, kept up by the Romish clergy, and which has much more important ulterior objects than the destruction of the Irish Church; an Institution which is assailed, solely because it is an obstacle to the attainment of those ulterior objects.

The Whig party make up the residue of the majority, being much the most numerous part of it. The movement is entirely theirs, and the result, whether victory or defeat, will be theirs also. If the final result shall be victory, the Conservative Ministry will no longer be an obstacle to the Whigs; and the Irish Church will cease to be an impediment in the way of the Romish hierarchy, when proceeding to enforce that imperative obligation, under which their Catechism declares that all men are, of belonging to what they pronounce to be the only true Church.

Into the councils of the Jesuit party which led to the prosecution of the seven bishops in 1688, the master mind of his generation, then Prime Minister, who was by his public profession a Protestant, was admitted; and he took the part of leader in the measures which brought on the Revolution. His singular abilities qualified him for that post, and he was too much of a statesman to allow his religion to stand in the way of his ambition. The adulation and art with which Sunderland ascribed to his royal master all the merit of reasoning him out of his Protestant heresy, and into the only true Church, by convincing him of the impossibility of finding salvation out of it, is described by Macaulay with a power peculiar to his pen. The persecution of the Church, in the prosecution of seven of its bishops, was preceded by the grotesque exhibition of the Prime Minister of England, taper in hand, and feet bare, knocking at the door of the Chapel Royal, humbly supplicating for admittance, as a poor and repentant sinner, who had gone astray, but who, by his royal master, had been brought back to the fold. The persecution of the Irish Church has not been *preceded* by such a touching ceremony, but whether the fall of that Church, and the ghostly reasoning of the Romish clergy, may not convert a Prime Minister of England, and reproduce the scene of 1688, is a thing which time alone can determine. Such a scene was not for the first time exhibited in the reign of James II.; a still more remarkable manifestation of the national conversion and repentance had been made in the reign of Mary, both in England and in Ireland, and a full description of it, as it took place in Ireland, is to found in the Act 3 & 4 Philip and Mary, Chapter 8, where the Irish Chancellor "devoutly, and right reverently, received the Pope's bull; and, upon his knees, to the good example of all others," in open Parliament, deliberately and distinctly, in a high voice, read the same to the Lords and Commons kneeling on their knees, "being repentant, for declaration of their repentance." In which posture the reading of the Latin Bull must have kept them for an hour, judging from the length of it.

The notion of tranquillizing the Romish clergy of Ireland, or of stopping their agitation by concessions, until the nation kneels to receive the Pope's Bull, and Condonation of the heresy which is now assailed, is perfectly visionary. Destruction of the State Church is but a step towards repeal of the Union ; and repeal of the Union will be but a step towards a counter-reformation; and for the means of conjecturing what that will lead to, I refer all readers to the history of Philip and Mary's reign, and to that of James II., and to guard against any prejudiced or Protestant account of those times, I will be satisfied with that of the Rev. Roman Catholic Doctor Lingard.

CHAPTER VI.

WHAT IS TO BE DONE WITH IRELAND?

The first step towards obtaining a reasonable answer to this question is to investigate the present condition of the country, and, if possible, discover the nature and the causes of the maladies, if any, which are injuriously operating upon it. Justice for Ireland is a constantly repeated demand, but no one has attempted to define what justice for Ireland means. The misgovernment of Ireland is unceasingly complained of, and past times are alone referred to in support of the complaint. There is no act which an honest man can do with a quiet conscience that every inhabitant of Ireland is not at perfect liberty to do, without any danger of being questioned by the Government or the Laws. If this be not liberty, I know not what liberty is. Every form of religious worship is allowed, and protected; and no man labours under disability of any kind on account of his religious convictions. If this be not perfect toleration, it is difficult to understand what toleration means. Trade and commerce of every kind is as free from restraint in Ireland as it is in England. There is no impediment to manufacturing industry, except what arises from the moral and social habits of the people themselves, and these habits are not within the sphere of Government influence. The acquisition of national wealth, which means the accumulation of property in the hands of individual owners, must ever depend upon individual thrift and ability; and beyond protection of person and property, and impartial administration of justice, the less Government interferes with the operations of industrious classes, by which alone wealth is produced, the better for the interests of the country.

It may be asked, if there be no misgovernment, why does Ireland not thrive? My answer is: I do not assert that there is no misgovernment; and I do assert, that, notwithstanding the misgovernment which does exist, whatever may be the extent of it, Ireland has thriven, and is thriving. It may then be asked, if Ireland has thriven, and is thriving, why is she not quiet? My answer is: because those who are quiet are despised and ignored, if not occasionally mulcted and punished; and those who are seditious and clamorous are feared, respected, and rewarded; and herein consists a principal part of the misgovernment which really exists.

I have shown what the agriculture of Ireland was in the last century, and what was the condition of the rural population. What is the agriculture at the present time, and what is the condition of the rural population, may be fairly inferred from the following facts:—There are over 650 estates of all magnitudes, from £100 to £20,000 a-year, under the control and management of the Court of Chancery. The total rents of these amount to £494,056 a-year, payable by 28,581 tenants. These estates are in all parts of Ireland, not only in all the provinces, but in all the counties, without exception. 452 of them are under my jurisdiction, the rents of which amount to £330,809, paid by 18,287 tenants. I have been now nearly eight years in office, during which time the rents have been paid, without murmuring or complaint worth noticing. The pressure of legal remedies for these rents has been very little used; the number of evictions absolutely trifling; and of between 400 and 500 receivers who collect these rents not one has ever been assailed, or interfered with, or threatened in the discharge of his duty, as far as I have been able to discover; and I am the person to whom the Receiver should apply for redress, if anything of the kind occurred. It is very well known that my ears are open to any just complaint from any tenant, and yet I am very seldom appealed to, considering the great number of tenants; and whenever a complaint is well founded, it is promptly and effectually redressed, at scarcely any expense of costs. I believe the other three Masters would make substantially a similar report to this in respect of the estates under their jurisdiction.

One of the estates in my list is now in the market for sale. The rental is over £13,000 a year. The tenants number 2500; they are all, or very nearly all, tenants from year to year, and I believe have been so for very many years, if not generations. The average rent payable by each is under six pounds a year. Four lots have been sold in the present year; and these are the first sales made. Two of them are subject to a head rent equal to about a fourth of the rents paid by the tenants. These lots were the first sold, because the owner set the smallest value upon them. Three of them fetched over thirty years' purchase of the yearly profit rents; the average rent payable by each tenant being about £5. The fourth lot is held by small cottiers at rents which average only £2; and this lot fetched twenty-three years' purchase. This estate has been under a receiver for three years, and I have never had one complaint from a tenant, nor one application for abatement of rent. I have not been able to discover the faintest trace of any harshness or oppression practised by the owner or his agent against one of the numerous tenants before the estate came under the Court. There are many other estates under me, paying rents from £500 to £20,000 a-year, in all the four provinces, and what I have stated of this estate may be said of every one of them. Clamour, agitation, or violence of any kind, I have never had to deal with amongst the tenantry of any one of these estates since I came into office, and it assuredly must be difficult to reconcile this fact with what we constantly hear about the landlord oppressions and tenant grievances of Ireland.

Many estates have come into Chancery during the eight years that I have held my office. In some cases, but not in many, the tenants owed considerable arrears, sometimes existing from the famine years; and which were irrecoverable: I have had to deal with these according to circumstances; and in some cases to abate the old rents, and remit arrears, and expunge them. Except in one case, and that of very recent occurrence, I have never failed to get the consent of all parties interested to let me, with the aid of the receiver, adjust the rents and arrears fairly and equitably, and bring them within the ability of the tenants to pay and live. I have never failed to make an adjustment satisfactory to allparties. The result of my experience is a firm conviction, that a special law of tenure for Ireland, diverging from the law of England, with which, since the reign of King John, it has been substantially identical, will be a special mischief, and be injurious to both landlord and tenants in this country, in many ways which will not be foreseen. There have been several Acts passed specially for Ireland, affecting the relations of landlord and tenant: and I do not remember any that did not produce more evil than good. The Act of 1826 against subletting was the result of English anger against Irish middlemen. It was soon found to be mischievous, and was repealed by an Act of 1832, of which, though less absurd than the Act of 1826, I know no good effects ; and it frequently operates unjustly, and begets inconvenience and difficulty in dealing with the devolutions of the tenant's interest, and in making it justly liable to his debts.

I have already noticed the signal cruelty of the Act for sale of incumbered estates, by which the hereditary property of ancient families was transferred to purchasers at less than half its value, and the just demands of creditors in numberless instances defeated ; sometimes to the ruin of widows and orphans, whose money and means of support had been lent on what was good security, if not damaged by that destructive enactment. English gentlemen are continually liable to be misled by exaggerated and often false statements of particular cases, which are most unjustly assumed to be mere examples of general oppression ; and a remedy is enacted, suggested by such special cases, and adopted without due regard to its more extensive and mischievous general effects.

As an instance of such legislation, I would refer to the Act 9 & 10 Vic., cap. 111, sections 10 and 12, requiring written particulars of rent for which a distress is made, and a written warrant when not made by the landlord or his known agent in person. The extent of litigation founded on mere formal crotchets, raised on these sections, and the number of cases in which justice was defeated, and fraud protected under these enactments, for many years, would be scarcely credible, while the cases in which they could possibly be useful can rarely happen at all.

Ireland since the Union is properly part of the United Kingdom. Although separate Legislatures had created some differences in the laws of the two countries before the Union, yet they were, as to laws of general operation (and especially the laws of land tenure), substantially the same. When a general Act was passed for England, it was soon followed by a similar Act for Ireland ; and so also after the Union, when a new Act was by a special clause confined to England, it was, in a short time, followed by a like enactment for Ireland. It is often difficult to discover why Ireland should have been excluded in the original legislation in many of these cases. If Ireland was merely the name of an English county, in place of being the name of a kingdom united to England, it would have all the benefits and all the protection which emanate from the care and caution which English gentlemen use in legislating for their own country, of which they have competent knowledge to guide them. The belief in England that Ireland requires exceptional legislation is one of the most prolific sources of mischief to it. This belief is founded upon constantly repeated complaints of undefined injustice, undefined oppression, undefined violation of national rights towards Ireland ; complaints which would have been just in the last century, or the centuries before it, but which have had no foundation whatever for the last forty years. These complaints come not from the people at all: they are fabricated, and uttered, and published by men who have some personal views to promote by exciting popular commotion, and discontent, which they produce without difficulty by ascribing the poverty resulting from ignorance and sloth to misgovernment and English oppression. English people have abundant proofs that the poverty exists, but they have no means of knowing the true causes of it. They cannot detect the falsehood of ascribing it to their own misrule; and by force of mere repetition, this imputation has at last struck the conscience of the English public. That Ireland was misgoverned in past times cannot be denied. Unacquainted as the English people are with the real causes of Irish poverty, they have been brought to believe that it is the effect of misrule; and they take blame to themselves for having permitted this cause to exist. The misrule and oppressions thus admitted are all ascribed to the English faction which formerly existed in Ireland, and abused the powers confided to them. This English faction were Protestants, and it is easy to assert that this Protestant faction still exists. There is no difficulty in thus persuading the English people and public to lay all the blame of the misrule which now touches their conscience upon the Irish Protestants of the present time. The remorse of the English people is thus turned into resentment against the Irish Protestants; and the national conscience of England must be relieved by doing some signal act of justice to the oppressed Irish. That the oppressed Irish were formerly the Roman Catholics of Ireland appears a self-evident proposition; and by the same process of reasoning which has brought the blame of the oppressions inflicted in past times upon the present generation of Protestants the title to redress is derived to the existing Roman Catholics, and the signal act of justice is therefore assumed to be due to them.

When it is considered that, of the oldest Irish Protestants now living, a large majority long, and at last successfully, exerted all their power and influence to emancipate the Roman Catholics—that of the Protestant opponents of that measure who still survive there are very few, if any, who have not long since changed their opinion, and approved of that act of justice—when it is considered. that, for at least forty years, no Protestants of Ireland, old or young, have been guilty of the smallest act of oppression to Roman Catholics—that no oppression, or disability, or other wrong, has been inflicted upon Roman Catholics by any party whatever for the last forty years —that of Government patronage, during that long time, much more than was justly due to them has been exercised in favour of Roman Catholics, in affected consideration of ancient injustice to past generations—nothing can be more grossly or more palpably unjust and oppressive, in the face of these facts, than to spoliate the property and rights of Irish living Protestants, and to call this spoliation and oppression an act of justice towards Ireland. To suggest this act of injustice, in the shape of special legislation for Ireland, is not answering the question, "What is to be done with Ireland?" upon a candid, a wise, an honest, or a prudent consideration of the present condition and the existing circumstances of the country.

If the English colonists who settled in Ireland, and

who at the Reformation became the Protestants of Ireland, were now living, and on their trial for the oppressions which they are alleged to have inflicted on the Irish race, the English nation is estopped from being their accusers. They came here as the soldiers and servants of the English Crown and English nation, and in this country acted upon the authority of English rulers, and in execution of commands which it was their duty to obey. They were sent to subdue Ireland to gratify English ambition—a mission not to be executed by gentle means. The final result has been the annexation of Ireland to the English nation and Throne; and if responsibility for the violence and oppressions by which this final result was accomplished attaches anywhere, it must attach upon the English nation itself, and not upon the Protestant part of the Irish people. But to talk of responsibility now for the violence of past times, and of redressing the injuries inflicted in past centuries; to make a show of rendering compensating justice now to the supposed injured race, at the expense of the present generation of those assumed to be the dominant party is the highest degree, not only of injustice, but of folly and absurdity; and any suggestion of it by those in power cannot be made without the danger of throwing society back into confusion and sanguinary strife.

Ireland being now a part of the United Kingdom, and fully entitled to the benefit of the English Constitution and English laws, nothing can be more obvious than that the proper mode of dealing with it is to treat it as part of the English nation. To enact laws for it which the English people repudiate for themselves is to deny to it the benefits of the union with England. The allegation that exceptional legislation is required, by special circumstances which are stated to exist in Ireland, is not supported by any credible evidence whatever, and is contradicted by the policy and the practice of three centuries.

By an Act of the Irish Parliament (10 Hen. VII., c. 22) all Statutes previously enacted in England were adopted, and extended to Ireland, and the differences which now exist in the laws of the two countries are the effect of subsequent legislation. These differences have been long regarded as an evil, which it is desirable to remedy. In 1862 a Commission was issued to sixteen Commissioners selected from the Bench and the Bar in both countries for the purpose of discovering the differences in the procedure and practice which then existed; in order that uniformity might be restored, as far as practicable.

In 1850 an Act had been passed for Ireland by which the procedure and practice of the Irish Court of Chancery had been specially regulated. For the old dilatory and expensive suit by bill, an expeditious and summary proceeding by petition, and an immediate reference of the whole suit to one of the Masters, was substituted, at the option of the party complaining. This proceeding by petition was almost immediately adopted by all suitors, and was so obviously beneficial that the suit by bill very soon became nearly, if not entirely, obsolete. The summary petitions were set down for a merely formal hearing by the Lord Chancellor, and without discussion were by rotation referred in nearly equal numbers to the four Masters; the inutility of this merely formal hearing was soon self-evident; and a short and simple amendment of the Act, dispensing with it, was called for, and audibly demanded by the public voice. The cost of this useless hearing was a large percentage on the reduced costs of the cheap and expeditious Chancery suit granted to the suitors by this truly remedial Act. The Master heard the whole case, and made a final decree, in all respects as effectual as one made by the Chancellor in a plenary suit, on bill and answer, and a mass of testimony taken in the most expensive and dilatory fashion, at the expense of victimized suitors for justice. I made myself between ninety and a hundred of these decrees every year, in some cases for large demands, amounting from £5000 to over £40,000, at an expense not exceeding, on both sides, in most cases twenty or thirty pounds, and within two or three months; and, if the petitioner was active, in a still shorter time, after the suit was commenced. From these decrees there was a right of appeal, which the appellant might bring to a hearing in a few days, and generally did so within a very short time. The appeals were not one per cent. of the number of decrees, and I do not recollect more than two or three cases in which the decree was not affirmed. The costs of the appeal were very trifling, compared with the old procedure. According to my experience no shorter, cheaper, or more effectual remedy could be imagined than that provided by this Act; and I never heard of any complaints coming from either petitioners or respondents. The Bar, and more especially the senior Bar, suffered by it; for I very seldom had before me more than one counsel at a side. In cases where no valid defence existed, the respondent seldom had counsel at all. Solicitors also suffered by it, for the briefs were but a few pages, and the counsel being few, the briefs were also few.

The ruinous expenses of the old procedure by bill and reference to the Masters, not for decision, but for a dilatory report, had become a topic of general complaint and scandal to the administration of justice in England. By an Act, passed in 1852, the office of Master was abolished in England, on the assumption that much of the delay and expense had arisen from the dilatory practice on references to them. I am not sufficiently acquainted with the operation and effect of the reconstruction, under this Act, of the Court of Chancery in England. But, from every thing I have heard, I infer that no such saving of time and money to suitors was effected by it as the Act of 1850 had accomplished in Ireland. The old form of suit by bill was still retained, and to this form much of the old expense is necessarily incidental. Centuries elapsed before the abuses of the old procedure were so exposed as to compel a change; how long it will take to discover whether the change was an improvement no one can yet pronounce.

An Act to regulate the procedure in the Courts of Common Law in England was passed in 1852, and without any discoverable reason for so doing it excluded Ireland from its operation. A special Act for Ireland was passed in 1853, widely differing in its provisions from the English Act. By this separate legislation, both for courts of equity and courts of law, the procedure and practice of law and equity in the two countries rapidly diverged, and created sensible inconvenience. The new procedure in the Irish Chancery was an unquestionable benefit to suitors, but seriously reduced the incomes of the inner Bar. The Irish Common Law Procedure Act, on the contrary, worked injuriously to suitors, and created difficulties in bringing cases to trial on the merits never before experienced.

When these several Acts were for ten years in operation, the Commissioners were appointed in 1862.

On the 27th of July, 1863, they made their report, and unanimously commented upon the common law procedure in both countries, as it existed under the new Acts, in the following words :—"We have carefully considered the working of the system of pleading and practice introduced into Ireland by the Irish Common Law Procedure Act of 1853, and find that it has not been satisfactory, nor has it been attended with such advantage as would justify a continuance of a diversity of practice in the two countries. And we have come to an unanimous resolution, that the system of practice and procedure of the courts of common law in England and Ireland should be, as far as practicable, assimilated. In adopting that resolution, we feel that we are only, in effect, restoring that substantial uniformity which existed in the course and practice of the superior courts of common law in both countries from the reign of King John to that of King William IV."

In respect of the divergence which had been created in the practice and procedure in the courts of equity in the two countries, the Commissioners did not report that the working of the Irish Chancery Act had not been satisfactory. They say:—"We have come to a unanimous resolution in favour of this assimilation" (i. e. which had been previously recommended by other Commissioners), and they add: "We think it is of paramount importance to restore and preserve, as far as possible, a uniformity of system in the equity jurisprudence of the two countries."

Some very strong evidence had been given to them of the injurious operation of the Irish Common Law Procedure Act, and they, accordingly, reported that its working was not satisfactory. Without any such condemnation of the Chancery Act, they merely resolved in favour of assimilation of practice and procedure.

When the Whig Government was in office, and the Conservative party in opposition, the Irish law officers brought in a bill to remodel the Irish Court of Chancery. By this Bill many existing offices were to be abolished, and the officers superannuated—three of the Masters on full salaries, and subordinate officers upon reduced pensions, of which they, with much apparent justice, complained. Many new offices were created, at great cost to the country; but with a liberal donation of patronage to the Government. When the Bill was thus introduced by the Whig party, in 1864, it was assailed by the leading professional orators then in opposition, and was pronounced by an independent member, who was not a lawyer, and who had no personal interest to restrain the impulses of an honourable mind, to be "the perpetration of a Government job." Leave was asked by a leading conservative lawyer to bring in a rival Bill, by which to supersede that which had been so designated a Government job.

The rival Bill was recommended by an assurance that it did not create any new place. Leave to bring it in was granted on the 1st of February, 1865. The Government Bill was vigorously opposed by all the Conservative Irish lawyers, and it was effectually baffled, and postponed from session to session, until 8th June, 1866, when the promoter of the rival Bill stated to the House that an arrangement was likely to take place; that the consideration of the rival Bill should be postponed for the present; that he intended to assist in passing the Government Bill, and in making it as useful as possible. Before the Bill, even with this assistance, could become law, the change of Ministry became inevitable on the 19th, and took place on the 26th of June. The promoters of the Whig Bill went into opposition, with their tongues tied from abusing their own Bill, when taken up by its former opponents. The law officers of the Whig Government had introduced also a Bill for the purpose of restoring the desired uniformity in the Common Law Procedure, and of repealing the Act which had not worked satisfactorily. By this Bill no new places were to be created, and the reform to be effected by it would not bestow patronage on the Government, or cost the country anything. The effort to promote this Bill was languid and short. The same causes which had delayed the Chancery Bill also delayed this Bill, and no one has since thought it worthy of any notice. The Act of 1853, the working of which was by the Commissioners unanimously reported to be unsatisfactory, still remains in full and mischievous operation. The Chancery Reform Bill had a different fate. It was promptly taken up by the Conservative successors of the former promoters, and, as these former promoters were estopped from abusing their own offspring, it speedily became law, and suitors in Chancery are now under instruction in the school of experience, which is commonly found to be a dear school.

The old procedure in equity, both in England and Ireland, had grown enormously expensive, both of time and money, to the ruin of suitors for justice. To remedy this, the two distinct Acts before mentioned were passed for England and Ireland, creating considerable differences in the mode of administering equity in the two countries. The principles of equity jurisprudence were not at all affected by the changes in procedure, and continued the same as before. The operation of the Act of 1850 for Ireland was to shorten the duration of suits, and to diminish the costs beyond all expectation. A few easy and obvious amendments, which became apparent in the working of the new system, would have made it as perfect as any human device for the administration of justice can be. I have no doubt that the suitors will soon find reason to lament, that the Commissioners did not recommend assimilation by adopting the principle of the Irish Act, and making the English procedure in equity analogous to the Irish, in place of adopting the contrary course. The new system will revive to a very large extent the expenses and the delay formerly so loudly complained of in Chancery suits. It will, however, restore their briefs to the senior Bar, and bring back to solicitors and their clerks the labour of preparing them.

The conscience of England has been recently struck with remorse for ancient wrongs inflicted on Ireland. The infliction of those wrongs is imputed to a dominant party, and this aggressive party of former times is identified with the Irish Protestants of the present day. The Roman Catholics of former times were the sufferers, and those are identified with the existing generation of Roman Catholics. Both generations, the oppressors and the oppressed, have passed away. No greater blessing could be bestowed on their posterity than oblivion of wrongs and sufferings which it is now impossible to redress. The wrongs and the sufferings of former times are no longer perpetrated by one party or endured by the other. Nothing now takes place in the least resembling them. The traditional memory of them is, however, kept fresh and galling, by the persevering imputation of English misrule, made in general terms, and never defined beyond a vague assertion, that it exists in the law of landlord and tenant, in the system of National Education, in a State Church, and in a Protestant University. If not in these, it is *in nubibus*—no matter in what, for the agitator's purpose. While the public mind is worried to very weariness by this general complaint of misrule, the misgovernment which really exists passes without notice or censure. The ignorant masses, whose poverty stimulates their attention to the unscrupulous sophistry addressed to them by pretending patriots, are easily excited to commotion when some sinister purpose is to be answered by an exhibition of Irish discontent, or when some party tool is seeking a seat in Parliament.

In a free country individual rights must be respected, and parties must be heard in assertion and defence of them. Complicated laws and intricate questions are an inevitable consequence of the discussions which must be permitted on all disputed questions relating to person or property. It is of the highest importance to the community that these questions, when brought before legal tribunals, shall be decided according to justice and according to established law. Every unjust and illegal decision is a demoralizing lesson, contradictory of the social maxim that "honesty is the best policy." When the laws have grown to gigantic dimensions—when, by inevitable complications, the administration of justice according to them has become a work of great difficulty, demanding an amount of ability and learning which can be possessed only by those who have devoted their lives to laborious study and reflection, the interests of society are deeply concerned in the selection of the men to whom this arduous duty is assigned.

The discussion of the questions in controversy between litigant parties demands knowledge and ability nothing inferior to that required for the right decision of them, which must ever, in a high degree, depend upon the learning and talents of pleaders and advocates. To compel the parties to conduct their own cases would be, in numberless instances, to secure a triumph to fraud and injustice, cleverly advocated, over the just rights of the weak and simple. No other means of avoiding this intolerable mischief have yet been discovered than to permit the parties to be represented by professional advocates, whose abilities are equalized by study, by training, and by practice. Next to the importance of learning, ability, and integrity, on the bench of justice, is the importance of learning, ability, and a high tone of moral sentiment in those who are permitted to exercise highly cultivated skill and talents in advocating the rights of litigant parties, and in swaying the judgments of those whose duty it is to decide according to law and justice. From this necessarily tolerated profession the judges must ever be selected; and this is but one of the many social reasons for raising and keeping up the standard of forensic dignity and morality.

In the wavering balance before alluded to, by which possession of power is determined between the two great English parties, every vote has an appreciable influence, and every flippant speaker is an useful ally. To determine the choice of a borough, or even of a county constituency, demands other arts than learning, veracity, and high moral sentiment and worth. To confine the selection of men for the judicial office to that minority of the legal profession who have been successful at contested elections is to divert and misapply the most efficient means of raising that important body called the Bar to the standard of moral and professional excellence by which the best interests of society demand that it shall be measured and estimated. So to exercise the power entrusted to the Sovereign for protection of the people may well deserve the name of misrule; and no argument can be necessary to prove its baleful effects.

It must not be supposed that I intend, in the least degree, to disparage any man, or class of men in existence. I do not mean to express any commentary upon men; I speak only of a principle adopted for party purposes, by the application of which the government of Ireland is affected, and which cannot be disregarded in candidly answering the question—"What is to be done with Ireland?" I am only accounting for the difficulties in governing Ireland derisively suggested by the parties who have asked this question, and who labour to trace those difficulties to laws and institutions which have had nothing to do with the production of them, but which, for party purposes, it is convenient to assail. I am reasoning against the demolition of ancient and useful Institutions, and against exceptional legislation for Ireland, by which the difficulties will be increased and multiplied, and every existing evil aggravated. I am commenting upon a vicious system. I am not throwing blame upon men evoked and brought into notice by that system, many of whom may perhaps be as ready to condemn it as I am, if they had not been driven or induced to take advantage of it. To shut up every road to the Bench, except that which passes through the House of Commons, is much more injurious to Ireland than the same principle of selection can be to England. When an Irish barrister gets into Parliament, he must give up the greater part of his practice, when he has practice to give up; for he cannot serve his party in London and his clients in Ireland. An English lawyer is not in the same dilemma, and may retain his practice, keep up his legal knowledge, and acquire professional experience sufficient to qualify him for the judicial office, while he devotes a portion of his evenings to parliamentary duties. The effect of bestowing the judicial office on men who never had, or on men who have lost their practice, is to deprive laborious aspirants of the accession of business descending on them when a lawyer gives up a large professional income for a seat on the Bench. It keeps old men at labour disproportioned to failing strength, and continues them an obstacle in the way of rising talent, while it deprives the country of their services in an office that cannot be otherwise worthily filled. It would be tedious, and it would be invidious, to trace all the social evils, great and small, which flow from this system of misrule. It has its share in creating agitation by promoting agitators, but this is the least important of its bad effects.

The evil has been much increased by modern facility in travelling, which makes a seat in Parliament tenable to a class of men who were formerly entirely excluded.

Occasions arise, but they are rare, in which the party in power may think it expedient to promote a man recommended only by his position in the profession; but such exceptions are no more than sufficient to prove the rule of which the country has just reason to complain, and the vicious application of which produces one of the real grievances which escape notice in the clamour raised by priests and patriots and party leaders against laws and institutions, upon the stability of which the peace and prosperity of the country essentially depend.

The law which regulates the relations of landlord and tenant has been substantially the same in England and in Ireland since the reign of King John. The condition of the tenantry is not the effect of this law, but of habits which legislators have no power to alter; which time, advancing civilization, and imported knowledge are slowly, but quite certainly reforming. Emigration is not the effect of this law, and no change in the law will stop or lessen it. The uncertainty and feeling of insecurity created by threatened changes, undefined and vague as they are, operate to deter landlords from making contracts of permanent duration, and fill the tenants with alarm, which increases their disposition to emigrate. It is fifty years since the Government adopted the opinion that emigration was the best solution of the Irish difficulty, and encouraged it by all the means it could apply. This policy was aided by steam navigation, and the increasing facilities of transit; and, like other remedies, this produced an unforeseen disorder worse than that which it was expected to cure. Repulsion from home was at first counteracted by love of kindred and the pain of separation; desire to rejoin the emigrants in their new settlements is now an overpowering attraction to the new world.

The attention which English legislators have been recently giving to the suggestions of Irish agitators and their associates in England is doing incalculable mischief, by destroying confidence in established laws and vested rights; and by exciting fears and apprehensions in the minds of all classes whose present position can be altered for the worse.

The tenantry, for whose assumed grievances the sympathy of England is claimed, have no confidence in the changes which are proposed, and vaguely promised. They experience, and they feel the effects of the caution which the fear of those changes has already produced in their landlords.

When a man who has acquired some fame, and who knows less of Ireland than he does of Peru, challenges the public attention with the question, "What is to be done with Ireland?" and dogmatically answers the question by asserting that "the rule of Ireland now rightfully belongs to those who, by means consistent with justice, will make the cultivators of the soil of Ireland the owners of it; and that the English nation has got to decide whether it will be that just ruler or not," every present owner of the soil must be startled with the authoritative enunciation of this Communistic dogma, while every cultivator who has sufficient intelligence to read must feel and understand the absurdity of expecting any good from it. That it forebodes legislative tampering with existing laws and vested rights is too evident and too certain, and past experience of such tampering is sufficient to make every man tremble whose property and rights are subject to it.

Hitherto we have been accustomed to believe that the rule of Ireland rightfully and lawfully belongs to the Queen, Lords, and Commons of the United Kingdom; and we had no apprehension that the English nation had before it a contest in which to decide whether these three estates shall be the ruler, or some unknown body of men who will undertake the task of making Irish peasants the owners of the soil which they cultivate, by some means which those unknown rulers shall, in their discretion, consider to be consistent with justice. Absurd as this is, yet coming from a pen, which, when writing on other subjects, has attracted some notice, it indicates, that we are drifting towards something dangerous to property, to liberty, and to peace. When we see the publisher of this Communistic doctrine leagued with the party who are boldly, and if not factiously, at least by efforts hardly ever used before, aspiring to the government of England, and with a heterogeneous majority trampling on the present ministry, not for any acts of misgovernment or misconduct, but for refusing to attack, and for professing a resolution to defend the ancient and established laws and religious institutions of the country, it is natural to feel some alarm for the safety of property and rights—it is impossible but to fear that, in defence of property and of rights, of religion, and of liberty, a sanguinary contest is before us with ruthless and licentious invaders, as yet unknown and unascertained, but now invited to the assault by aspirants to offices hitherto reserved for the defenders of law, of order, of property, and of religion.

Certain constituencies in Ireland are notoriously in the power, and under the absolute sway of the Roman Catholic clergy. These are principally county constituencies, the right of voting in which is founded on tenure of land. It is easy to persuade the tenants, that the law is unjust which enables the landlords to determine the right of the tenants, in order to recover either the land or the rent. In other cases, the right to newly value the land and raise the rents, or resume possession. Nothing can be easier for a patriot, or a priest than to persuade tenants that this is a bad, and an unjust law, and that it should be repealed and altered. If the landlord determines the tenancy in exact conformity with the terms of the contract; and if each party, at such termination of the tenancy, has had, and has got all that his bargain entitled him to get, and no more, it is impossible to say, with any colour of truth or justice, that any hardship or wrong is inflicted in such a case on the tenant. In order to take the tenant's case out of this simple position, which is, in nearly every instance, its true position, an additional allegation is introduced—viz., that during the terminable right of holding, the tenant has made improvements, either in confidence that he would not be disturbed, or forgetting that the power to evict him was in the hands of the landlord. This is a mere invention, fabricated for the purpose of giving colour for legislative interference. For one case in which the tenant makes improvements on a terminable or precarious tenure, 500 occur in which he exhausts and deteriorates the land, and leaves it reduced to half its original value. The class of tenants who have ability to improve, have also intelligence and prudence to be secure before they make the expenditure. But for the purpose of persuading the tenants to vote for the man of the people, who promises to repeal the bad law, and to take the power of eviction out of the landlord's hands, it is not necessary to do more than to abuse the law and revile the landlords. When the constituency is Roman Catholic, the word of the priest in support of the candidate, and in condemnation of the law, is decisive, and wholly unquestioned.

In addition to, and entirely independent of this temporal motive, the clergy, by teaching the Catechism from which I have before quoted, have acquired an irresistible power over the minds of those who believe it. There may be a few educated Catholics who do not believe some of the dogmas of this Catechism, but that all those who follow their priest to the poll believe it is as certain as that they live. One of these dogmas is the absolute necessity for confessing sins, and another is that th priest has power to *forgive* them. To exclude all doubt as to the sense of this word "*forgive*," it is printed in Italics, in the Catechism from which I quote.

It is therefore quite certain, that the men who are returned to Parliament by these constituencies are the representatives of the Roman Catholic priests, and of no other constituents whatever. The voters are mere puppets, and nothing else. As before observed, the men so returned must be unanimous and energetic on every question espoused by those on whom they depend for their seats.

When the rest of the House is almost equally divided, an alliance between one of the divisions and this compact body becomes not only formidable, but decisive. Destruction of the Irish Church is the great object of the Romish clergy; destruction of the landlords' rights is the object of the tenant voters. The holy alliance first takes up the Church question. This is the policy of the Whig aspirants to office, presenting as it does a prospect of success, because upon this the Ministry must oppose them. If this resistance of the Ministry can be overborne by a majority however heterogeneous, the Ministry are out, and the Whigs are in. The abolition of the Irish Church presents therefore a question in which the Whig party has as strong an interest as the priests, to whom the true Whigs of the seventeenth century were the determined enemies, and against whose machinations the bulwarks were erected which the mercenary place-hunters are now assailing. If the opposition, by defeating the Ministry, can get in upon this question, then the land question will have its turn, and will be dealt with from the commanding position of the Treasury Benches. If the Irish Church can be abolished, and its endowment confiscated, in contempt of 700,000 intelligent and energetic Protestants, by a Whig opposition, it is hard to understand how Irish landlords can be protected against the assaults of a Whig Ministry.

What is to be done with Ireland? The question thus asked by one of the holy alliance is answered by the clerical portion of it, and the answer is:—"Make it our battle field, and we must get the victory." The Church is first to be demolished; then will come the landlords, whose property was so mercifully dealt with in 1849, and the following years. The National Schools come next, of which 4000 are already in the hands of the Romish clergy—they will have but little difficulty in getting hold of the remaining 2600. These Schools will furnish students to the Romish University, which will soon rear its head; and if the rising generation, high and low, do not learn the Catechism of Doctor Butler, revised and edited by the four Romish Archbishops, it will not be the fault of the holy alliance.

Special legislation for Ireland, under these circumstances, is a formidable spectre, and the union with England begins to assume an entirely new complexion. The assault upon the Church property of the Protestant people is assuredly ominous to that property upon which the tenantry, who are the tools of the Romish clergy, have been taught to set their minds. No one can be surprised that this English party strife upon the Irish battle field has created alarm in the minds of all who see and understand the danger which it threatens to everyone who has anything to lose which he cannot remove from this battle field to some place of safety. Land cannot be removed, and when patriot representatives of priests are leagued with a heterogeneous majority, cemented by one common purpose of overthrowing a Ministry, and getting into power, are pledged to legislate for fixity of tenure, for tenant right, for power to the tenant to improve his landlord out of his estate, landlords must take alarm; they must be deterred from parting with the possession of their land, except upon terms which secure to them the power of resuming it on short notice, the moment an empirical Bill appears likely to become law. While this is the effect upon landlords, no confident expectation of good is excited in the tenants. The most intelligent of these distrust the vapouring promises of agitators, and when they find the landlord determined to take, and hold a position in which he can protect his property from the operation of any spoliating enactment, the tenants who have eyes to see, and who have had sufficient thrift to preserve the means of emigrating, or whose friends in America will remit these means, adopt the provident course of flying from a country in which their footing has been taken from under them by an agitation hitherto wholly barren of anything resembling wholesome fruit. The class of tenants who are thus prompted to fly are those which it most severely damages the country to lose. In the eight years that I have had before me, every year, the names, and to a very great extent, the individual condition and circumstances of near 19,000 tenants, holding under the Court of Chancery, on a tenure described by the words—"For seven years pending the cause," it has often struck me as a remarkable fact—how very few of them have emigrated. When a tenant under the Court desires to emigrate, he applies to the Receiver, and through him to me, for liberty to substitute another in his place, and this liberty I have never refused. It has also happened, that an unthrifty tenant desirous to emigrate, but not having sufficient means, and believing that the Receiver would think it for the benefit of the property to get rid of him, has applied to the Receiver to give him a help towards the expenses of transit, as a consideration for a quiet possession of the land; the Receiver has in those instances applied to me for leave to do so, stating his opinion, that the property would be served by it. Leave to do this,

I have given, when recommended by the Receiver. These two classes comprehend all emigrations from the estates under my jurisdiction, except those of absconding tenants, of whom there have been a few, and a few only. Counting all these, I do not believe that, in the eight years, fifty tenants have emigrated off the 450 estates, and out of nearly 19,000 tenants, holding under the Court of Chancery, which is practically the landlord of these tenants; and not being affected by threatened legislation, has continued to grant the usual leases for seven years, pending the cause. No person, I think, can fail to see that this is a very suggestive fact, and that stopping the pernicious agitation is the best means of stopping the hemorrhage which is exhausting the strength of the country.

How then is the agitation to be stopped? This, I think, and I hope, is a question which the English people and their honourable and high minded representatives in Parliament will be inclined to substitute for, or to ask in addition to the question at the head of this chapter. To this question I will endeavour to give the best and the truest answer which my experience and my knowledge on the subject will enable me to give.

Until it is perfectly known to all Englishmen who exercise the franchise, and to those who are elected to serve in Parliament, that the same toleration of all creeds and forms of worship which exists in England, also exists in Ireland; that the same equality of rights in all classes, and in all persons, exists in both countries; and that no sects, no classes, no men labour under any disabilities in Ireland which do not also affect the inhabitants of England in like cases;—until this is known in England, those who possess the power of legislation will be exposed to the machinations of crafty pretenders, and agitation will be an attractive trade. If Englishmen of all parties were once convinced of this great truth, that the blessing of equal laws and equal rights is as perfectly established in Ireland as it is in England, they would no longer think it just or useful to enact special laws for Ireland, which can have no other effect but to destroy the equality which already exists; they would no longer attend to the suggestions and demands of agitators, and the trade would soon become a bad one, and would die a natural death. This is my answer, and the only one I can give to the question—"How is agitation to be stopped?"

The dealings of landlords with their tenants, although regulated by the same general laws throughout the realm, must yet vary and be modified, according to local circumstances, local customs, and many causes which render expedient such deviations as the general laws admit of. Great variety in these dealings is to be found in England, in different counties, and even upon neighbouring estates. Let any candid Englishman consider how he would regard a proposition to enact a special law by which to restrict him, or the landlords of his county, from dealing with his or their tenants, within the limits of deviation allowed in other parts of England; and let him then, in the English spirit of fair-play, ask himself, whether he knows the special circumstances under which landlords in Ireland have to deal with their tenants sufficiently to justify him in imposing shackles upon the Irish landlords, which the general laws do not impose? Let him use his reason and judgment, as if he were a juror, acting upon evidence, and ask himself whether he can, with any regard to justice, act upon the testimony of some men who have got their seats by abusing landlords, and provoking towards them the hatred and hostility of tenants, for the purpose of destroying the landlords' influence, and giving effect to that of the priests and their landless tools. Until English gentlemen, entrusted with the power of legislators, and having the destinies of Ireland in their hands, and at their mercy, shall think it base and dishonourable to gain a majority for their party by an alliance with these tools, and by aiding in special legislation for a country of which they know nothing, except from those who misrepresent and traduce it, Ireland will continue to be the ruined battle-field for English party strife, and no man can feel secure in the possession of anything that he has. Let every upright and honourable Englishman (and I trust and would fain believe that such are the great and overwhelming majority who serve in Parliament) ask himself whether the experience which he has of his own tenantry, rich, intelligent, emancipated from priestly influence, confiding in their landlord, and enjoying his confidence in return, orderly and obedient to the laws, without the refuge of the confessional and absolution to blunt the stings of conscience when they commit crime, even when that crime is the murder of a landlord, let him in the spirit of English candour, and English fair play, ask himself if such English experience qualifies him to devise endurable special shackles for the landlord of an Irish tenantry; and thereby to destroy that identity and uniformity in the laws of the two countries, which has substantially existed for seven hundred years.

What is to be done with Ireland? Do with it as you do with England. Enact no special laws for Ireland that you would not enact for England. Be deaf to the speeches of patriots, who represent no constituencies but Romish priests. Think not that you can quiet these by any concessions short of a counter-reformation, and short of placing in their hands the executive power of the Sovereign, whereby to enable them to enforce that obligation which their Catechism dogmatically imposes, of belonging to their Church. Make no alliance with these men, or their representatives, for party purposes, and agitation will soon become a bad trade, and Ireland will cease to be England's difficulty, when it ceases to be the battle-field for English party strife.

If you be offended and disgusted, as every upright and honest man ought to be, at the jobbing so constantly imputed to Ireland; if you believe it to be still true that Ireland is a nation of jobbers, as Lord Cornwallis seventy years ago asserted, do not shut your eyes, as he did, to the fact that Ireland supplies only the material, and that the jobbers are of genuine English manufacture.

If you believe that the prosperity and the morals of a civilized nation must mainly depend, as they clearly must, upon an able and upright administration of law and justice, tamper not with the members of an honourable profession, from which the ministers and functionaries must be selected from whose ability, learning, and integrity that greatest of all national blessing must flow, or not exist at all.

In dealing with Ireland, do not ignore that great body of the people by whose intelligence and labour, mental and bodily, the business of the country is carried on, and its prosperity, such as it is, has been produced. When you are called upon to destroy the Irish Church Establishment, be not blind to the fact, that of this great body of the people, the Protestants, whose worship and tolerant religion you are so called upon to persecute, are very nearly one half of this efficient body of the people. That very nearly the other half are Presbyterians, and other dissenters from the Romish creed; and that nine-tenths of all the residue (who are falsely called the people) are those who are priest-ridden, and whose ignorance, sloth, and want of thrift constitute the great impediment to Ireland's progress; and that you have no power whatever to remedy the moral defects of these, which must be left to time, aided by the efforts and example of those whom you ignore, and whose emancipated intellect, and energetic labour has raised Ireland from the famine and desolation of bygone centuries.

Those who are attracted by the seeming fairness of leaving every congregation to support their own clergy, should learn how this voluntary system has worked, and what are its fruits in the States of America. Of this, no better illustration can be given than the sect of Mormons, who adopted the brutish and brutalizing principle of polygamy; and with it also adopted a scriptural principle that, " work is worship"—another form of expressing that, "in the sweat of thy face shalt thou eat bread." By their polygamy they scandalized the fanatics of the other sects, who surrounded their first settlement; by their devout and devoted toil the Mormons had made for themselves an Eden in the wilderness. The polygamy taught by their apostle, who was an offspring of the voluntary system, provoked the intolerance of their fanatic neighbours, whose intolerance sprung from the same parent; and they were, by pitiless violence, driven in the depth of an American winter from the homes which they had built, and the fields and gardens which they had toiled to cultivate. Aged men and women, infants and mothers—the whole nation of them were driven at the point of the sword, with no provision but the clothes which they wore, to face the desert, and travel hundreds of miles in cold and hunger to look for a new settlement in a wild so dreary, that even the savage Indians abhorred and deserted it. There they had nothing to contend with but the natural sterility of a waste deserted by all other living creatures. Notwithstanding their brutish domestic principle, the dogma that work is worship subdued the barren earth, and a new Eden spread and gradually expanded over a wild where no animal had lived, no plant had grown. Far remote from the habitations of all other human beings, they were not observed, and escaped persecution, until, having subdued the earth, they had increased and multiplied, and replenished what they had subdued. Now again, when discovered, they are objects of furious detestation to the fanatics of other creeds, who thirst for their blood, and would sweep them from the earth but for 20,000 rifles in the hands of resolute fighting Mormons.

Polygamy is but one of the multitude of absurd and even loathsome religious vagaries which have sprung from the voluntary system to plague society in the Western world. The merciless fury and fanaticism of other sects, from which each has to defend itself at the point of the bayonet, is another offspring of the same system. Let those who war against a State Church, who would spoliate the endowment of an independent clergy, reflect that where there are as many absurd creeds as there are raving fanatics, and where these are as numerous as the stars, there is no State Church, and every congregation supports its preacher. Let the English people, who are now invited to force this system upon the Irish nation, compare the toleration and state of religious feeling in England, various or even conflicting as it is, with that which pervades every nation in which there is no moderator in the institution of an established State Church, and where all the preachers are made dependent on the influence which they can exercise over the minds of those who listen to them, and they must be sensible of the grave injury which they are prompted to inflict on this country, in violation of their solemn compact with the Protestants of Ireland.

NOTE TO PAGE 173.

It has been asserted that the ratio of the Protestants to the Roman Catholics has diminished, and this alleged diminution is taken as a proof that the mission of the Church has failed, and that, therefore, it should be abolished. The population in 1672, as stated by Sir William Petty, consisted of 100,000 Protestants of the Church of England; 100,000 Presbyterians, Independents, Anabaptists, and Quakers, being of the English race; 100,000 Scotch Presbyterians; all the rest, numbering 800,000, were Irish Papists. If the three denominations of Protestants be classed together, and compared with the Papists, their ratio was then as 3 to 8. If the Protestants and Presbyterians of 1861 be classed together, their total in 1861 was 1,289,206; the Roman Catholics in 1861 were 4,505,265; therefore, all Protestants were to Roman Catholics in 1861 something more than 1 to 3½, which is a less ratio than 3 to 8; and it is true to say that the ratio of *all* classes of Protestants to the Roman Catholics has diminished. But this diminution is entirely owing to the slow increase of the Presbyterians and other Protestant dissenters since 1672, when they amounted to 200,000, and were to the Papists then as 1 to 4, they are now to the Roman Catholics only as 1 to 7. The clergy of the Established Church are not chargeable with the relative falling off of the Presbyterians, and they are entitled to the credit resulting from the increase of the ratio of their own congregations from 1 to 8 as it was in 1672, to 1 to 6½ as it was in 1861. The Church of England Protestants having increased from 100,000 to nearly 700,000—viz., seven-fold, if the Presbyterians had increased in the same proportion from 1672, when they were, English and Scotch, 200,000, they would now be 1,400,000, instead of being less than half that number. The distinction between English and Scotch Presbyterians has long since ceased. The cause which prevented the increase of the Presbyterians appears from the letter of Primate Boulter, of 23rd November, 1728, already quoted at page 142, in which he states the great emigration of Protestants from the North of Ireland, of which nearly all the Protestants were Presbyterians. Thus the assertion that the ratio of Church of England Protestants to the Roman Catholics has diminished is entirely unfounded, the fact being that this ratio has increased from being 1 to 8 to be now 1 to 6½, which is a substantial augmentation.

THE END.

www.ingramcontent.com/pod-product-compliance
Lightning Source LLC
Chambersburg PA
CBHW031402270326
41929CB00010BA/1292